*"Don't forget to
be kind to strangers,
for some who have
done this have
entertained
angels without
realizing it!"*

—Hebrews 13:2, *The Living Bible*

We Didn't Know They Were Angels

Hospitality Even When It's Inconvenient

Doris W. Greig

Nearly 300 family tested recipes

Regal Books

A Division of GL Publications
Ventura, California, U.S.A.

Published by Regal Books
A Division of GL Publications
Ventura, California 93006
Printed in U.S.A.

Scripture quotations in this publication are taken from:
KJV—King James Version, Authorized King James Version.
NASB—New American Standard Bible. © The Lockman Foundation 1960,
1962, 1963, 1968, 1971. Used by permission.
NIV—Holy Bible: The New International Version. Copyright © 1978 by the
International Bible Society. Used by permission of Zondervan Bible Publishers.
Phillips—The New Testament in Modern English, Revised Edition, J.B. Phillips,
Translator. © J.B. Phillips 1958, 1960, 1972. Used by permission of Macmillan
Publishing Co., Inc.
TLB—From The Living Bible, Copyright © 1971 by Tyndale House Pub-
lishers, Wheaton, Illinois. Used by permission.

Library of Congress Cataloging in Publication Data

Greig, Doris W., 1926-
    We didn't know they were angels.

    Includes bibliographies.
    1. Hospitality—Religious aspects—Christianity. 2. Cookery. 3. Greig,
Doris W., 1926-
I. Title.
BV4647.H67G74   1987   241'.671   86-31451
ISBN 0-8307-1145-7

2 3 4 5 6 7 8 9 10 / 91 90 89 88 87

Any omission of credits or permissions is unintentional. The publisher and
author request documentation for future printings.

Rights for publishing this book in other languages are contracted by Gospel
Literature International (GLINT) foundation. GLINT also provides technical help for the adaptation, translation, and publishing of Bible study
resources and books in scores of languages worldwide. For further information, contact GLINT, Post Office Box 488, Rosemead, California, 91770,
U.S.A., or the publisher.

Dedication

To the hundreds of houseguests and others God has sent into our lives who have ministered to us as "angels," and to whom we have had the privilege to minister.

To our children, Kathryn, Bill III, Gary and Jane, who set extra places at our table, gave up their beds and in many other ways lovingly and warmly received these "angels," many of them strangers.

And last, but not least, to my husband Bill who encouraged me to open my heart, and our home—often at the last minute—even when, "We didn't know they were angels!"

The Greig Family
Christmas 1963

Gary, 5, Jane, 2, Doris, Kathy, 10, Bill and Billy, 6.

Contents

Part 1

1
Wieners and Beans—or Pride!
"Because of Yvonne our family was able to put hospitality into God's perspective."

2
Hospitality—A God-given Opportunity
"We need to grab opportunities to share our home, our friendship . . . our love with family, friends and a hurting world."

3
Mary, Martha and Me
"In God's economy we are all useful in the different forms of Christian hospitality."

Foreword

We Didn't Know They Were Angels really touched my heart. Doris Greig is a gifted author who is not afraid to expose her own weaknesses and inner struggles. As I read her manuscript, I found myself becoming excited about what can be accomplished by simply opening one's heart and home to others. What an example of Christlikeness she sets!

As well as challenging her readers spiritually, Doris offers very practical suggestions for effective hospitality. These hints, which come from years of experience, are supported by Scripture, which she presents with refreshing insights.

We Didn't Know They Were Angels challenges the contemporary Christian woman to practice what Doris calls "relaxed availability," to redeem the time that she has been given wherever she might be—in her own home, in her community or in a crowded airline terminal.

Preface

Dear Reader,

It is my prayer that this book, which contains many stories about our family and the guests God has sent our way, will be a blessing and a help to all who read it.

Each chapter provides scriptural basis for the "whys" of Christian hospitality. *We Didn't Know They Were Angels* deals with the gift of hospitality that certain Christians have been given by God, as well as the call to *all* Christians to extend the love of God in the many other forms of Christian hospitality.

This is not a how-to book for successful dinner parties, church socials and other such functions. But I have offered some suggested menus and favorite recipes gathered over a period of 35 years simply because I love good and easy food. Adapt them to your needs, and enjoy them!

God may be sending some "angels" your way. Will they be a blessing or a burden to you? May God give you the eyes to see not only the benefits in the giving of yourself to these angels, but also the inexpressible joy of receiving from them, too!

Doris W. Greig

Part 1

1

Wieners and Beans—or Pride!

It was a Monday afternoon; I had been washing and ironing clothes for our family all day long. As I worked, I prayed for myself, my husband and our four children. I removed the sheets from each bed, washed and dried them and returned them to each of the children's rooms and to our own bedroom. And as I did, I prayed for each family member, smoothing the sheets on their bed and fluffing each pillow. I lifted that person's needs to the Lord, giving Him thanksgiving and praise for each one.

I talked to God about my dreams for our family and for each child in it. I prayed that our family would be so filled with the love of Christ that it would "ooze" out of the doors of our house to fill the neighborhood, the school, the community and the world with the sweet fragrance of Christ. "Follow God's example in everything you do just as a much loved child imitates his father. Be full of love for others, following the example of Christ who loved you and gave himself to God as a sacrifice to take away your sins. And God was pleased, for Christ's love for you was like sweet perfume to him" (Eph. 5:1,2, *TLB*).

As I ironed shirts, blouses and dresses, I prayed again for

each person in our family. I prayed that God would shape and form them into the people He wanted them to be, that they would walk faithfully with the Lord all the days of their lives, and that they would reach out to others with the love of Jesus Christ.

By now, the children, ages 5, 6 and 10 years, had arrived home from school one by one; they walked the two blocks to our home. They knew this was laundry day; if possible mother was not to be disturbed. My 10-year-old daughter Kathy was caring for her two brothers, Billy and Gary, and our active 2-year-old Jane, who had followed me about the house all that day while I worked. It was a welcomed breather that I had looked forward to all day.

I was particularly thankful because there seemed to be a greater spirit of peace and cooperation than usual, and I knew I would manage to get my laundry completed in time to cook the wieners and beans for dinner.

I had planned to fix carrot sticks, open a large can of apple-sauce and serve the dinner at our usual hour of 6 P.M. It was not a fancy dinner, but I knew the children especially would enjoy the hot dogs. My husband was always appreciative of any meal I served him.

The phone rang at about 4:30. It seemed an uncalled-for interruption in my hectic schedule. I wanted to get the ironing done before I prepared the meal. Kathy answered the phone and told me her daddy wanted to speak to me. As I walked to the phone, I wondered what on earth he could want at this hour. After Bill told me the reason he had called, I felt like a bomb had exploded in the kitchen and hit me!

Bill, in an excited voice, told me he was sitting in his office with a woman from South Africa. "Will it be all right if I bring her home for dinner?" he asked. "She has not been in an American home yet, and would really enjoy seeing our home. She wants to get acquainted with you and the children," he said.

My first reaction was to scream or cry! How could he do this to me, I wanted to shout. It was at that moment all my spirituality went down the drain. As calmly as possible, I tried to explain to Bill that this was my "laundry day," and I had wieners and beans planned for dinner. I told him I didn't have the time or the energy to go to the store for anything else, nor did I have any other food to supplement or make any change in this "slapped together meal."

He on the other hand was so enthusiastic when he heard that we were having wieners and beans; I couldn't believe it! He's got to be kidding, I thought. He told me Yvonne would be thrilled to have wieners and beans because they were typically American and she probably had never tasted them. He was a super salesman—he guaranteed she would love my dinner! I had my doubts.

I frantically fished for another excuse to get out of this dinner visit. I told Bill that the house was a horrible mess, that I wasn't exactly neatly dressed and that the kids were dirty from playing in the backyard. Again, he tried to encourage me. He told me that families around the world, even in South Africa, are like this, and Yvonne would feel right at home with us. He said, "Not to worry, Doris."

Well, as you may have gathered by now, I have a husband with a God-given gift for extending hospitality to anyone, anytime. He personifies the members of the Body of Christ who are given special ability to provide a warm welcome and an open house for those in need of food or lodging. I was a new Christian, and wasn't so sure God had called *me* to this ministry however! Yet, if my husband had the gift, wasn't I, his partner, to support him in exercising it? Thus, I began to send up "arrow prayers" to God after agreeing to have this stranger from South Africa into my home for an "exotic American dinner" of wieners and beans.

"You've come a long way, baby," I said to myself, as I ran the bathwater for the children and laid out clean pajamas for the smaller children to climb into after their baths. They all pitched in before dinner to help pick up the house and re-establish a measure of decency and order. Actually "a measure of decency and order" was all we ever had at our house. Can anyone ever have everything sterile and pristine with four children, two cats, one dog and numerous smaller animals, like rodents and snakes in cages and jars, plus playmates of all ages romping through the house?

I was too tired to even think of setting the dining room table. Some of the children were still in the milk-spilling stage anyway, so I decided I would be asking for a disaster on a Monday night when everyone, including Mother, was tired. So I chose not to eat in the dining room. Thus, our "committee" of five decided to set the kitchen table with our prettiest plastic mats, plastic dishes and our everyday stainless flatware.

When I had explained to the children where our dinner guest lived, they wanted to know if she was Black. I honestly said I didn't know, I hadn't asked, and that it really didn't matter. She was one of God's people, far from home, and would enjoy being with an American family for an evening. The children enjoyed setting the table. They picked a few flowers from the yard and arranged them in a small vase for a centerpiece.

As I scurried about, I refused to allow myself to dwell on the fact that the kitchen floor should be swept, and that all of the furniture in the house needed dusting. There wasn't time! I decided, "Why spoil the whole evening by getting grumpy over details that really won't count through time and eternity anyway?" I really sensed the Holy Spirit guiding my mind into right thought patterns and bringing everything into a proper perspective as far as this evening was concerned.

I thought of God's promise in Zechariah 4:6, " 'Not by might nor by power, but by My Spirit,' says the Lord of hosts" (NASB). God was letting me know that this evening was in His hands. I didn't have to fret that I did not have the might nor the power to have a model home, model children or a model meal for this guest. God was allowing me the privilege of experiencing His power and might to make the evening pleasant and memorable not only for Yvonne, but also for our entire family.

MY PACESETTER

The Lord is my pacesetter,
    I shall not rush.
He makes me to stop
    for quiet intervals.

He provides me with images of stillness
        which restore my serenity.
He leads me in ways of efficiency
        through calmness of mind,
            and His guidance
                is peace.

Even though I have a great many things
        to accomplish each day,
I will not fret
        for His presence is here.

His timelessness, His all-importance
        will keep me in balance.
He prepares refreshment in the midst
        of my activity by anointing my mind
            with His oil of tranquility.

My cup of joyous energy overflows.
        Surely harmony and effectiveness
            shall be the fruit of my hours,

And I shall walk in the pace
        of the Lord

And dwell in His house
forever.

—Author Unknown[1]

True hospitality, no matter what form it takes, is always a gift from the Holy Spirit. I sensed God's supernatural help in overcoming my insecurities and fears of what Yvonne—this unknown person, unknown entity—would think of me, my children, my house and the meal I served.

"Who gave me that fear and insecurity in the first place?" I asked myself. It certainly wasn't God. This fear is a "Snare of the devil" (2 Tim. 2:26, NASB). I recognized that I had been under attack, but as I relied on the Holy Spirit and remembered that "Greater is He who is in you than he who is in the world" (1 John 4:4, NASB), I felt a peaceful calm filling my mind and body. I knew the Lord was at work within me. Actually, I began to look forward to the dinner hour!

As I look back on this experience, I can see the hand of God on my life—shaping and forming me into His image. He worked in my life through this growing experience of trusting Him in the circumstances of that Monday laundry day so long ago. "And we know that all that happens to us is working for our good if we love God and are fitting into his plans. For from the very beginning God decided that those who came to him— and all along he knew who would—should become like his Son, so that his Son would be the First, with many brothers" (Rom. 8:28,29, TLB).

Just as God does not make His spiritual children all alike physically, He formed us differently for various uses in the Kingdom of God. Your call may not be to allow your furniture to get worn and your dishes broken by hosting a lot of people for dinner. But remember hospitality comes in many forms.

Sometimes hospitality means weeping with a friend or a neighbor, or staying up extra late just to listen to the story of the pain in someone's life. It may be watching the neighbor's children when their mother is ill, or taking food to the home of a new neighbor. Hospitality can take many shapes and forms. We need to pray, "God, please make me willing to see, and then grasp, the opportunities you send my way. I trust your Holy Spirit to give me the wisdom and strength I need from you for each opportunity you call me to participate in this day and this week. By the power of Jesus' name, I commit my life to you as your servant."

Would you like to hear the outcome of the Monday laundry day opportunity the Lord gave me? Yvonne came! She was young and full of fun, and the children liked her immediately. As I dished up the beans and stuffed the hot dogs into their buns, put the applesauce and carrot sticks into pretty serving bowls, Yvonne showed the children pictures of Johannesburg, South Africa. She told them about the climate, people, plants, animals and churches there.

What a blessing it was for my children to be exposed to another country and culture through her sharing that evening. In the few brief moments before I called them to dinner, my children were given a larger view of the world through Yvonne's pictures and conversation.

> *Do not forget to entertain strangers, for by so doing some people have entertained angels without knowing it.*
> —Hebrews 13:2, *NIV*

I called to them in the living room, "Dinner is served!" The children joyously led Yvonne to the kitchen and we all sat down to the table. It looked quite pretty with the flowers the children had arranged, and the soft glow of the candles I had added at the last moment. The hot dogs on a platter and the beans in the casserole actually looked and smelled pretty good.

Yvonne immediately admired the applesauce bowl, an antique I enjoyed using. She was so excited about her "American dinner." Imagine, she had never had hot dogs and baked beans before! She exclaimed over them; she actually "oohed and aahed."

"These are so wonderful," she said. "I love your American food!" The children were impressed by her enthusiasm and ate with greater appreciation their standard Monday night fare. They were pleased to have been "my helpers" in hospitality that night.

Whenever I have seen Yvonne in years since, she has always reminded me of that "delightful evening" when she was introduced to our family. Yvonne never fails to mention how good the wieners and beans tasted, and what fun it was to be counted as worthy to be treated "just like family." As she reminds me of this, I realize that my pride almost kept me from this "choice experience," as she defines it.

I am also reminded that my pride almost kept me from enjoying that evening too. It was a growing experience for my children as their world view was enlarged. And for me, it was a growing experience in letting go of non-essentials and trusting God to meet me where I was and enable me by His power to enjoy that evening. I almost missed the joy of getting to know Yvonne, sharing my family with her and giving her a little glimpse of our American home and culture. It was either wieners and beans or pride. I am so glad that with God's guidance, I was able to set aside my pride and instead chose to serve wieners and beans!

Earlier that day I had prayed for my children. I had asked God to mold them into His image. What I now realized was that He not only "molded" them that evening, but also He was in process of molding me into a usable vessel for His glory. To think I almost missed the "Potter's touch" on my life that day because of foolish pride!

Yes, Yvonne was like an angel sent to us by God. And because of her our family was able to put hospitality into "God's perspective."

Have Thine Own Way, Lord!

Have Thine own way, Lord! Have Thine own
Way!
Thou art the Potter; I am the clay
Mould me and make me After Thy will,
While I am waiting, Yielded and still.

Have Thine own way, Lord! Have Thine own
way!
Search me and try me, Master, today!
Whiter than snow, Lord, Wash me just now,
As in Thy presence Humbly I bow.

Have Thine own way, Lord! Have Thine own
way!
Hold o'er my being Absolute sway!
Fill with Thy Spirit Till all shall see
Christ only, always, Living in me!

—George C. Stebbins[2]

God Is Calling You

1. How do you currently turn everyday household duties into opportunities to think about and pray for members of your family?

2. List a specific need for each family member. Lift those needs to the Lord when you are scurrying about your busy day.

3. Think of a situation where you were called upon at the last minute to either have someone into your home for dinner or extend hospitality in some other manner, such as drive someone to the doctor or keep someone's child. How did you react?

4. Can you think of a time when pride stood (or nearly stood) in the way of your extending warm and generous hospitality to someone you know or to a stranger, thereby removing the blessing of giving and receiving God's love through ministering to someone else?

Notes:
1. Author unknown. From *The Hurrier I Go* by Bonnie Wheeler (Ventura, CA: Regal Books, 1985), p. 40.
2. George C. Stebbins, "Have Thine Own Way, Lord!" ©1935, Hope Publishing. Public domain.

2

Hospitality—A God-given Opportunity

Recently, while waiting to board a plane in Chicago for Los Angeles, I observed a tall, thin, sophisticated-looking woman enter the terminal with a very handsome, well-dressed man who looked very much like her.

I wondered who they were, why they had been in Chicago and what their destination would be. They stood in line together, and as they approached the ticket agent, he instructed the woman to move three desks down into another rather long line. Her companion seemed a little upset at their separation, and I wondered why. As soon as he had completed his own ticketing details, he rushed over to the willowy brunette, took her bag and waited in line with her until her business was completed. I never expected to see them again, but enjoyed pondering what their reasons were for being at O'Hare Airport in Chicago.

I find it helps to pass the time while waiting in airports to observe people and wonder about their everyday lives. I often find myself sending up "arrow prayers" for those who seem to have immediate needs.

Since our plane was almost an hour late, Bill and I walked

to a restaurant at the center of the terminal and had a quick lunch. When we walked to the gate and waited in the very crowded lobby area for the call to board our plane, the two people I had observed earlier were nowhere to be seen. Thus I slotted the "unfinished story" in my mind and gave it no further thought.

After quite a long wait, we finally were allowed to board our stop-over flight to Denver. We stowed our carry-on luggage, then found our assigned seats at the back of the plane. We sat down, fastened our seatbelts and began to watch the passengers as they came down the aisle to find their seats. It was enjoyable to observe their various responses to locations and seatmates.

Imagine my surprise as I saw the sophisticated-looking couple walk down the aisle. *There certainly is a strong resemblance,* I thought as I saw them approach. The most delightful surprise was that they sat down in the only other two seats in our row. This lovely lady was seated next to me, and the man had an aisle seat. He made sure his companion was comfortably seated; they both seemed to collapse in their seats.

From their conversation, I gathered that they had come from separate cities to Chicago to be by the bedside of their dying mother. They spoke of going to the hospital daily with their father in his car, and pondered what they would do when he became ill. Would they rent a car or take a taxi back and forth to the hospital? I sat there wondering to myself, *Where is your father now? How is he doing?* No mention was made of where he was living, or how he was coping with the loss of his wife. With a vivid imagination, I wondered if they had closed the family home and put their father in a small apartment or home for the aged. No mention was made of other family members. There appeared to be only two children and here they were seated at my left en route from Chicago to Denver!

I'm telling this story because I heard some of the saddest words I have ever heard spoken during the conversation between this brother and sister. She said to him, with such pain in her voice, "I really feel badly about the timing of this. I had planned to bring Mother to San Francisco to hear the symphony rehearse." I wasn't surprised at what she said, as she looked very much like a musician or an art patron. "I wanted to take her to see those lovely old Victorian houses there in the city, because she would have enjoyed it so much." She stopped with these few words and breathed a long, sad sigh and the conversation concerning their mother's death ended.

There was no more talk about their mother and no more discussion of their father. It was as if they had dismissed the topic from their minds for all eternity. They now commented on the food served, down to the smallest detail. They compared flight numbers and departure times of the planes they would be boarding in Denver.

I wanted to shout, "But, what about your dad? Don't miss another opportunity! Is he able to travel? What would he like to see in San Francisco? What would he like to do with you, his precious children, before he leaves this earth? And if he cannot travel, will you go to him while he is alive and share your lives with him?"

Of course I did not say these things aloud. It seemed their priority was to communicate about the life and death of their mother and complete that chapter of their lives.

They did not discuss their spouses, although each wore wedding bands, their occupations, their finances, their health, their children (if there were any), their hobbies or any other topic. It was almost as if two strangers had looked into each other's eyes for the first time in many years, as they stood by the bedside of their dying mother in that Chicago hospital.

Unfortunately there seemed to be no joy at simply being together again, nor did I sense any anticipation of another meeting. This sister and brother did not discuss the desire to visit one another soon. Before they ended their conversation about their father they only talked about how to handle the details "when Dad gets sick, is hospitalized and then dies."

My heart ached for these two, a brother and a sister, who might not see each other again until their eyes meet across the bed of their dying father in a nursing home or a hospital. This time together could have been such an opportunity for a new beginning of family fellowship. Instead, as our plane made its stop in Denver these two bounded out of their seats, grabbed their luggage and headed for different gates to catch their planes: She to San Francisco, he to Phoenix.

They were like ships passing in the night—hardly aware of each other's lives, and not really caring very much about each other's needs, heartaches or dreams. They didn't even appear to recognize their insensitivity to each other. It seemed they didn't know what they were missing.

This story basically deals with opportunities that this brother and sister managed to ignore—the opportunity to show love and fellowship to their father while he was alive, and the opportunity to share anew their lives with each other. Their mother's death had brought them together after what seemed to be many years of little or no communication. Here was a God-given opportunity, and it appeared to pass by unobserved by either one of them.

> *We often face tremendous opportunities that are cleverly disguised as impossible circumstances.*

Missed opportunities! We all have them in our lives. We need to learn to grab them. Opportunities to share our home, our friendship, our money, our time, our love with family, friends and a hurting world. We need to pray that God will open our eyes to the opportunities He puts in our pathway, often through adverse circumstances, and then ask Him to make us joyfully willing to use these circumstances to bring glory and honor to our heavenly Father. And at the same time bring love and joy to others.

When I think of hospitality, I am reminded of Jesus' words in Matthew 25:31–40: "When the Son of Man comes in his glory, and all the angels with him, he will sit on his throne in heavenly glory. All the nations will be gathered before him, and he will separate the people one from another as a shepherd separates the sheep from the goats. He will put the sheep on his right and the goats on his left. Then the King will say to those on his right, 'Come, you who are blessed by my Father; take your inheritance, the kingdom prepared for you since the creation of the world. For I was hungry and you gave me something to eat, I was thirsty and you gave me something to drink, I was a stranger and you invited me in, I needed clothes and you clothed me, I was sick and you looked after me, I was in prison and you came to visit me.' Then the righteous will answer him, 'Lord, when did we see you hungry and feed you, or thirsty and give you something to drink? When did we see you a stranger and invite you in, or needing clothes and clothe you? When did we see you sick or in prison and go to visit you?' The King will reply, 'I tell you the truth, whatever you did for one of the least of these brothers of mine, you did for me'" (NIV).

Hospitality is not just giving dinner parties and having houseguests! Jesus Christ describes not only feeding the hungry, quenching the thirst of the thirsty and inviting the stranger in, but He also includes servanthood acts of hospitality such as clothing the needy, looking after the sick and visiting the prisoners.

The Encyclopedia Britannica Dictionary defines hospitality in this way: "To be hospitable is to be disposed to behave in a warm way and manner, and to entertain with generous kind-

31

ness." My mind went back to the airport where we sat waiting for our plane. I was observing the people who were to be my fellow passengers.

An older woman with her very elderly mother was brought by an electric cart to our crowded gate. The man who drove the cart got down and practically lifted the little old lady down the stairs and carefully led her over to our seating area. He shouted as he came, "Will some kindhearted young person please give up their seat for this frail little lady who needs to sit down?"A young woman seemed to "eject" from her seat immediately, and waved the man over to her chair. Slowly, the little lady shuffled through the crowd as the man gently supported her.

This young woman exhibited exactly what my dictionary defined as hospitality right there in the crowded airport terminal. She behaved in a "warm way" immediately and responded without hesitation to the "opportunity" when it was presented. She gave up her seat without grumbling, and with "generous kindness," not even pondering any inconvenience it might bring her way. I observed her as she stood visiting with the daughter of the elderly lady, and it was obvious that she was enjoying the experience of giving her seat to this very fragile old woman. She must have looked like an "angel" of mercy to the woman in need.

I wondered, Is she a Christian? Certainly she was exhibiting the kind of hospitality every Christian is called to give. She may not have a home where she can entertain houseguests or have lovely dinner parties, but she was exhibiting a form of hospitality that all Christians are called by Christ to practice by the power of the Holy Spirit within us. She gave of herself immediately as the opportunity presented itself. I could see it brought joy to her to do this.

Christians have this promise: "For it is God who is at work in you, both to will and to work for His good pleasure. Do all things without grumbling" (Phil. 2:13–14, *NASB*). Verse 15 instructs us in this way, "That you may prove yourselves to be blameless and innocent, children of God above reproach in the midst of a crooked and perverse generation, among whom you appear as lights in the world."

The young woman in the airport was a "light of hospitality" to the whole lobby full of people. She did not grumble about having to be inconvenienced by giving up her right to sit down in that hot, crowded waiting room until her late plane arrived and was ready for her to board.

We need to ask ourselves what kind of "light" we are as Christians in our homes, our neighborhoods, our communities or wherever we find ourselves. Are we as quick to see and then respond to human need as this girl was? And if we are, do we do it to bring glory to ourselves, or to our Lord? Are we sensitive and available to Christ when He provides an opportunity to be hospitable?

Jesus said in Luke 14:12–14, "When you give a luncheon or dinner, do not invite your friends, your brothers or relatives, or your rich neighbors; if you do, they may invite you back and so you will be repaid. But when you give a banquet, invite the poor, the crippled, the lame, the blind, and you will be blessed. Although they cannot repay you, you will be repaid at the resurrection of the righteous" (NIV). He was telling us to extend hospitality without any thought of a return or a reward here on earth.

Will Christ be able to say to us the words He spoke in Matthew 25:34: "Come, you who are blessed of My Father" (NASB). Will we choose to be blessed by the Father by making ourselves available to be used as a vessel of Jesus Christ to be "His light" in a darkened world that is hungry and thirsty to know the Saviour? Are we anxious to be His light to a world of people whose hearts are restless and who are strangers to God? Will we view the world through the eyes of Christ and allow Him to use our hands, our feet, our hearts, our homes and our resources to feed the hungry and quench the thirst of those who physically and spiritually are so needy?

Will we eagerly welcome the strangers and invite them not only into our homes, but into our hearts? Called and empowered by the Spirit of God, will we make conscious choices so that we may have a part in clothing the poor and visiting and ministering to those who are sick and imprisoned?

God calls each one of us as Christians to be hospitable in some way. How will you respond? The choice is up to you!

Dear Lord,

It's Christmas Eve.
I've just finished wrapping Mom's gift.
It's a color TV and it was expensive!
She lives alone on a small Social Security allot-
    ment.
It will help her "while away" the lonely hours.

But, Lord, this year
I have decided to give Mom another gift–
A more important gift!
The gift of myself!

Lord, I will be available
To drive Mom to the supermarket,
To the doctor and the dentist.
I will take her to the art gallery
    she has longed to visit.
I will invite her for dinner more often,
And not just on holidays or other
    special occasions!

Lord, by your Spirit
Help me to overlook her forgetfulness

And questions repeated over and over again.
Let me turn my schedule over to you
So that by your plan, I'll have time for Mom!

Also, Lord, please
Remind me to tell Mom that I love her!
Help me to hug her often
To touch her hand
And kiss her cheek
While I still have her here to love.

God Is Calling You

1. When was the last time you found yourself waiting in an airline terminal, doctor's waiting room or parking lot outside your child's school? Did you use that opportunity to send up "arrow prayers" for those seated around you and those passing by?

2. As we look back upon the sister and brother in this chapter, can you think of opportunities you have missed in your family relationships? Are there opportunities in your life right now that you could take hold of to mend a broken relationship or see to the need of an elderly family member?

3. What kind of "light" are you in your home, your community, your workplace, the world? What steps could you take to make your "light" more visible to those around you?

4. God calls each one of us to be hospitable in some way. How will you respond to that call in the next week to not only those God has placed in your immediate surroundings, but also to those "strangers" He will bring into your midst?

3

Mary, Martha and Me

Erma Bombeck once said that a mother has to make a decision early in her life. She either goes down as the world's greatest cook, or she sets an example of sharing for her children by accommodating every surprise guest they bring home for a meal. She made her decision. That's why she says there is an entire generation out there who believes Mrs. Bombeck serves half-macaroni and half-spaghetti with a sauce so pale it won't stain a tablecloth—and chicken parts that aren't identifiable even to another chicken!

She goes on to talk about the company who drops in while dinner is cooking. They won't go and they "won't stay." She pleads, "I've got plenty." They accept. She then goes to the kitchen where she drops on her knees in front of the oven containing two stuffed peppers and prays, "Lord, I know you haven't done it for a long time, but I'm begging."

Certainly many of us have sent up similar "arrow prayers" at just such times, and though Erma's example is an extreme one, we've all been there from time to time. Yet, we need to keep in mind that people who just drop in really are usually much more hungry for fellowship in a home where hospitality reigns, rather than a large meal.

Bonnie Wheeler, in her book *The Hurrier I Go*, summarizes what true Christian hospitality is:

Hospitality

Sure, I believe in hospitality, Lord.
Just not *my* house.

We can't afford the fancy foods,
My dishes don't all match.
The living room sofa needs repairs
And what would I do with the kids?
You just don't understand, Lord.

But, my child, I do understand.
I never had a house, but I turned no one away;
When I fed the multitudes, it was with the plainest
    fare—
Borrowed fish and bread.
We had no dishes and no place to sit, but the
    ground.

It's you that don't understand, child.

Hospitality is not giving the fanciest food,
On your finest plates,
In an immaculate, childless home.
My kind of hospitality is a special kind:
Not things, not possessions, not treasures.

My kind of hospitality is sharing—
Yourself,

As I did.[1]

Often we think of hospitality and simply link it up with dinners and parties, yet the Encyclopedia Britannica defines it this way: "To be hospitable is to behave in a warm way and manner." Second it says, "To entertain with generous kindness." So, to be disposed in a warm way and manner is just as important as to entertain with generosity! And then, a third thing that I have added for the Christian (not found in the dictionary) is that hospitality involves "sensitivity and availability." If we are not sensitive to opportunities, then we are not available to them.

There is an old Chinese proverb that says "Time is a river in which no man steps twice." In today's fast-paced world, an opportunity can rush by very fast; we must reach out and touch it, and use it to bring glory to God, for "no man steps twice" in the river of opportunity either.

At Christmas we celebrate the birth of our Saviour Jesus Christ, who later gave Himself as a sacrifice. This showed His love for us, and we are told in God's Word to be full of love for others. God was well pleased with Christ, and His sacrificial offering of His life upon the cross was sweet perfume to the Father. We are to be His sweet perfume to a hurting world around us today.

"Be full of love for others, following the example of Christ who loved you and gave himself to God as a sacrifice to take away your sins. And God was pleased, for Christ's love for you was like sweet perfume to him" (Eph. 5:2, *TLB*).

From time to time we all hurt. Every person who is honest enough to admit this will tell you that there are hurts that need the ministry of the Lord through God's people. Those who are not yet in the family of Christ need us to be His hands, His feet, His eyes, His ears and His voice to help them find God's love.

We are challenged to minister hospitably to a needy and hurting world in James 1:22–25, "But prove yourselves doers of the word, and not merely hearers who delude themselves. For if anyone is a hearer of the word and not a doer, he is like a

39

man who looks at his natural face in a mirror; for once he has looked at himself and gone away, he has immediately forgotten what kind of person he was. But one who looks intently at the perfect law, the law of liberty, and abides by it, not having become a forgetful hearer but an effectual doer, this man shall be blessed in what he does" (NASB).

Verse 27 says, "This is pure and undefiled religion in the sight of our God and Father, to visit orphans and widows in their distress, and to keep oneself unstained by the world." An "effectual doer," as this verse promises, will be blessed by God; we can count on it!

Hospitality is a two-way street. At times we give hospitality, and other times we receive it. Perhaps after cooking a Thanksgiving dinner for family and friends you decide "it was a privilege" and at the same time "an exhausting experience." There are times when we all think, "I don't want to be sweet perfume; I am too tired."

There have been times when I have had the same emotions. I've thought, *I'm too tired to behave in a warm manner to anyone who comes to my door today and needs to talk. I am too tired to entertain in a generous, kind way.*

Yes, through the years I have felt these emotions from time to time. *I'm too tired to listen to her,* I thought when she came to my kitchen door and wanted to have a cup of coffee and cry over something she needed to share. *I'm too tired when my husband asks me to entertain his business guests.* I have felt too tired to be available and sensitive. On those days I could only serve, pray and weep with the hurting by the strength God gave me. The promise found in Philippians 4:13, "I can do all things through Him who strengthens me" (NASB), has proven God's faithfulness to me over and over again.

The story is told of a husband describing his wife in this way, "Oh, I call her an angel, because she's always up in the air about something and harping!" You know, I have been guilty of that. I've been guilty of missing God's blessing because I've been "up in the air" about inconsequential things, and "harp-ing" about them! God needs to remind me again and again to trust in Him, His promises and His power to keep them.

We need to keep in mind God's economy, and this little verse expresses trusting God—one day at a time—to supply our emotional and physical strength to grasp the opportunities He sends our way:

> *Yesterday is a cancelled check. Tomorrow is a promissory note. Today is ready cash. Use it!*

We each have different goals, energy levels, personal needs and priorities around which we must pray and ask God to orga-nize our thoughts and daily activities.

I am reminded of how differently Mary and Martha responded when Jesus came to visit their home. Mary must have been a sanguine personality. I can see her calmly and joy-ously sitting at Jesus' feet as she absorbed all of His wonderful words (see Luke 10:39). Martha was probably a choleric per-sonality who was dashing about with a very high energy level, and perhaps a quick temper.

It was Martha who welcomed Jesus into her home (see Luke 10:38). As the hours passed by, she began to feel that Mary was not doing her share of the work in serving the Lord Jesus. So she lost her cool and said to the Lord, "Sir, doesn't it seem unfair to you that my sister just sits here while I do all the work? Tell her to come and help me" (Luke 10:40, *TLB*).

This seemed a strange request to make of a houseguest, especially our Lord! My conclusion is that only a pure choleric would snap and speak to a guest like that, rather than go qui-etly to her sister and ask for some help in the kitchen.

We must not compare ourselves to others, we Marys or Marthas, as we measure our own Christian hospitality. This was a mistake Martha made: Choleric Martha wanted Jesus to make her sanguine sister, Mary, just like herself. God does not make us like cookie-cutter gingerbread men, all looking and acting alike. We need to affirm each other—whether we are Marys or Marthas! In God's economy we are all useful in the different forms of Christian hospitality.

For instance, listening is "behaving in a warm way," which is a part of biblical hospitality that Mary was called to do. Serving actively is also biblical hospitality in action; Martha was called to do this. Martha demonstrated hospitality in action, while Mary showed her hospitality by listening to the Lord.

I am reminded of the story of the man walking in the desert when a voice said to him, "Pick up some pebbles and put them in your pocket, and tomorrow you will be both glad and sorry." The man obeyed. He stooped down and picked up a handful of pebbles and put them in his pocket. The next morning he reached into his pocket and found diamonds, rubies and emeralds. He was both glad and sorry. Glad that he had taken some—sorry that he had not taken more.

And so it is with the truths from Christ that Mary received as she sat at her Lord's feet. They were far better than diamonds, rubies or emeralds! As Mary undoubtedly shared some of the "gems" the Lord had spoken as she sat at His feet, I am sure Martha wished that she had stopped to listen awhile and hear some of these treasures firsthand.

Perhaps she thought, *Oh, I wish I had brought the apples in a bowl and sat at Jesus' feet peeling and slicing them while He spoke.* And often I have wondered if Mary had hurried to help Martha in the preparation and serving, if there would not have been plenty of time for both of them to sit at Jesus' feet and drink in His rich words of life. Certainly, cooperation is necessary in any family if all are to enjoy the rich blessings of giving and receiving hospitality.

Mary was glad she sat and heard the Lord Jesus' treasured words that day. And like her, we need to take time to listen to the Lord, in prayer, through reading His Word and through the words of others. As we do, we will be prepared to serve, as Martha served. In whatever area of Christian hospitality God has planned for us to serve, He has promised to equip us with His Spirit. We need to claim the promises from His Word for our daily lives in order to have the strength and wisdom for every opportunity God sends our way.

Growing a Friendship

Friendship is like a garden
It needs my tender, loving care.
Help me to plant it,
water it,
cultivate it,
weed it.
Watch it grow!

But if you begin to neglect it,
One day you look up and see—
barren spots
dry spots
hard ground
dry weeds
and all the glorious colors gone.

It seems the same with you, Lord.
Fellowship with you
needs tender loving care
if our love is to grow!
My heart is the garden
Plant your Word in it, Lord;

Water it with your Holy Spirit
Cultivate it daily . . .
but that's my part isn't it, Lord?

Weed out my garden, Lord
I want to watch it grow
and bloom in friendship
first with you,
then with others.

—Doris W. Greig

There's a humorous story of a lady who invited guests on a blistering hot summer day. Her little 4-year-old son was in the kitchen with her as she was getting ready, and when they sat down to dinner, she turned to her little boy and said, "Would you like to say the blessing, Dear?" He said, "Mommy, I don't know what to say." She said, "Just say what I would say."

And so he said, "Oh, Lord, why did I have to invite these people here on a hot day like this?" That's what he heard his mother say! Hospitality, however we display it, is catching too, isn't it? Our children, spouses and friends begin to realize whether we have a hospitable household, no matter how we exhibit our hospitality.

Many times I have said to God, "You know I am too frail. I am not a good vessel. Can't you give me another assignment?" And the Lord, not always in audible ways, answers back, "Don't you realize you are the only material I've got to work with in this situation? I made you for this situation! My sweet perfume through Jesus Christ won't go out to this lonely world unless you make yourself available to me, today, in this situation."

And I say, "But I'm too frail! I'm just too tired!" Or "I've got too many little kids tugging at my skirts." Or, "You know I have

a bad heart, and not a lot of energy. I'm growing older, Lord."
At every stage of life we have different excuses. But, I want to
tell you that God is not looking for superstars. He's looking for
empty vessels. Empty vessels to fill with the love of Jesus
Christ.

God never fails to remind me of two of my favorite verses
when I think of the empty vessel. "Christ in you, the hope of
glory" (Col. 1:27, *NASB*), and "I can do all things through Him
who strengthens me" (Phil. 4:13, *NASB*). These are God's
promises to enable us to be used in whatever He calls us to do.

Now, He isn't going to ask you to do anything He won't
give you the strength for. But we do have to offer ourselves,
and I haven't always offered myself willingly. I haven't always
yielded my poverty, my frailness, my weakness to God's
power. You know, God's power has gotten trapped inside me
sometimes. He hasn't always been able to use me. I've not
always behaved warmly in the situation; I've not always entertained with kindness.

The following "Prayer of Welcome," seen inside the door-
way of The Old Rectory at Crowhurst, Sussex, England, never
ceases to challenge me to look to the Lord for His empowerment for all who come through the door of my life:

> O God, Make the door of this house wide
> enough to receive all who need human love and
> fellowship, narrow enough to shut out all envy,
> pride and strife. Make its threshold smooth enough
> to be no stumbling block, but rugged and strong
> enough to turn back the tempter's power. God,
> make the door of this house the gateway to Thine
> eternal Kingdom, through Jesus Christ, our Lord,
> Amen.

When we offer ourselves to Jesus Christ as an "empty vessel" to be used by Him, He tells us, "I am with you; that is all

you need. My power shows up best in weak people" (2 Cor. 12:9, *TLB*). Weak people, that's what we are. And the apostle Paul went on to write in 2 Corinthians 12:9, "I am glad to boast about how weak I am; I am glad to be a living demonstration of Christ's power, instead of showing off my own power and abilities" (*TLB*).

So, we are called to be hospitable in Christ's strength, by His power and not by our own. As we give ourselves to God, we discover that He gives back to us a wonderful present of His power and the ability to demonstrate Christ's love to those He sends our way. A side benefit of being hospitable was described by Robert Lewis Stevenson, when he said, "A friend is a present you give yourself." God has given many friends to those who will open their hearts and their homes.

He has some friends all wrapped up just for you. By sharing your life with others in an open and inviting manner, you will be discovering the treasures of friendships God has planned for you to enjoy!

> *Those who make the worst use of their time are the first to complain of its shortness.*
>
> —Jean de La Bruyere

God Is Calling You

1. Have you ever had company stop by just as your family was about to sit down to the dinner table? How did you respond to that situation?

2. We know that God desires us to be a combination of both

46

Mary and Martha in our daily walk with Him. If you are a Mary, how can you become a little more like a Martha? And if you are a Martha, how can you become a little more like a Mary?

3. Can you think of a time when God wanted to open a door for you to be hospitable to someone, but you didn't allow His power to work through you? If the opportunity arose again, how could you handle it differently remembering that God will never call you to do anything He has not already equipped you to do?

4. Reread the "Prayer of Welcome" in this chapter. Now write your own prayer of welcome adapting and personalizing it to reflect your heart and home.

Note:
1. Bonnie Wheeler, *The Hurrier I Go* (Ventura, CA: Regal Books, 1985), p. 118. Used by permission.

4

The Princess and Her Siamese Cats

The doorbell rang early one Saturday morning. I was busy ladling out the pancakes for our traditional leisurely Saturday morning breakfast with the children, now 3, 6, 7 and 11 years old. My husband went to the door and came back with a puzzled look on his face. He was holding a yellow envelope in his hand; I recognized it was a telegram.

As I set a platter of fresh blueberry pancakes on the table, he sat down and opened the telegram saying, "I wonder who would be sending us a telegram?" I leaned over his shoulder thinking it could be an emergency message from some family member.

The telegram read as follows: "Shushila Uberoi arriving Sunday morning, 10 A.M., Los Angeles International Airport, via Indian Airways. Please meet her. STOP. Needs shelter for a short time. STOP. Letter follows. Signed Roy and Coral Baker."

My husband and I looked at each other, amazed! At once, we realized that we had been sent an unexpected gift from India by our long-time missionary friends. Apparently there was a good reason for this journey, but we had no idea why she was being sent to us.

She was a stranger; what did she look like? Was she an angel sent by God? I immediately wondered if she liked children, since we had four in our home. Three or four weeks with a stranger who did not like children could be difficult.

Fortunately, by this time we had added a guest room off our garage, so I had a place where I could put this "stranger" being sent our way. In other years when we had houseguests, I had to bunk the children together in one or two bedrooms in sleeping bags while we gave their bedrooms to our visitors. It was a relief to know that I did not have to upset the family routine with this sudden appearance of yet another houseguest!

Somehow I knew this was not going to be a short visit, a quick prayer or an hour of listening to someone. I felt like old Abraham, being called to share my tent, food, family and friends with this person for a short time. It turned out that God called us to share our home and our hearts with Shushila for nearly six months. Looking back, we see the blessings this brought to all of us. She was certainly like an angel to us.

> *Never let your brotherly love fail, nor*
> *refuse to extend your hospitality to*
> *strangers—sometimes men have*
> *entertained angels unawares.*
> —Hebrews 13:1,2, *Phillips*

We read of Abraham's hospitality in Genesis 18:1–14:

"THE LORD APPEARED again to Abraham while he was living in the oak grove at Mamre. This is the way it happened: One hot summer afternoon as he was sitting in the opening of his tent, he suddenly noticed three men coming toward him. He sprang up and ran to meet them and welcomed them. 'Sirs,' he said, 'please don't go any further. Stop awhile and rest here in the shade of this tree while I get water to refresh your feet, and a bite to eat to strengthen you. Do stay awhile before continuing your journey.' 'All right,' they said, 'do as you have said.' Then Abraham ran back to the tent and said to Sarah, 'Quick! Mix up some pancakes! Use your best flour, and make enough for the three of them!' Then he ran out to the herd and selected a fat calf and told a servant to hurry and butcher it. Soon, taking them cheese and milk and the roast veal, he set it before the men and stood beneath the trees beside them as they ate. 'Where is Sarah, your wife?' they asked him. 'In the tent,' Abraham replied. Then the Lord said, 'Next year I will give you and Sarah a son!' (Sarah was listening from the tent door behind him.) Now Abraham and Sarah were both very old, and Sarah was long since past the time when she could have a baby. So Sarah laughed silently. 'A woman my age have a baby?' she scoffed to herself. 'And with a husband as old as mine?' Then God said to Abraham, 'Why did Sarah laugh? Why did she say "Can an old woman like me have a baby?" Is anything too hard for God? Next year, just as I told you, I will certainly see to it that Sarah has a son'" (*TLB*).

I could relate to Sarah as she laughed, in her case at her age and inability to have a baby. At my age I wondered how I could handle a guest from the Indian culture for even three weeks. As

I went on making blueberry pancakes for the family, I thought a lot about Abraham and Sarah, and the three men who were sent from God unexpectedly. Abraham had opened his heart and his tent to these men—just as I should do for Shushila.

Abraham had a servant heart, as he asked them to rest in the shade of a tree and got water to bathe their feet. He was sensitive to their tiredness, and urged them to stay awhile before continuing on their journey. I compared this to Shushila's circumstances, and decided that indeed she probably will need a three-week rest before she goes on her journey. Little did I realize that her rest would be several months. Had God sent someone to announce this visitation to me I might have laughed like Sarah, or cried!

After clearing up the breakfast dishes, I took a look at the Scriptures and realized that not only had Abraham invited them in to stay and rest before continuing their journey, but this old man had quickly run back to the tent to encourage Sarah to prepare the best food for them while he hurried to the herd and selected a fat calf for the meal. It appears that he served the best he had to these strangers.

If God could enable Abraham, who was nearly 100 years old, and his wife Sarah to be so gracious as to provide their very best food and restful, comfortable surroundings for the three strangers, I decided that He could enable me to be gracious to my "stranger" too. I chose a Scripture verse that I would use over and over again in the next six months: "Is anything too hard for God?" (Gen. 18:14, TLB).

Bill and I decided that he would drive to the airport on Sunday morning to meet Shushila while I took the children to Sunday School and church. The children were really excited at the prospect of a houseguest from India.

By now they realized God had given us the gift of hospitality to the peoples of the world, and they had enjoyed visits from people from many different continents. Never before, however, had we had a houseguest from India.

After church, we hurriedly piled ourselves into the car and drove home to see if Father had returned with Shushila. When I parked in the driveway, it was as though the car exploded as the children tumbled out and ran to the front door, calling to me to hurry with the key so they could see if Shushila was there. She had not arrived yet, so we began final dinner preparations and waited for them to return from the airport.

Then we heard the front door open and voices. All of us ran to the front door to greet our guest, and were impressed to see her in a beautiful silk sari, long dangling earrings, with her hair pulled up into the traditional Indian bun, many rings on her fingers and Indian glass and gold bracelets tinkling on her arms. As she greeted us, she had the traditional Indian accent and looked so much like an Indian that I found it hard to believe she had been born and raised in Texas! While she appeared to have ample means, she really only had what she was wearing and what little money and belongings she was able to bring with her.

Slowly, after she had time to eat and relax, she shared her story with us of how God had led her back to the United States. She spun a fascinating story that afternoon while the younger children napped.

She had been raised in a home where her stepfather beat her until finally she had been sent to live in a foster home for the last years of her high school education. In this home, her foster parents encouraged her to attend college. So Shushila went on to the University of Chicago, then worked in New York before going to India.

She told us that she had been hired as a reporter for a newspaper in India, and had written for Nehru when he was head of India's government. She apparently lived in the jet set of the upper strata of society in India and through this group of people met a handsome young prince. She had been in India only a short time when she married the prince, a Hindu and head of a princely state of India. The main palace was in Cooch

Behar and had over 300 rooms! As I looked at our simple, rather frayed household, I wondered how she was going to cope with us here. I thought of the very small guest room she would occupy.

Shushila went on to tell us that the prince also had a palace in the woodlands of Calcutta, and one palace in Darjeeling with 42 other houses on the property where friends and servants lived. It became very obvious as she talked that she had lived like a princess (and that all of her jewelry was real). She also mentioned the fact they had traveled to Europe frequently for weekends, or during the monsoon time to escape bad weather. They shopped for clothing in Paris and enjoyed health spas in Germany. It was nothing to fly to Vienna for a concert or to spend a weekend!

However, one day the prince's elder brother tried to get him to sell a large plot of private land in Calcutta that had been left jointly to them by their grandfather. Both brothers needed to give consent for the sale of this property. Since the prince would not consent, his brother, who was heavily in debt due to drugs, women and gambling, had the prince killed while Shushila was in London on a shopping expeditior.. He was hit on the head, and the palace was set afire. His death had been called accidental, by fire. The older brother sold the land in Calcutta not long after and was able to pay off some pressing debts.

Shushila also shared with us the interesting fact that the prince's family destroyed the will, which the prince had made after their marriage that provided for Shushila's welfare with much wealth in the event of her husband's death. The family brought out the old will that gave her nothing as the wife of the prince. She had lived as a princess in India; now she was not given a penny and was practically a pauper.

For seven long years Shushila was a widow receiving only a little help from some of the prince's relatives, as well as from friends in India. She lived in a Bombay hotel most of the time.

a guest room occupied for any length of
. Maybe your family has a symbol, such
ready to "perk up" a discouraged neigh-
er children, the symbol of your hospital-
ar around which your children's friends
oard of puzzles and games to enjoy

have a popcorn popper that calls the
und a common bowl and visit. Another
ould be a Ping-Pong table or a basket-
ay where people can laugh, shout, jump
se, the dining room table where people
r's eyes and listen as they eat together is
spitality in any home.
ave a fireplace or an outdoor fire pit
bors can gather on a cool evening to
l cozy and secure in revealing inner
. Each family, and person, needs to ask
ind of hospitality they are to share with
God sends to their door.
of *Open Heart, Open Home*[1], a book
"True hospitality is a gift of the Spirit."
that, when needed, she has received
eating heart to heart human bonds."
Your Spiritual Gifts Can Help Your
at while all Christians do not have the
e responsible to have a role in enter-
people over for dinner, occasionally
he night, taking a visitor out, hosting
ur car, making sure that new people
unity, are all included in our Christian
s come easily, and we never feel that
o it as well as, we should. But we do
agner is clarifying the point that there
by the Holy Spirit and exercised in

Then she met her second husband, Mr. Uberoi, a very wealthy manufacturer of pharmaceutical drugs. He was widowed, had several children and was a great deal older than Shushila. It was more a marriage of convenience for them both. They lived luxuriously in the whole top floor of an apartment building that Mr. Uberoi owned. Again Shushila's life-style reverted to the elegance and wealth she had known with the prince. She flew to Europe for her perfume, designer clothes and concerts. However, there was a hunger in her heart for "something more."

One night she had a dream in which Christ was beckoning to her; she responded in faith to Him. Shushila's mother had been a Christian, and she had planted in Shushila the seeds of the gospel message. Shushila had attended a church during her childhood. Even though the home was an unhappy arena, she had the teachings of Christ from the very beginning, from her mother and her Sunday School teachers. Now, at the age of 50, she turned to the Lord in simple, childlike faith. I was reminded of Proverbs 22:6, "Train up a child in the way he should go: and when he is old, he will not depart from it" (KJV).

She longed to read a Bible, but none was available. Shushila told her Sikh husband about the vision, and he was very sympathetic to her faith. He urged her to call the missionaries who recently had rented one of his flats. She called the flat and that is when she came in contact with Roy and Coral Baker. They arranged to take her to a Bible-teaching church, and brought her a Bible. This was a miracle in itself, since Bombay was a very large city with very few Christian churches in it. Part of the miracle was the fact that these missionaries had rented the flat about one month before Shushila had her dream.

Shushila's husband had a very serious heart condition and knew he did not have many years left. When he saw how lonely she was for her family, he urged her to return to the

United States. He could not predict how she would be treated after his death, so he wanted to be assured that she was settled back in her own country before he died. He did die not long after she returned to this country. Since he knew all about her vision of Christ, it is possible that he came in faith to the Lord Jesus. We do know that he was happy for Shushila's faith and encouraged her in it.

The story Shushila shared with us that Sunday afternoon would have been blessing enough from God for opening our home to her for any length of time. For indeed we were hearing the wonders God was performing in our generation!

Eventually Shushila found work at my husband's office. When it became evident she would stay on in Glendale, we began to collect furniture from friends and thrift shops for an apartment for her. After six months, she was able to rent an apartment and be on her own. We became her family in Christ, and she was an "auntie" to our children, spending Sundays and holidays with us.

In the meantime, our children learned much about Indian culture, and I learned how to wear a sari and do a little Indian cooking. We all learned much about the Indian life-style and thought patterns (which were very different from ours).

We also learned a new tolerance—Shushila was a heavy smoker when she first arrived. I was very thankful for the separate guest room where she did most of her smoking. In time she was able to quit smoking for her health's sake, but we learned patience and acceptance as the Lord made our hearts tender toward this new Christian.

One thing I neglected to mention is that when Shushila came from India, she brought with her two Siamese cats. They were "her children" since she had never had any children by either of her husbands. She said she could not leave them behind in India. Since these Siamese cats had never lived outside, she decided they would live in the guest room with her!

Now, these cats were not calm by nature, and we had

grasscloth on the walls of the guest room. Can you guess what happened to our walls? When the cats got lonely for Shushila, they would chase each other around the room and climb up and down the grasscloth walls! It was obvious, as I cleaned the room, that the grasscloth was going to have to be a casualty of our call to Christian hospitality. But really, when we weighed the blessings that God brought our way through Shushila, the grasscloth was not an important commodity.

> *God often comforts us, not by changing the circumstances of our lives, but by changing our attitudes toward them.*

Whenever I think of Shushila, I think of Matthew 25:35, "For I was hungry, and you gave Me something to eat; I was thirsty, and you gave Me drink; I was a stranger, and you invited Me in" (*NASB*). Yes, Shushila was hungry, to know more of Jesus Christ; and thirsty, to drink in His Word and learn to pray and trust God. She was the stranger whom God sent to us to invite in, and because we were allowed that privilege, we were indeed blessed by the Father (see Matt. 25:34). Many hours were spent with Shushila around our kitchen table pouring over God's Word, discussing it "precept upon precept" and then praying together that God would do His work in all of our lives.

Abraham had his tent, and we had our guest room! Not everyone is called to share their tent, or their guest room, for six months. But God will enable us to enjoy the time, and bless us in the service that He calls our families to.

Your call to hospitality may be symbolized by something

entirely different than a guest room occupied for any length of time by a houseguest. Maybe your family has a symbol, such as a coffeepot always ready to "perk up" a discouraged neighbor. If you have younger children, the symbol of your hospitality may be a cookie jar around which your children's friends can gather or a cupboard of puzzles and games to enjoy together.

Your family may have a popcorn popper that calls the neighbors to gather around a common bowl and visit. Another symbol of hospitality could be a Ping-Pong table or a basketball hoop in the driveway where people can laugh, shout, jump and play. And, of course, the dining room table where people can look into each other's eyes and listen as they eat together is a familiar symbol of hospitality in any home.

Your family may have a fireplace or an outdoor fire pit where friends and neighbors can gather on a cool evening to dream dreams and feel cozy and secure in revealing inner thoughts to one another. Each family, and person, needs to ask God to show them the kind of hospitality they are to share with others, "the strangers" God sends to their door.

Karen Mains, author of *Open Heart, Open Home*[1], a book about hospitality, says: "True hospitality is a gift of the Spirit." She goes on to explain that, when needed, she has received supernatural help for "creating heart to heart human bonds."

C. Peter Wagner, in *Your Spiritual Gifts Can Help Your Church Grow*[2], states that while all Christians do not have the gift of hospitality, they are responsible to have a role in entertaining guests. "Having people over for dinner, occasionally putting a person up for the night, taking a visitor out, hosting church parties, loaning our car, making sure that new people are oriented to the community, are all included in our Christian role. None of these things come easily, and we never feel that we do as much of it, or do it as well as, we should. But we do make an effort." Thus, Wagner is clarifying the point that there is the Christian gift given by the Holy Spirit and exercised in some lives, but every Christian has "a role" given by God in the field of hospitality, though it may not be an outstanding gift.

He points out the way Christian roles operate alongside spiritual gifts. This is vividly illustrated by the gift of giving. There is no question that every Christian is to give part of his or her income to the Lord. According to the Bible, every person should set definite giving goals and give with cheerfulness (see 2 Cor. 9:7).

Wagner says that this is a Christian role, and there are no exceptions. "Rich Christians should give, and poor Christians should give. Young marrieds who have low income and high expenses should give alongside more mature people who are financially secure." He goes on to state, "The gift of giving is the special ability God gives to certain members of the Body of Christ to contribute their material resources to the work of the Lord with liberality and cheerfulness."

The same definition could be given for hospitality. The gift of hospitality is the special God-given ability to certain members of the Body of Christ to open their hearts, homes and other resources with liberality and cheerfulness to all people in need. Alongside the gift is "the role" of sharing as a Christian as much as God enables you to share, thus exercising some form of hospitality to which God definitely calls you.

Our family has never regretted "the role" we played in Shushila's life and spiritual development. It was truly a privilege and a blessing to be able to sit at the table and read and discuss the Bible with her for many hours during those six months. It is not often that an opportunity to nurture a "new babe in Christ" comes along in such a way.

We felt that God gave us the time to feed her from His Word before she was launched out into the world from the little nest she had in our guest room.

It has been some 20 years since Shushila's visit. She is still walking with the Lord, growing up in Christ and trusting Him by faith. We thank God for the time He allowed us to invest ourselves, our home and our hearts in her life!

> *Everyone is trying to accomplish something big, not realizing that life is made up of little things.*

God Is Calling You

1. Have you ever had a Shushila in your life, that is, someone who came into your home for a short time, but ended up staying much longer than you had expected? Thinking back over the experience, was it a time of nurturing for both you and your guest? Was it a time used to share the love of God, as well as your home and food? If you could relive the experience, would you do things differently?

2. Have you ever had the opportunity to share your life with someone from another culture? You may not ever have the experience of having someone from another country live in your home for a time, but there are several ways to share cultures with others such as inviting someone who may be visiting your church from another country to your home for dinner. Or you could go to the local college and invite a foreign student to spend an evening with your family. Can you think of other ways?

3. You may not be called to have an extended houseguest. The author listed several other symbols of hospitality you may have in your home, such as a coffeepot, popcorn pop-

per, cupboard of games and puzzles or a fireplace. What symbols of hospitality do you feel God has called you to use in this type of ministry?

4. Can you think of someone God has brought into your home to whom you were able to witness or encourage in his or her Christian walk? Perhaps someone you opened your heart and home to came at just the time you needed an extra dose of God's love and healing!

Notes:
1. Karen Mains, *Open Heart, Open Home* (Elgin, IL: David C. Cook Publishing Co., 1980).
2. C. Peter Wagner, *Your Spiritual Gifts Can Help Your Church Grow* (Ventura, CA: Regal Books, 1979).

5

Caring for Caterpillars

There is a saying: "If you ever want to love a butterfly, you have to first care for a lot of little caterpillars." Caterpillars here applies to other people's children, your own children and their friends. Even after 33 years, I find myself being hospitable to my children's friends. My son calls periodically from Glendale and asks, "Mom, is it OK if I bring my girlfriend home this weekend?" And I always say, "Sure, that's fine."

Recently, we had our two granddaughters, Shelley, 5, and Kimmie, 3, spending a few days with us. At the same time, a young seminarian working at the church was staying in one of our upstairs bedrooms; an out-of-state board member from my husband's business was staying in another. My son gave me one of those calls nearing the weekend, and I said, "Of course, come on along." It was obvious that we had run out of beds, so when they arrived I told our son Bill that he would have to sleep on the davenport in the living room. I put his girlfriend in the last guest room upstairs.

As I was bustling about in the kitchen the next morning getting breakfast for the little girls, the first ones up, Shelley said, "Grandma, there is someone asleep in the living room on the davenport. Is it your minister, or is it Uncle Billy?" I chuckled. They do look somewhat alike and are about the same age. I was able to assure her that it was her Uncle Billy. She responded, "Well, if it's Uncle Billy, I'll go and kiss him. But I didn't want to go and kiss the minister!"

You may be thinking, "My word, a commitment of over 33 years to caterpillars! I don't know if I am willing to make this." But you know, if you signed up to be a mother, it goes with the territory.

Christ calls you to this kind of commitment as a Christian mother, and I'll tell you why. Remember what I said, "If you ever want to love a butterfly, you have to first care for a lot of little caterpillars," and that means wiping their noses and running to the bathroom when they need help. And they aren't all your children you will be helping either, for mothers in the neighborhood will be delighted for you to care for their little caterpillars if you are willing. These mothers are glad to send their children with muddy feet, sticky fingers and high-pitched voices into your home. And you have the privilege of treating these children with a respect and dignity they may never receive in their own homes!

In addition, because these youngsters have become comfortable in your home, you will be able to establish a great communication with them as they become teenagers, and believe me God will never let any of your loving acts or words go to waste. Your life may be the only Christian witness these children will ever see. What a privilege and, at the same time, a wonderful God-given "responsibility-opportunity"!

> *When opportunity knocks at the door, some people are out in the yard looking for four-leaf clovers.*

A mother once wrote about her frustration concerning all the caterpillars she had around her house:

Is it defeat?
The endless spatters on the wall—
Crumbs and paper cups—
Half empty coffee cups—
Litter of living—
Why can't my house be
Spic and span and shining?
A testimony to organization
And order and efficiency?
There must be an answer.
Is it love?

—Linda Metzke[1]

If God calls you to nurture young children, teens or collegians, He will provide the power of the Holy Spirit to be a creative Christian friend and counselor. Some mothers of young children have Bible clubs, as I did, for their children after school. The first thing we would do at our Bible clubs is have punch and a treat, and then we would take 15 or 20 minutes at the most in the Bible. I had inexpensive little pocket Bibles for each child. I kept them in a special drawer where they knew they could always find "their" Bible. Most of the children who came into my home didn't have a Bible, or weren't allowed to underline verses in their Bible at home. As we sat around the kitchen table, we would underline verses and talk about them. If there were some special problems during the week, I would choose appropriate Scriptures. Every child was told how precious he was to God. Then after our little Bible lesson we would make cookies or a cake, and sometimes Popsicles for a treat later in the week. I always had "a hook"! Later the children would take their cake or cookies home to share.

At Christmastime we would make special items, string pop-corn and make popcorn balls. We made Christmas cards and decorations from the last year's cards. While doing all these things we would talk about the real meaning of Christmas.

The Lord will give some of you creative ideas for this kind of hospitality in your neighborhood. But, remember the "hook" needs to be there to get them to come to the Bible Club. After they participated in the "hook," they would play—and at 5:00, or earlier if their mothers wanted them home, the little caterpillars would go "crawling off" to their individual homes.

You may be sitting there thinking, This is too giant a com-mitment for me. I took it one day at a time. And that's all God asks you to do too! He says, "You're an empty vessel, you're weak, you're frail, but I'll give you enough strength for each day."

He gives strength to the weary. "And *to him* who lacks might He increases power. Though youths grow weary and tired, *And* vigorous young men stumble badly, Yet those who wait for the Lord Will gain new strength; They will mount up with wings like eagles, They will run and not get tired, They will walk and not become weary" (Isa. 40:29–31, *NASB*).

I am still able to say that after 33 years God has been faithful—and it works! It really works when you depend upon God one day at a time. By depending on the Lord one day at a time, then there will be no regrets for missed opportunities with the children in our lives.

To My Grown-Up Sons

My hands were busy through the day
    I didn't have much time to play
The little games you asked me to
    I didn't have much time for you.

I'd wash your clothes, I'd sew and cook
But when you'd bring your picture book
And ask me please to share your fun
I'd say, "A little later, son."

I'd tuck you in all safe at night
And hear your prayers, turn out the light
Then tiptoe softly to the door
I wish I'd stayed a minute more.

For life is short, the years rush past
A little boy grows up so fast
No longer is he at your side
His precious secrets to confide.

The picture book is put away
There are no more games to play
No good night kiss, no prayers to hear—
That all belongs to yesteryear.

My hands once busy now lie still
The days are long and hard to fill
I wish I might go back and do
The little things you asked me to.

—Anonymous[2]

Being a hospitable parent, grandparent, aunt, cousin or
friend of a child means never being so busy that you can't take
time to spend a few moments reading a storybook or listening
to a long rendition of a sports event. Later on you will be privileged to hear bigger and more important things, if you are willing to take time with these children and their friends when they
are young. That's hospitality! For an investment in the King-

dom of God, take the moments that God gives you with young people and make the most of them.

In Mark 10:14, Jesus said, "Suffer the little children to come unto me, and forbid them not for of such is the kingdom of God" (*KJV*). Mark 10:16 tells us that Christ took the children up in His arms and put His hands upon them and blessed them. Today we are the Lord Jesus' hands in our neighborhoods and communities. Many lives will never be blessed with the touch of Christ unless Christians are willing to use their hands to bless in various ways the many children whose parents are just too busy for them. What an opportunity to extend hospitality to children such as these!

There will be many humorous moments as we minister to these little ones. Once I remember opening the bathroom door after Bible club and finding two ducks swimming in my bathtub. The girls had decided to bring the ducks in and let them swim.

Another friend of mine tells about one particularly hectic birthday party. As she waved good-bye with great relief to the boys and girls, she went back inside and headed for the bathroom. She thought, *What a relief all the children have gone home!* She opened the door of her bathroom, and there stood little Jimmy, one of the neighborhood boys, vigorously brushing his teeth with *her* toothbrush.

Shocked, she said, "Jimmy, what are you doing?"

He looked at her calmly and said, "Its all right Mrs. Williams. I brush my teeth with this toothbrush every time I come over here." Now this really didn't seem too funny to my friend then, but by the time she bought her new toothbrush, she had recovered from the shock and decided it was downright funny!

She hid her new toothbrush and left the old one for Jimmy to use every time he came to their house. It has become a family joke and a source of wonderful laughter for the whole family through the years.

You will have things like that happen to you too. Be prepared! But it's OK. It all adds to your memories.

A real home is a hospitable playground. If God is calling you to this kind of hospitality and ministry, be careful to have a house or yard where children can play. If your home is going to be hospitable to children of all ages, you have to have a home where anything can get broken. If you have inherited china, beautiful vases and antiques, don't get them out until the children are older—or put them on high shelves where they will be safe. You want the children to be able to play in your house and yard, and not have to worry about them. Yes, children must learn respect for others' property, but accidents will still happen. If a dish does get broken, you must decide what is more important, the child or the dish.

You know, it's usually easy to pick out the children whose mothers are perfect housekeepers and who value their furniture, houses and their yards more than they do children. Do you know how? They're always being sent to play in your yard or to the school playground. What a privilege to extend hospitality to children like that who aren't comfortable in their own homes. They will probably never experience that kind of Christian hospitality anywhere else.

This is a cute little poem; you will know why I share it with you. In fact, one of these things I left undone many times. I'll let you guess which one!

> The beds are all made and the dishes are done.
> The kids are all shiny and ready for fun;
> The clothes are all ironed, no dirt on this floor.
> No doubt you've guessed I'm calling next door.

> —Anonymous[3]

You know, the floor used to get so bad in my house that one of my sons would walk barefoot across the floor in the morning and say, "Mom, my feet are sticking to the floor." This was probably the day after one of the Bible clubs had been there baking cookies or making Popsicles. I would say, "Oh, I guess today is the day I am going to have to scrub that floor!" I operated on the principle that I put down one time in this little poem:

> Come in! Sit down!
> My home is clean enough!
> No, it's not perfect!
> But I have time for friends!

Now, you may not be called to do all we have talked about. Remember, God calls and gifts each one of us differently. I am just sharing with you some of the "funnies" out of my life, as well as some of the creative ways God has allowed me to minister hospitably to children in my neighborhood.

Remember, one day at a time He will empower you with the ability to cope and to enjoy, and then to look back—as I now look back. I think about those years as some of the best years of my life, and yet I think of what Corrie ten Boom said, "The best is yet to come." There will be a grand reunion in heaven one day with all of the "little caterpillars" who came to faith in Christ and became "beautiful butterflies" to the glory of God!

With each year, your ministry of hospitality will change. Perhaps already you have gone beyond a ministry to small children, into another ministry to your neighbors and other adults in the community. But if you are a grandparent, aunt, cousin or friend, your ministry to young children will "begin again."

Increasingly, with the growing number of divorces, many children are living in single-parent homes. And since more and more mothers are working full time, children may not receive the close-level attention they need. Grandparents, and other Christian adults can fill in for absentee parents.

When grandchildren visit, there is the beautiful challenge of how to grow close to them, understand their feelings and build them up. A grandfather plays an especially vital role with grandchildren when there is no father. Why not use a notebook to record the story of a child's visit, making him feel very welcome and worthwhile. Before the child can write, ask him what he has been doing all day while Grandpa worked, and put down a few sentences in his own words, dating each story. Grandma can keep a diary, too.

Some pages will tell of making cookies with Grandmother, learning to sew and other fun things that Grandma taught. Other pages record sadness over the death of a pet, or loneliness. This will be an honest record of what happened on visits to grandparents, and years later the story will have rich meaning for the grandchild.

Long-distance grandparents can use letters, the phone or a tape recorder for communication. As grandparents keep in touch with their grandchildren, I believe these overtures of love and interest show real hospitality and will pay off in years to come. A letter, at least once every two weeks, is especially meaningful as children love to get mail. One grandmother I know, Maureen Murphy, chooses a book and records it on the tape recorder, ringing a bell each time the page should be turned. She sends the book and tape at the same time, thus having a private story hour with her grandchild, too. Visit them as often as you can, and invite them to visit you in return.

One day while visiting with my daughter Kathy and her three little girls, who were all under six years of age, the doorbell rang. I ran to answer it and there stood the lady mail carrier with a package. As I signed for it she said, "You must be the grandmother who writes all the cards and letters these little girls love to get."

I told her that both grandmothers send mail to them. She obviously enjoyed delivering that mail as she realized what joy it brought to the children.

If you don't have grandchildren of your own, why not

"adopt" one and begin to make some happy memories for that child.

One little girl wrote these words, "Grandmas don't have to do anything, except be there. They're old, so they shouldn't play hard or run. It is enough if they drive us to the market where the pretend horse is, and have lots of dimes ready. Or, if they take us for walks, they should slow down past things like leaves or caterpillars. They should never say: 'hurry up' . . . . Everybody should try to have one, especially if you don't have television, because grandmas are the only grown ups who have got time."[4]

This little girl knew that her grandma always had time for her, often devoting her days during those special visits to just being together—never mind the dishes and the housework for awhile. What a legacy of memories we can leave to our grandchildren as we open our hearts and homes to them. Wouldn't it be nice to someday get a letter like this:

Dear Grandma,

I want to thank you for the love you've given me through all these years, from toddler to teenager. Thanks, too, for the time you gave so that Mom and Dad could have time alone together. What fun I've had with you on those visits to your home, and on the weekends you've come to my home to care for us.

Thank you for letting me bake cookies in your kitchen and never complaining about the mess I made. Thank you for always having time to read me a story, or tell me one about when you were little. And for the fun things you shared with me about Mom when she was a little girl.

Thank you for the nights spent in your big bed when I was afraid. And for not being cross when I threw up on your comforter! Thank you for telling me about that special room Jesus had all ready for Grandpa when he went to heaven.

Yes, thank you for all the wonderful years of love and endless hugs. Thank you for always having time for me and just being there to listen to my dreams.

I love you!

As older people ministering to young children, we also have the tremendous opportunity to reveal the love of Jesus Christ. "All thy children shall be taught of the Lord; and great shall be the peace of thy children" (Isa. 54:13, *KJV*). If you have felt the call to minister to children, remember that prayer undergirds all that you do. "Don't worry about anything; instead, pray about everything; tell God your needs and don't forget to thank him for his answers. If you do this you will experience God's peace, which is far more wonderful than the human mind can understand. His peace will keep your thoughts and your hearts quiet and at rest as you trust in Christ Jesus" (Phil. 4:6,7, *TLB*).

A request in these prayers for children would be for faith in God. We know that life is hopeless without faith in Jesus Christ, and we want our grandchildren—and other children we minister to—to be covered with the righteousness of Jesus Christ.

Henrietta Mears, authority on teaching young people, once noted, "It's easier to teach the facts of Genesis than to help a youth discover why he is here and what Christ's will is for him." As adults ministering to children, we need to make a habit of talking about answers to prayer, of God's plan for the lives of each person in this world, and we must be willing to share our own faith. More valuable than money in the bank, securities, jewelry or real estate are the intangible spiritual assets we can share with children at every stage of their lives.

Henri Nouwen writes in his book *Reaching Out*[5] about the relationship between parents and children in terms of hospitality. He focuses in on the Bible's teaching that children are a precious gift from God to be loved and cared for, not something to own, rule and dominate. He further states that children are like strangers coming into our lives, with their own uniqueness of style, rhythm and idiosyncrasies. He states that it requires time, patience and energy to make them feel at home. Thus, the Scriptures call us to give to our children what every stranger needs—acceptance, love, time, safety, friendship, space and freedom.

By providing these needs, we are allowing our "little caterpillars" to develop, and one day they will break forth and fly away as "beautiful butterflies." One of the most powerful posters illustrating this fact has a picture of a child with the caption, "A child is someone who comes into your life for a brief time and then disappears into an adult."

Molding Life

I took a piece of plastic clay
And idly fashioned it one day;
And, as my fingers pressed it still,
It moved, and yielded to my will.

I came again when days were past;
The bit of clay was hard at last;
The form I gave it still it bore,
But I could change that form no more.

I took a piece of living clay,
And gently formed it day by day,
And molded with my power and art
A young child's soft and yielding heart.

I came again when years were gone,
It was a man I looked upon;

He still that early impress wore
And I could change him nevermore.

—Anonymous[6]

The caterpillar grows within the cocoon, and breaks forth into a beautiful butterfly. Remember if you want to love a butterfly, you must be willing to care for a lot of little caterpillars.

So we are privileged to minister to children who will emerge one day as beautiful butterflies gently formed by the Holy Spirit. Have you touched a caterpillar for Christ lately?

The New Generation

Is it any wonder, Lord,
    that the new generation
      is rebelling against
         their parents' double standard
           of morals
         and their parents' worship of
           money and material things.

Most of them have never been shown
    real love
      real concern
        real honesty
          real morality
            real worship of the true
            God
               Jesus Christ, Lord and
               Saviour.

Dear Lord, I pray that
    in their rebellion
      in their struggle

in their search
        for real meaning in life
May this new generation find
    by your Holy Spirit's leading
    the Truth
        in Jesus Christ.

And, Lord, somehow involve me
    in sharing you
        with this new generation.

—Doris W. Greig

God Is Calling You

1. Do you feel your home is inviting to the children and young people in your neighborhood? What steps could you take to make it even more inviting?

2. Have you ever opened up your home for a gathering of children such as a Bible club? What kinds of activities did you plan? Would you be willing to have a neighborhood Bible study for children or for adults in your neighborhood or community?

3. Is there a young person in your life right now, perhaps one of your own, a neighbor child or a Sunday School student, who could use a little of your time? How could you arrange time from your busy day to accommodate that need?

4. Lots of memorable things happen when you open your heart and home to youngsters. What are some of the most amusing times you can remember?

Notes:
1. Linda Kuzan Metzke, "Is It Defeat?" Used by permission.
2. Anonymous. From *The Hurrier I Go* by Bonnie Wheeler (Ventura, CA: Regal Books, 1985), p. 88.
3. M.M. Fay, "Neatness," from *Sourcebook for Mothers* by Eleanor Doan (Grand Rapids, MI: Zondervan Publishing House, 1969).
4. "Grandparents Are for Hugging," *U.S. Catholic*, August, 1982.
5. Henri J.M. Nouwen, *Reaching Out: The Three Movements of Spiritual Life* (New York: Doubleday, 1975).
6. Author unknown. From *Sourcebook for Mothers* by Eleanor Doan.

6

Some Became Butterflies— But Not Without Risk

I'll never forget preparing peanut butter and jelly sandwiches for my four-year-old Kathy and her five-year-old friend Louisa. My 15-month-old son was sitting in his high chair, banging his spoon against the tray to capture my attention.

Louisa was looking at me very seriously as I spread the peanut butter on one slice of bread and jelly on the other. She seemed a little worried; I wondered if her mother did it differently.

Then Louisa asked, "Mrs. Greig, are you going to have a baby?"

"Well," I said as I looked down at my greatly expanded waistline, "I certainly look pregnant, don't I. I must be pregnant."

Before Louisa could ask how babies were made, I decided I'd better call her mother and let her share with Louisa what she wants shared at this point in her life. I thought of different customs in different lands, and knew that Louisa's mother, a war bride, might want to handle the situation totally differently than I would in our home.

In the meantime, Louisa continued to peer at me inquisitively, leaning forward.

"Yes, Louisa, I *am* going to have a baby in about one week."

Still in a serious mood, she looked at me and said, "Do you know that your baby will be Chinese?"

What did she say? I wondered if I had heard her correctly. I had been so involved in making sandwiches that I had lost the trend of conversation.

"Why is that?"

And Louisa said, "Because every third baby born into the world is Chinese, Mrs. Greig! Didn't you know that?"

"Well," I said, "I didn't know that. But Louisa, I think that means that one out of every three babies in the whole wide world are Chinese, but in our family we will probably have another little girl just like Kathy, or a little boy just like Billy."

"Are you sure, Mrs. Greig?" And I could see the wheels turning in her head. I knew that she would go home to her mother and ask for an explanation, so I served the sandwiches and ignored the topic of conversation, feeling that we had covered enough of it in my kitchen! Later, I called her mother and we both had a good laugh over Louisa's theory. I'm sure mother and daughter had a good talk that day.

Our children and their friends can really bring a lot of life and laughter, as well as fingerprints and scattered toys, into our lives. But their candid comments make it all worthwhile.

We Christians have the privilege of treating children, our own and our neighbors', with respect and dignity, no matter what the topic of conversation may be. So I'm glad I didn't laugh at Louisa and say, "You're so foolish, Dear." I could have gone into a long technical explanation of why we would not have a Chinese baby. But Louisa was one of my "little caterpillars" and to her I was a reflection of Jesus Christ, His dignity and His love.

When Louisa attended school in the fall with my daughter, she came to our home every morning one half hour early just to sit at our breakfast table and have family devotions with us. If she hadn't had breakfast, she would eat with us; sometimes she'd have a second breakfast. We would read a little Scripture from *Little Visits with God*[1], and discuss what the Lord had in mind for our day. We would pray together as a family.

Make Us Hungry

Breakfast as usual
    at seven-thirty
And then our family time
    with you, Lord.

But what went wrong this morning?
    seven personalities were involved
        bumping together
            two adults
            five children.

Attitudes were crackling!
    with:
        indignation
        jealousy
            resentment
                impatience.

There was cereal spilled all over the floor!
    one boy wanted only cranberry juice
    one girl wanted his glass, too
        No one wanted to share
            not even a grapefruit!

The telephone jingled
    Just as we began to read your message
        I should have taken it off the hook!
And then the doorbell rang

Just as we joined hands to pray.

Lord, I guess there are mornings like this in every
     family,
   but please help me not to get discouraged
        and help us all to love one another more!
Lord, make us all hungry for you in the morning.

—Doris W. Greig

Louisa participated in our family devotions and joined in discussion and prayer all the way through sixth grade. We had a chance to introduce wonderful biblical concepts to her, this precious child sent to us by God. Yes, she strayed a bit in her teen years, but when she married and had her own little one, she and her husband began bringing her to Sunday School, just as she had come to Sunday School and church with our family. Those teen years had been painful for me, as well as for her mother. I feel that God has privileged me to be her spiritual mother, and with this privilege came many joys as well as pain.

I am reminded of the Lord Jesus' words from Matthew 25:45: "He will reply, 'I tell you the truth, whatever you did not do for one of the least of these, you did not do for me'" (NIV). Also, His words in Matthew 25:40 challenge every Christian to minister to the children. "I tell you the truth, whatever you did for one of the least of these brothers of mine, you did for me" (NIV).

As a young mother, I was tremendously blessed by a book called *Bless This Mess and Other Prayers*, by Jo Carr and Imogene Sorley from which the following poem is taken:

Thank you Lord,

For these other people's children—
With whom my son plays baseball,

With whom my daughter shares confidences,
With whom my small ones play
    And squabble
And learn that life is composed of relationships.

The things they learn at the hands of their peers
        I could never teach them.
The joys—and the heartaches—
    Dished out by their friends
Add color and life to their childhood.
And—much more.
Now is their training ground.
    Now is their time of becoming.
What they become, Lord, is deeply affected
    By these other people's children.

So they, too, become my responsibility.
And—may it be so—my blessing.

They are mine to instruct
    And chasten
And love, while they are at my house.
They are mine to befriend,
And mine to act responsible before.

Bless them, Lord,
And my own.
And me.
                                    Amen[2]

    Throughout the years, we have had several foster children
in our home. Most of them came as very scraggly little caterpillars. And not always did we get to see the finished product.
    Both junior-high-aged brothers who lived with us for some
time were returned to their mother before we could see if they

developed into "beautiful butterflies." However, we felt privileged to sow the seed of God's Word in their hearts. We had done as much as we could with the opportunity God gave us. We then had to learn to release these boys to the Lord, praying for them, as they returned to their mother.

They were 13 and 14 years old when they came to us, and there were many times when we had frustrations, as their cultural background was very different from ours. One thing the Lord showed us through this experience was that each person is created in God's image, and deserves His love, given in dignity and warmth.

> *The most important thing in child training is love.*

The Lord Jesus Christ gives us the Good Samaritan story as a model of hospitality. As we read this passage in Luke 10:25–37, He guides us to visualize loving hospitality. Jesus portrays the Samaritan disrupting his schedule to carefully treat the wounds and take the injured man from a totally different culture and race to the inn. Christ's description of the Good Samaritan disrupting his schedule to carefully treat the wounds of this man is a beautiful expression of hospitality.

There are thousands of children in our world today who need to have their "wounds" ministered to by Christians. Some of us will be called to provide a home for foster children. Some of us may be privileged to adopt a child; God blessed our family with a fourth child in this way. Others of us will minister to wounded neighborhood children in various ways.

There are many children who are abused at home,

neglected spiritually and very lonely. They are in need of Good Samaritans today. Whenever I read this passage in Luke, the words almost jump off the page as I read Jesus' admonition: "Go and do likewise" (v. 37, *NIV*). This is a call in our day, just as it was in the day when Christ walked this earth!

When our little Kathy was three and a half, we took a foster daughter into our home. She was a great help to me since I was five months pregnant with our second child and had been ordered by my doctor to stay off my feet most of the time. At the same time, Dick and George Kraft, sons of missionary friends in Taiwan, China, were spending the summer with us. Attending high school at Wheaton Academy, they needed a summer home. Not knowing that I would be expecting a baby and threatening to miscarry that summer, we had promised to take them.

Ray Netherly, a Campus Crusade for Christ worker, was also staying with us and driving into Minneapolis from Mound, Minnesota, almost daily. He was forming the first chapter of Campus Crusade for Christ at the University of Minnesota. Unknowingly, we had also invited Ray to stay with us. Needless to say, we had a very large old home to house everyone in.

Our foster daughter Mary was almost 16 years old when she came to us. I began to instruct her, discipline her and love her with the love of Christ. That summer she attended Sunday School and church with us, and sat in every morning for our family devotions with our "family at large."

At suppertime and when we did the dishes, we had many discussions and were able to sow the seed of God's Word in her. We felt that God wanted us to keep Mary in our home as one of our children, but suddenly one day her mother appeared out of nowhere. She was a carnival worker, and wanted Mary to go with her. The Welfare Department agreed to this, and just that quickly Mary packed her bags and left us. That was the last time I ever saw my little "caterpillar," and I can tell you that I shed many tears that day and in the weeks ahead. We have never seen Mary again. Yet, I feel the time we invested in her was not wasted. And only in eternity will we find what became of Mary.

When God calls us to this kind of ministry, we have to be willing to risk a broken heart. Christ Himself had a broken heart over those who would not listen and believe He was the Messiah, and surely, if our Saviour had a broken heart, He will enable us to carry that same broken heart to the throne of the Father for His healing touch. "I want to know Christ and the power of his resurrection and the fellowship of sharing in his sufferings" (Phil. 3:10, *NIV*).

Several years ago my husband had a junior-high-age boy in Sunday School in our little church in Mound, Minnesota. The boy's parents, who were not Christians, moved to Minneapolis from our small town of Mound on Lake Minnetonka. This was some 20 miles from the city.

We would often invite this young man to spend weekends with us so that we could encourage him in the Lord, take him to church and Sunday School and show him what a Christian home was like. This boy was one of the "caterpillars" we asked the Lord to help us develop into a beautiful "butterfly"; this ministry went on for approximately three years.

Then, one day my diamond engagement ring disappeared on the weekend he had been visiting us. We hated to think that our guest might have taken it. In fact, it was a very painful thought, and yet we had to report the loss to the police. As they questioned us about the people who had been in our home during the time the diamond had disappeared, we had to be honest and tell them about this young man. My ring was gone for a period of about six months, and I had resigned myself to the fact that I would never see it again. It was difficult, but I had to think about what was really important in life. I told myself, "Rings do not have eternal value!"

This story does not have a happy ending. The young man was found in Minneapolis, wearing my ring; the police later returned it to me. Unfortunately, he was not repentant, and was unwilling to return to our home. So we have not seen him to know if he later developed into a butterfly or not. It's not always easy to know if everyone you invite into your home is going to be an angel. You have to deal with a lot of caterpillars! And, some of them are going to break your heart. Yet some, through your nurturing, will break through that cocoon and you will be rewarded by seeing a beautiful butterfly fly out, a new creature in Jesus Christ.

Another person God sent our way was a burned-out missionary from India. He came back from his third term in India with some strange delusions about himself. I can remember his coming to our house with briefcase in hand.

My three little ones gathered around him at the table by our poolside as he opened his briefcase. He proceeded to tell them that he was a private detective now and wanted to show them his gun. He removed a water gun from his briefcase and proudly displayed it to them. I immediately went into the house to hide all the knives in our kitchen! At the same time, knowing he was hungry, I prepared him a meal from the best of what I had in the refrigerator and took it out to him.

I did not feel free to ask him to spend the night in our home, since my husband was away on a business trip. He assured me that he had a motel in downtown Hollywood.

Not long after, he returned. This time Bill was home. We invited him to stay in one of our bedrooms, and arranged for him to have a complete physical with our Christian family doctor. It was diagnosed that he needed psychiatric care, and since he was from another country, where he could get free treatment, a group of Christian businessmen agreed to collect money for a return ticket to his homeland.

While he was packing to go home, I walked down the hall and glanced into the bedroom. He was folding my children's Mickey Mouse sheets and pillowcases. I thanked him for stripping the bed, and then noticed that he had all of the Mickey

Mouse sheets from the linen closets already in his suitcase! He explained to me that they did not have Mickey Mouse sheets where he was from and so he was taking them all home with him.

This is one of the "strange strangers" I have entertained. Here again, I didn't argue with him for I felt that the issue of the sheets was not that important. We continue to pray for our friend and hope that he received the psychiatric help he needed. Until heaven, we leave him at the foot of the cross with Christ, who is his Saviour, and entrust him into His care.

God is a gracious host, and we see a model of His hospitality in Psalm 23. In this Psalm He graciously extends generous hospitality to all Christians and treats them as His royal guests. With a generous love and open heart, God spreads a table before us to eat until we are full! He protects us against our enemies, physically and emotionally. He provides refreshing and cleansing with oil. He quenches our thirst with a cup of water so full that it overflows as we bring it to our thirsty lips. Thus, we see the qualities of the perfect host. As we look at these qualities of God, the gracious Host, we know that we can take our emotional wounds to Him and He will refresh and renew us.

That summer with Mary, God's words in Psalm 62 meant a lot to me: "My soul finds rest in God alone; my salvation comes from him. He alone is my rock and my salvation; he is my fortress, I will never be shaken" (vv.1,2, *NIV*).

"God, my gracious host, help me to endure the pain of seeing Mary return to the carnival life with her mother," was my heart's cry that next fall and winter. Another passage of Scripture in which God is the perfect Host ministered to my life at this time. It gave rest for my weary soul. "Come to me, all you who are weary and burdened, and I will give you rest. Take my yoke upon you and learn from me, for I am gentle and humble in heart, and you will find rest for your souls. For my yoke is easy and my burden is light" (Matt. 11:28–30, *NIV*).

As I have read these Scriptures over and over throughout my lifetime, I recognize that I am not alone in any situation, circumstance, place, time or experience. I am never apart from the Lord. "For Thou art with me" and within me! Every Christian has the privilege to claim these promises for themselves. The Lord Jesus promised, "Never will I leave you; never will I forsake you" (Heb. 13:5, *NIV*).

We as Christians have the Holy Spirit within. We are simply His outer garments. We need to pray each new morning, "Jesus, here I am reporting for duty. Thank you for this new day and for promising to be with me in it. I want to be your clothes today. Just walk around in me, dear Lord. Let your light shine through me as love in action today."

Some wonderful "caterpillars" came into our home during their sophomore, junior and senior years of high school, and developed into "beautiful butterflies"! We had friends who were missionaries in Guatemala who wanted their daughters to re-enter the public school system in California before going on to college here. They had attended a Christian mission school in Guatemala most of their lives. Phyllis Shackelford came to live with us for two years, and after she went on to college, her sister Janet arrived. Following Janet came Charlotte. They were close to the age of our oldest daughter Kathy and became a tremendous blessing in our household as the girls fellowshiped with one another. They could stand together as Christians, and not feel lonely during their high school years. These girls were like ministering angels to our household. To this day, we do not fully realize the blessings they brought to all of us!

Providentially, God knew my future and realized that I would be put to bed with a very irregular heartbeat for nine months the year Janet was with us. Janet and Kathy ran the household during the time I was bedridden. Not only did they learn how to market, wash, iron and cook, but they learned to serve the Lord in this way. They did it with "heartiness to the Lord" and it was a good year in our family.

Even the junior-high-age boys learned to cook, bake cakes and cookies and take care of their own clothing. God never wastes anything. He took our trials and turned them into triumph! The caterpillars in our household that year blossomed out and became beautiful butterflies serving the Lord together. This poem expresses some of my emotions as I lay bedridden with heart problems that year:

Patience! Courage! Fortitude!

Dear Lord, give me
    patience
    courage
    and fortitude.
Gary's in the kitchen again
    whipping up his favorite recipe
      or some cookie or cake.
Oh, he's such a flamboyant cook, Lord!
    the kitchen will soon be covered
    with a mosaic of
      sugar
        flour
          shortening
            and maybe eggs!
And after he's cleaned it all up, Lord,
    the kitchen will still be slightly covered
    with his mosaic of
      sugar
        flour
          shortening
            and maybe eggs!!!
Lord, help me to be glad
    for this boy who loves his home
      who feels free to create in my kitchen
      some delicacy that

his boyish stomach desires.
Dear Lord, one day he will grow up
and the mosaic will no longer be there.
Thank you, Lord, for my flamboyant cook
and the mosaics he creates!!!
—Doris W. Greig

If you are in difficult times and wonder why God, your hospitable Saviour, has allowed this problem in your life, trust Him to bring comfort in your life and sustain you. He can bring triumph out of your tragedy. In Psalm 23 God, the ultimate Host, promises that He will restore your soul and guide you in righteousness. As you trust God the Father, you can echo the words of the psalmist, "Even though I walk through the valley of the shadow of death, I will fear no evil, for you are with me; . . . You prepare a table before me in the presence of my enemies. You anoint my head with oil; my cup overflows. Surely goodness and love will follow me all the days of my life, and I will dwell in the house of the Lord forever" (NIV). Trust God, the perfect Host!

God may be calling you to minister to the type of caterpillars I have described in this chapter. You will not know whether He is calling you or not unless you are willing to invest time in fellowship, prayer and in listening to God. Invite the Holy Spirit to show you God's direction for your life. Be a good listener, and He will reveal to you through circumstances and conversations if this is to be your kind of ministry. Remember that risk is a part of this ministry. If He calls you to this task, God will enable you and you will see the wonderful miracle of His hand forming little caterpillars into beautiful, mature butterflies!

Looking back over the years when we have been privileged to have many, many little caterpillars in our home, God has shown me that I need never feel unimportant or non-essential. Little souls, so precious in His sight, so ready to copy us and so eager to learn are set before us as a gift from God. What we do, how we act and what we say is so important. It is only through Christ's wonderful guidance and the Holy Spirit's power that we can be the kind of reflection of His love that is worthy of imitation. Little eyes are watching, little ears are listening and little minds are constantly absorbing.

We need to ask ourselves if our "caterpillars" are growing in wisdom and understanding of God from what they see and hear from us (see 2 Tim. 1:5). God has chosen some of us to be His hospitable hosts—molders of men and women. What a responsibility! What a privilege! "Therefore be imitators of God, as beloved children; and walk in love, just as Christ also loved you, and gave Himself up for us, an offering and a sacrifice to God as a fragrant aroma" (Eph. 5:1,2, *NASB*).

"For I am mindful of the sincere faith within you, which first dwelt in your grandmother Lois, and your mother Eunice, and I am sure that it is in you as well" (2 Tim.1:5, *NASB*). The apostle Paul wrote these words to Timothy. At times we feel that we have very little influence and worth. This Scripture reminds us that although we may have moments of doubt concerning our influence and worth, with God's hand on our lives our ministry can be a significant one to all of the little "caterpillars" He puts into our lives.

Many days seem difficult and tedious, but thank God for the tedium! Remember that trying moments, sleepless nights, the long, seemingly endless hours of work that never seems to diminish in a household are just a part of spinning a cocoon that will produce a beautiful butterfly or two or three or more!

There will be times when you will wonder how you will ever live through it all. And yet, there is the undergirding peace and incomparable bliss in nurturing "caterpillars."

"Be sober in all things, endure hardship, do the work of an evangelist, fulfill your ministry" (2 Tim. 4:5, *NASB*)

God Is Calling You

1. Have you had children in your life, your own or otherwise, whom you have been privileged to see blossom into beautiful "butterflies"? Can you recall specific examples where you were uncertain as to the outcome of someone's life only to find that God, in His infinite love and wisdom, guided the process of his or her life from a funny little "caterpillar" to a beautiful and glorifying "butterfly"?

2. Have you ever been privileged to provide a home for a foster child? Have you ever considered a foster child, or perhaps adopting a child? What would be the first step you would need to take if you feel God calling you in this way?

3. What qualities listed in this chapter make up the "Perfect Host"? How can you apply these qualities to your life that will in turn allow you to effectively reach out to others with the same love of our Perfect Host?

4. Whenever you reach out to others and involve yourself in their lives, there will be risk involved. Can you think of experiences you have had that did not work out as you would have hoped? If given the opportunity to do over, would you handle those particular situations any differently? Were you able to hand those unpleasant situations over to the Lord and say, "Thank you, at least, for what part I could play in that person's life."

Notes:
1. Allan H. Jahsmann and Martin P. Simon, *Little Visits with God* (St. Louis, MO: Concordia Publishing House, 1957).
2. From *Bless This Mess and Other Prayers* by Jo Carr and Imogene Sorley. Copyright © 1969 by Abingdon Press. Used by permission.

7

The Canon Came to Dinner

Late one Friday afternoon, the telephone rang. It was my husband asking me if he could bring a Canon home for dinner! *A cannon?* I thought to myself—picturing a large, black cannon with a pile of big black cannonballs sitting beside it.

I said, "Cannon?" Bill realized that I had a different interpretation of what he was bringing home for dinner. So he said, "I'd like to bring the Canon Harry Sutton home for dinner." I said, "Oh . . . oh!" when I realized that this was not the cannon I had imagined. This Canon was a Church of England Rector from London who was visiting the United States studying the Jesus People movement.

My husband went on to say, "After dinner we are going to go out to Chuck Smith's Calvary Chapel." It was the '60s and I knew great things were happening there. A lot of hippies were coming to know the Lord, and were being baptized in the ocean. They were coming to church in their jeans and T-shirts. Some wore tennies; others were barefooted. I had seen pictures and read about the revival in *Life* magazine.

Well, the Canon came in full regalia! His black suit and collar "turned backwards" really impressed our children. They noticed his English accent too. He looked so proper, I wondered how he would respond to tennies, jeans and T-shirts and maybe even barefooted kids at the Calvary Chapel service.

The children were very surprised when the Canon began to tell jokes at the dinner table. He was fun! He laughed a hearty belly laugh that rolled out so joyfully. Even though he wore a black suit with the white collar "turned backwards," they decided this Englishman really had a great sense of humor. I don't even remember what I served for dinner, but I do remember that we had a good time at the table, and I guess that's the most significant part of a meal, isn't it?

Often we had guests that came and went like this, and I was getting accustomed to serving them whatever family fare I had planned, not feeling guilty that I didn't have a fancy meal for them. Ruth Graham made a comment once about her home that has really helped me to feel comfortable entertaining guests, even when my house isn't perfect and my meal doesn't look like it has been catered by the best restaurant in town. Ruth told my friend Jean Wilson, "I decorate my house with cobwebs." In other words, she was saying she never was ashamed of a cobweb here and there, a little clutter now and then. These are not the things people are really looking for when they come to your home.

> I have to break
> My shell
> Not only to reach out
> To you,
> But to let you
> Enter my world
> To share me
> My life
> My risks
> My assets
> My liabilities.

If I do, it may be easier
For you to let me
Enter your world.
It takes courage to reach out.
It takes courage
To let me enter.
It is like
A leap in the dark.
Familiar landmarks
Are not at hand.

Each reaching out,
Each entering
Is unique.

—Albert J. Nimeth[1]

As I read these words, I realized that it was only by the mercy of God that I had been able to "break my shell" and allow people to enter my world, "to share me, my life, my risks, my assets, my liabilities." And it has been worth it!

While reading the Bible from the standpoint of hospitality, I realized that there have been other people who have broken out of their shells and opened their hearts and homes to strangers. As a result they have experienced God's blessing upon their lives.

Job is an example of this. He states in Job 31:32, "But no stranger had to spend the night in the street, for my door was always open to the traveler" (NIV).

In Acts 16, Lydia, the woman who dealt in purple cloth from the city of Thyatira, opened her heart to the Lord and responded to Paul's message. In verse 15, we read these words: "When she and the members of her household were baptized, she invited us to her home. 'If you consider me a believer in the Lord,' she said, 'come and stay at my house.' And she persuaded us" (*NIV*). These passages from both the Old and New Testaments illustrate how the Lord gave courage to reach out to strangers.

And so, our family's opportunity had come to open our world to the Canon. We had our dinner and quickly stacked the dishes. Later, we all piled into the car and headed down the freeway toward Calvary Chapel in Orange County. In the car we discovered that the Canon liked to sing; and he asked the children for their favorite songs. We had a great time singing all the way down to Calvary Chapel. We sang some secular songs and some hymns. The long journey seemed to slip by all too quickly.

Think of how unhappy I would have been if I had withdrawn to my tower, filled the moat and pulled up the drawbridge around my home! I would have limited God in all that He did that evening at Calvary Chapel.

We arrived at the church and the Canon wasn't at all shocked by what he saw. In fact, he was tremendously enthused and excited by the number of young people holding their Bibles and waiting in line to get in. During the service he sang the Christian folk music with wonderful zest. He hadn't even seemed to notice how these young people dressed or wore their hair.

Our children caught the spirit from him too. By now they were junior high and senior high age, and the experience was a tremendous blessing to them. This was the beginning of many trips with our children to Calvary Chapel to enjoy worshipping with the Body of Christ there.

Yes, the Canon from the Church of England loved this worship experience. He raved about it all the way home, and told us how he was going to put a chapter in his book about this very special evening. He was traveling around the country, observing what God was doing in the different churches of the United States.

It turned out to be a marvelous evening for our entire family. We all tumbled into bed, blessed from the evening, ready for a sound night's sleep. When Saturday morning came, the Canon appeared at the breakfast table, still full of enthusiasm and humor. Our children were blessed to know this man of God. Truly the Canon was like an angel to us as he helped us see and experience what God was doing in the Body of Christ at Calvary Chapel.

> *Don't forget to be kind to strangers, for some who have done this have entertained angels without realizing it!*
> —Hebrews 13:2, *The Living Bible*

Through this experience, they caught a small glimpse of how Christians around the world are "rooted and grounded" by the love of Christ. I thought about this after the children had gone off to school, and my husband and the Canon had gone off to the office. I had just been reading an article about the huge redwood trees of California, which still amaze mankind. The article said the redwoods are the largest living things on earth, the tallest trees in the world. Some of them are 300 feet high and over 2,500 years old.

I had always thought that trees so large must have a tremendous root system that reaches down hundreds of feet into the earth. I found out that isn't so. They have a very shallow root system; the redwoods' root system all intertwine; they are locked to each other. When the storms come, the winds blow and the lightning flashes, the redwoods still stand because they

99

are locked to each other. They are not alone, for all the trees support and protect each other. Each tree is important to all the other trees in the forest.

As I pondered this truth about the redwoods, I decided that through the Canon's visit, God had given me and my family a spiritual glimpse of the root system of Christians all around the world. In the Church-at-large there is the root system intertwined on the solid foundation of Jesus Christ. My family had experienced this in Christian fellowship with the Canon, and at Calvary Chapel.

Our fellowship with the Canon was possible through the bond of Christ. It seemed to me that the evening had been a perfect illustration of 1 John 3:23, "And this is His commandment, that we believe in the name of His Son Jesus Christ, and love one another, just as He commanded us" (*NASB*). We had sensed the love bond of Christ with this brother in Christ whom we had never met before. Without Christ as the foundation, the Church is powerless. By our love, we must show the world the difference Jesus makes!

Undoubtedly the Christian believers who gathered in Lydia's home for dinner and to stay at her house sensed this same fellowship because of their common faith in the Lord Jesus Christ. Their roots were intertwining within the soil of God's marvelous love. The Holy Spirit later gave Paul these words in Ephesians 3:17–19, "And I pray that Christ will be more and more at home in your hearts, living within you as you trust in him. May your roots go down deep into the soil of God's marvelous love; and may you be able to feel and understand, as all God's children should, how long, how wide, how deep, and how high his love really is; and to experience this love for yourselves, though it is so great that you will never see the end of it or fully know or understand it. And so at last you will be filled up with God himself" (*TLB*).

Later the next day, as I was working around the house, I stopped to read an article someone had written about keeping entertaining simple, which certainly applied to that quick dinner before we went to Calvary Chapel. The article suggested that if you are busy, as most families are, a simple menu is best. Plan to serve food that can be prepared ahead. A roast placed in the oven at low temperature before Sunday School is done when church is over, ready to set on the table. I usually include potatoes and carrots with the roast. Along with a salad and dessert, the meal is complete. I have heard of people who put in a large casserole before church, and if there are visitors they meet on Sunday morning, they invite them to come for dinner. This is hospitality in action!

Other suggestions are to stay away from last minute preparations as much as possible. Do ahead all that you possibly can. I cut up my salad ingredients the night before and put them in a serving bowl and wrap it in plastic. The salad is as fresh as if you had just tossed it. There is also an easy-to-prepare, 24-hour salad with the dressing layered over the top; the recipe is found in the Recipe Section later on in this book.

Entertaining guests should really become a family affair, and early on I involved my whole family in this process. Even as preschoolers, they learned to put the napkins next to the fork and knew where the salt and pepper were to be put on the table. By performing these simple tasks, they were learning that they had a part in our home's hospitality. As the family grew older they helped put the dinner on the table and cleaned up afterwards. How I miss that help now! Their help made entertaining a joy for the whole family, because they felt involved and important. And Mom should never be left alone in the kitchen, because it means she spends all of her time preparing and doesn't get to share in the visiting.

When you start entertaining company, don't get discouraged if you are a nervous wreck at first. One of these days you will "break out of your shell" and find that when people just drop in it doesn't bother you as much. In fact, I like it when I don't have much notice, because there can't be any complaints about the food or the situation of the house! It is truly potluck. A canned chicken, or some type of canned meat with instant mashed potatoes and a nice canned or frozen vegetable and applesauce is always a good meal to fix in a hurry, without a lot of fuss. Keep these, or other such items, on an "emergency shelf" in your kitchen at all times. The Girl Scout motto "Be Prepared" really is a good one to follow.

Ken Taylor and his wife had ten children. Ten children! That's why he wrote *The Living Bible*; he got so tired of reading the *King James Version* and having them squirm and wiggle and not understand it.

Mrs. Taylor said she was never ashamed to serve just home-made soup and biscuits to her guests. She keeps the soup and biscuits in the freezer. Do you know what I've got in my freezer now? Homemade soup and homemade muffins. And if some-one comes unexpectedly, I can always heat the soup on the stove and warm the muffins in the oven or microwave. Remember, it's the fellowship that counts. Another good rea-son to have something fixed and frozen is that if you hear of a sick friend or neighbor, you have a meal already prepared to take to them. That's hospitality!

So if God calls you, don't feel like you have to serve an ele-gant seven-course dinner to be hospitable.

Of course, you may have some catastrophes. I'm going to tell you about one I had. It was a Sunday dinner, and there were 12 people coming. My daughter was home from college with her roommate. Her fiancé was also with us. In fact, he was in the room Shushila had recently moved out of. One of my lit-tle neighborhood "caterpillars" was coming to church with her fiancé and they were going to come to dinner also. I had a houseguest from England who would be with us. We had "adopted" Auntie Kay Coppleman from our church, and she always came for Sunday dinner. And there were five of us still at home.

I always counted on my oven for Sunday dinner. It had a

great timer on it—set it and forget it. And I had this wonderful recipe for an oven-baked chicken dish—rice, water, mushroom soup and onion soup. (See recipe section.) You put the chicken on top, bake it, and it's delicious! Gelatin salad and a tossed salad made the day before completed the meal. So, with 12 people for dinner, I thought *this will be a good menu, easy to fix, and it will be all ready when we get home.*

So, after serving the family breakfast I hurriedly cut up the chicken, arranged the rice, soups and water in the roaster and put the chicken on top. Then in perfect confidence I set my wonderful oven timer and went off to Sunday School and church. I hurried home before the rest of the family with Jean Wilson, my guest from England. As I unlocked the front door, my heart sank to my feet when I walked in and I could not smell the chicken cooking. For some reason, the timer had not worked that Sunday.

OK, here's the catastrophe—12 hungry people and raw chicken. The table was not set either. I had expected to assign that task to some of the children while I put the finishing touches on the dinner. Now what?

First of all, I prayed, "Lord, help me." And then I organized my guests.

You know, that was one of the most fun dinners I can remember; my children often remind me of it too. I don't remember all of the other Sunday dinners, because they were so much like a lot of other Sunday dinners. But that particular Sunday when the timer didn't work was one of the most memorable, fun Sundays we have ever had!

I remember Jean, with her lovely English accent, saying, "Oh, Doris, we'll just wash the rice off the chicken, then fry up the chicken." And I said to her, "Oh, sure, and we'll boil up the rice with the mushroom soup and water"—and we did.

We giggled like schoolgirls and had a great time getting dinner together. My senior high boys arrived home and set the tables. In fact, everyone pitched in. Auntie Kay put the "serviettes" on the table. She was from Canada and always called the napkins "serviettes."

So you see, catastrophes aren't always bad; they truly can unite the family. The guests can enjoy them too. Expect catastrophes, and then make them fun. It's our attitude that counts, isn't it? We can either fly around in the air and harp about it, or we can admit that we have a flop on our hands, then make the best of it.

Ruth Harms Calkin has written about just this sort of thing in *Lord, It Keeps Happening and Happening*:

The One Fixed Pole

Dear Lord, forgive me
For my foolish, desperate attempt
To win Heaven's blue ribbon
For the management
Of my own small world—
When deep in my bewildered heart
I know, I do know
That the one fixed pole
In all my hectic confusion
Is the faithfulness
Of the living God.[2]

I have found God is faithful to provide the strength and wisdom we need to deal with our catastrophes, as well as the smoothly organized dinners. God works miracles today in our "catastrophes" even as He did for the widow of Nain in 1 Kings 17. Our problem is that we don't always recognize the miracles that God works, and the wisdom and strength that He gives us.

Ponder these words from 1 Kings 17:13–16: "But Elijah said to her, 'Don't be afraid! Go ahead and cook that "last meal," but bake me a little loaf of bread first; and afterwards there will still be enough food for you and your son. For the

Lord God of Israel says that there will always be plenty of flour and oil left in your containers until the time when the Lord sends rain, and the crops grow again!' So she did as Elijah said, and she and Elijah and her son continued to eat from her supply of flour and oil as long as it was needed. For no matter how much they used, there was always plenty left in the containers, just as the Lord had promised through Elijah!" (*TLB*).

As I have read these words many times over, I believe the message God has given me is: Don't be afraid! And, through this story He has illustrated how He will meet our needs to feed anyone He may send into our homes.

You may ask, "How can I afford this? Food costs so much!" This is true, but the Lord has promised to give back to us more than we give to Him. We can never outgive the Lord! He will give us creative ways of entertaining without straining our budgets.

We can start by asking a couple of families over for a picnic, and ask them to bring a dish to pass. Our family has discovered that people just like getting together and enjoy furnishing part of the meal. Everybody loves to taste someone else's cooking from time to time, and exchange favorite recipes.

The Bible has much to say about hospitality. In Romans 12:13, Paul talks of practicing hospitality. Titus 1:8 suggests that we should be lovers of hospitality. Jesus commanded us to serve if we wanted to become great (see Matt. 20:26). And Paul spoke in Philippians 4:15 of the church becoming partners with Him in giving and receiving.

So much can be shared over a sandwich or a dessert and a cup of coffee. It is a way we can share our love and concern for others. In 1 Peter 4:9 we are told to cheerfully, without grudging, share our homes with those who need a meal or a place to stay overnight.

I heard the story not long ago of a stingy rich man who sat at his dresser for his meals, and ate his tasty and expensive foods from his dresser drawer so that if a visitor came in he could shut the drawer and not have to share his food. Can you imagine such a lack of hospitality? Yet, aren't we guilty of this sometimes? If we have a nice home, but we hate to have company because it means too much work—the house will get dirty and messed up—we are doing the same sort of thing. Or, we may feel our home is not as nice as someone else's, so let *them* have the company.

Some of us intend to practice hospitality, but time slips by and we just don't get around to it. With busy lives, it's easy to neglect entertaining.

It's a good idea to sit down at the beginning of each month and plan to entertain at least once during that time, if not more often, someone the Lord has placed on your heart. Don't keep putting it off or you never will use adequately the time or the dwelling place God has given you. Since everything we have belongs to Him, we need to use it to His glory!

Over the years, I've heard so many people say, "I just don't enjoy having company. I must not have the gift of hospitality." This could be true of both statements. Change is hard to make for everyone, but if you really want to be used by God you will make the effort. You may find it difficult at first. In fact, I used to have the jitters for days before entertaining guests. Don't get discouraged if you are nervous for a while and uncomfortable about sharing your dinner table. Try it. You may find that you'll like it! And people are really starving for this kind of love.

And remember that God has promised to answer our prayers for His help in any situation. "All things, whatsoever ye shall ask in prayer, believing, ye shall receive" (Matt. 21:22, *KJV*).

If we make the effort to share our lives with others, and if we ask the Lord for His empowerment through the Holy Spirit, then we are guaranteed to receive all of the resources we need for every situation. Our God is faithful! "Faithful is He who calls you, and He also will bring it to pass" (1 Thess. 5:24, *NASB*).

106

God Is Calling You

1. It is not always easy to open up our world and allow others to enter. Maybe this has been difficult for you to do. Have you called upon God to help you open up more and more in order for Him to show His blessings not only to those He will bring into your midst, but also to you, His very precious child?

2. Sometimes we get caught up only in what is happening in our little corner of the world. We do not always see how God is doing His mighty work in other areas of the world. How can you and your family avail yourselves to see what God is doing in the Body of Christ as a whole?

3. It's always easier to readily open our homes to others if we have foods and menus fixed ahead. What are some of the little helps you have found over the years to help make last-minute entertaining more enjoyable and hassle-free? What are some of the things you could begin to do to become more hospitable?

4. There will be catastrophes when you entertain. But they can be turned into enjoyable moments. Can you recall times when circumstances were less than desirable, but eventually turned into blessings for all?

Notes:
1. Albert J. Nimeth, from *Tenderly I Care* (Chicago: Franciscan Herald Press, 1977). Used by permission.
2. From: *Lord, It Keeps Happening and Happening.* By Ruth Harms Calkin. Published by Tyndale House Publishers © 1984. Used by permission.

8

Life Is but a Weaving

Reaching out to the elderly and handicapped is taught by Jesus as an act of true hospitality in Luke chapter 14. Christ challenges us to invite the poor, crippled, lame and the blind to our party—not just our friends, relatives and the influential people from our neighborhoods and communities who will probably repay us with an invitation in return. He challenges us to see the "overlooked people" in our communities and reach out to them with loving hospitality.

The poor, crippled, lame and blind, old or young, often see life only from the wrong side of the tapestry. From the underside, their lives appear to be in constant chaos. God wants to use His people to help them get the perspective from His side, the top side, which is a beautiful picture of what God has planned for each and every one of us. If we take this challenge from Luke 14, we will be used to bring that beautiful picture on the top side of the tapestry in view for those who are feeling discouraged, lonely and unloved.

This poem expresses what God wants every human being to see in the midst of sorrow:

My life is but a weaving, between my God and me,
I do not choose the colors, He worketh steadily,
Oft times He weaveth sorrow, and I in foolish pride,
Forget He sees the upper, and I the underside.

Not 'til the loom is silent, and shuttles cease to fly,
Will God unroll the canvas and explain the reason
   why.
The dark threads are as needful in the skillful Weav-
   er's Hand,
As the threads of gold and silver in the pattern He
   has planned.

—Anonymous[1]

We can help those who see only the "wrong side" of their lives realize that God sees His side all the time! One day they shall see the beautiful embroidery work from His side, and thank Him for it. Those of us who can see His pattern in the great lines of the Bible need to share with those who feel hopeless. We need to bolster their faith, for faith is like radar that sees straight through the foggy areas of our lives. Faith is the reality of seeing spiritual things the human eye cannot see. We can be enablers to help those without Christ come in faith and know His love and direction for their lives. Then they can find the blessings of Christian fellowship and the meaning of God's grace in times of need.

Sometimes we are afraid of ministering to the people God names in Luke 14. It is so easy to plead a multitude of demands on our time. Yet, friendships cannot survive and needs will not be met if we are not willing to be God's servants, available to take the initiative. We need to be willing to write that letter, make that phone call and stop for a visit even if it isn't "our turn."

Being available means altering plans to accommodate someone else's need. Being available means listening not only to what your friend is saying, but to what she is not saying. Or to hear what she is trying to say and cannot.

Sometimes we are unavailable because we are afraid of getting hurt. So we withdraw. Sometimes we fear the handicapped and elderly, not knowing how they will respond to our overtures of friendship. We have to be willing to let down the bridge and open the gate of our lives to them. We have to risk it! We must see ourselves and our love as a gift from God to the other person. The old saying "Nothing risked, nothing gained" applies here.

> Accepting a friend
> As he is
> Is not to give him
> A license
> To be ugly,
> Mean and
> Despicable.
>
> Acceptance
> Gives a friend
> Support
> "But it also challenges him
> To become
> What he can become—
> A noble,
> Fine person.

—Albert J. Nimeth[2]

This should be our objective as a friend of any handicapped or elderly person: "For you were called to freedom, brethren; only do not turn your freedom into an opportunity for the flesh, but through love serve one another. For the whole Law is fulfilled in one word, in the statement, 'You shall love your neighbor as yourself' " (Gal. 5:13,14, NASB).

Biblical hospitality is illustrated in the Old Testament

through King David as he rescues the son of his beloved friend Jonathan. Mephibosheth was injured while being rescued by his nurse at the height of battle (see 2 Sam. 4:4). In 2 Samuel 9:1: "David asked, 'Is there anyone still left of the house of Saul to whom I can show kindness for Jonathan's sake?' . . . Ziba answered the king, 'There is still a son of Jonathan; he is crippled in both feet.' 'Where is he?' the king asked" (2 Sam. 9:3,4, *NIV*).

King David sent for Mephibosheth and encouraged him not to be afraid: "For I will surely show you kindness for the sake of your father Jonathan. I will restore to you all the land that belonged to your grandfather Saul, and you will always eat at my table" (2 Sam. 9:7, NIV). Thus, the grandson of Saul, the man who had tried to kill David, had become like one of David's sons (see 2 Sam. 9:11).

Here was the ultimate example of hospitality to the son of Jonathan, who could have been sentenced to prison or death because of his lineage through King Saul. This young crippled man was shown the love of God through David. "And Mephibosheth lived in Jerusalem, because he always ate at the king's table, and he was crippled in both feet" (2 Sam. 9:13, *NIV*). What an example for us to reach out to the lame, whether they are lame physically, emotionally or spiritually.

The fruit of the Holy Spirit is listed as love, joy, peace, patience, kindness, goodness, faithfulness, gentleness and self-control (see Gal. 5:22, 23). We are challenged by the last verses in Galatians 5, "Now those who belong to Christ Jesus have crucified the flesh with its passions and desires. If we live by the Spirit, let us also walk by the Spirit" (vv. 24,25, *NASB*).

The fruit can be seen in the Christian, but only when we are in contact with the Vine. "As the branch cannot bear fruit of itself, except it abide in the vine; no more can ye, except ye abide in me" (John 15:4, *KJV*). As Corrie ten Boom always said, "You are not good if detached." She called us to abide in Christ always.

Cowardly, wayward, and weak,
I change with the changing sky
Today so eager and strong,
Tomorrow not caring to try.
But He never gives in,
And we two shall win,
Jesus and I.[3]

Corrie said in her book entitled *Not Good if Detached*,
"Instantly I see it! Indeed I am not worthy at all. The branch
without The Vine cannot produce fruit, but I can do all things
through Christ who gives me strength. The strongest and the
weakest branches are worth nothing without The Vine; but
connected to it they have the same nature."[4] She always
pointed people to the Lord Jesus Christ. This should be our
ultimate goal too as we reach out in friendship to the handicapped and elderly.

In John 5 we read of the sick man near the healing pool at
Bethsaida who waited for decades for someone to help him get
into the pool. He waited and waited and waited! Nobody
cared. Until one day, unexpectedly, Christ appeared. Now, the
sick man, who represents all mankind before they come to
Christ, could tell someone his greatest need—"I have no one."
This hurt more than his ailment. He had no reproach or bitter-
ness in his words, just futility and helplessness.

Christ cared! He cared by the expression on His face, the
tone of His voice and the touch of His hand. There was no mis-
taking His genuine concern. If we allow the Spirit of God to use
us, there will be no mistake in our genuine concern for others.
We will move among people as Christ did, truly caring by the
expression on our faces, the tone of our voices and the touch of
our hands.

There are many people in this world who have no one.
They need understanding, help and encouragement. When we

113

have won the friendship and trust of those who are old and lonely, poor, crippled, lame or blind, we will, in time, win the right to share the love of our Saviour with them. We will seem like angels to them.

When those whom God calls us to be hospitable to see genuine concern in us, they will be willing to open up their bruised hearts and reach out, as the sick man did so long ago, to tell us their greatest need. It is at this point that we not only offer ourselves as hospitable friends, but also we have the living Lord Jesus to share. "Truly, truly, I say to you, he who hears My word, and believes Him who sent Me, has eternal life, and does not come into judgment, but has passed out of death into life" (John 5:24, *NASB*).

By His words: "Go in peace," "Be of good cheer" and "Have no fear," we can bring Christ's love, comfort and genuine concern to the needy. We can trust God to give us understanding and the knowledge of how to help and encourage all individuals He sends our way by the power of the Holy Spirit.

> *The deepest problems of our society are loneliness, isolation, and the inability to feel self-esteem.*
>
> —Harry Stack Sullivan

Chesterton says of St. Francis of Assisi: "To him a man was always a man, an individual, who did not disappear in a crowd. There never was a man who looked into those brown, burning eyes without being certain that Francis of Assisi was really interested in him—in his whole inner life as an individual, from the cradle to the grave, that he himself was being valued and taken seriously."[5]

114

Here is caring that is more than casual contact. Here is the pouring of one soul into another. Here is tact, sympathy, understanding, gentleness, humility and love. We, too, can ask for these gifts of the Holy Spirit and know that God will empower us to be as sensitive. "Christ in you, the hope of glory" (Col. 1:27, *NASB*).

If we are to care for the hurting, we need to identify with them, share their pain, touch their wounds, stand by in their bereavement and allow them the dignity of their emotions. We care when we do not want anyone to waste their suffering, or wallow in self-pity.

Clown Faces

Dear Lord,

My little Janie cuddles in my arms
            and says,
                "Let me paint a clown face
    on you, Mommy."

It was her own idea
        no one taught her this little game
            but we play it often together.

She paints my face
    in imaginary colors
        and I paint hers in turn.
We play this pointless little game
    over and over again.

Lord, grown up people play this
    in their game of life, too.
        They paint on a smiling face
        so that the world can't see their

115

```
    fear
       sadness
          defeat
             misery
                bitterness
                   and emptiness
                      in their hearts.

    Please, dear Lord, help me
       to see behind these grown-up clown faces
          show me the need of each heart
             that you send across my path
                by your Holy Spirit

    And, Lord, I ask you to show me
       how to help them
          drop their clown faces
             and reach out to you.
```

—Doris W. Greig

By itself, suffering is like an unsigned check—worthless! Too often, a cross remains just that—a cross. Of all the means of redemption, Christ chose suffering. Now, suffering is redemptive. Christ "signs the check," giving it value. "Now if we are children, then we are heirs—heirs of God and co-heirs with Christ, if indeed we share in his sufferings in order that we may also share in his glory. I consider that our present sufferings are not worth comparing with the glory that will be revealed in us" (Rom. 8:17,18, *NIV*).

We care when we ask those who are hurting to unite their aching hands with Christ's pierced hands. We care when we ask them to unite their broken hearts to Christ's heart. We care when we give some meaning to their suffering. We care not

116

only by words and deeds, but also through prayer.

Ruth Bell Graham wrote these words that express the heart cry of many who suffer:

> I cannot look you in the face
> God—
> these eyes—
> bloodshot
> bleary
> blurred
> shoulders slumped,
> soul slumped,
> heart too blank to care;
> fears
> worn out by fearing,
> life
> worn bare by living;
> —living?
> too old to live,
> too young to die.
> Who am I?
> God—
> Why?[6]

Many of us are afraid to listen to the fears of others. One of the most terrible aspects of the world today is that nobody wants to listen to anybody. When we are bereaved, alone, bewildered or frightened, nobody really wants to listen. Nobody has time to listen. Even those who love you don't seem to have the time. That is sad, isn't it? Perhaps we are guilty of the same action, shutting off hospitality to those who really need to come into our kitchen and sit over a cup of coffee and share their lives with us.

Sometimes we are afraid to listen because it may mean getting involved. It may mean re-evaluating our own priorities. It may mean sacrificing our own self-interests. Listening demands time and an abundance of patience. The demand seems even greater when we have no ready solution to the problems we hear, but we must ask God for the patience, because to listen is to care. We need to ask God to give us ears to hear what others want to say, what they are trying to say, and the reason why they need to say it. We need to listen to their silent cries. And we need to listen with attention. We need to be careful not to sound off with inane clichés. There are lonely, isolated, imprisoned people who need to share themselves with us. Will you open your heart and your home for this kind of sharing?

Recently, I heard a story that illustrates the terrible loneliness of many of the aged in our land today. There was a little old woman who lived alone in a dark, lonely room. It seems the neighbors paid little attention to her. She bothered no one until one day the newspapers were piled up outside her door. Curiosity prompted the neighbors to call the police. The woman was dead. "Dead for three days," the doctor said.

On her table was an open diary. For the past three weeks she had written in her diary: "Nobody came today." Next to the diary, a paper clipping was found. It said, "Six elderly people living alone found dead this year."

Many of the elderly in our land are forced to live alone because there is no one to care for them. They have no one to help them get institutional care. Many of them choose to live alone. Regardless of the reason, they are lonely. Loneliness is the ultimate poverty.

Science prolongs life, but science does not remove the anguish of loneliness. Now, in your church, in your neighborhood, in your community, there are people just like this little old woman who need your love. Not everyone is called to this ministry of hospitality, but some of you are feeling a tug in your hearts right now, thinking of a grandma, or a little old man down the street who may be newly widowed. Many times it is the man who is left behind that is more helpless and in need.

He needs to hear from your family. If the Lord is tugging at your heartstrings, you know He is calling you to this kind of hospitality friendship. Give your time, which is a gift from God, to invite the lonely into your home. Use your car to provide transportation for the elderly and handicapped. Thus, you will be given an open door to eventually share your Saviour with those who do not know Christ. And by allowing others to share more feelings than fact, you will brighten someone's day.

Share a bit of hospitality with pen, paper and a stamp. Writing takes time, but there are some ways to organize and do it painlessly. Stack your letters in two piles: one pile contains letters you want to answer when it is convenient; the other holds those that need immediate attention. Next, watch for small segments of time, such as waiting in a dentist's office, sitting and watching the news or waiting for the vegetables to cook at dinnertime. Have your stationery handy in a small box you can carry with you. Pull it out when you find a segment of time, and answer one letter at a time. You can also take advantage of other spare moments by carrying addressed, stamped envelopes and cards in your purse. In that way you can write a note and drop it in the mail immediately. And remember, people just need to hear from you; you don't have to write a book!

Writing is easier if you can think of it as a form of conversation. Don't just share facts and weather data, share your feelings to brighten someone's day. As you think of using letters as a form of hospitality, write them to encourage, praise, counsel and to give consolation. When distance separates you from a person, hospitality does not need to cease. Long-distance concern can be far-reaching through creative correspondence.

> *Handwritten hugs go where arms can't reach!*

Notes to those shut-ins and elderly people to whom God has called you to minister in your own community are always welcomed.

The telephone is another way of reaching out in hospitality to the lonely shut-in or the elderly person. Just the sound of a friendly, warm voice brings delight and healing into the days of many people. I have read of ministries where people volunteer their time to call the elderly and shut-ins once a day just to let them know they care about them, to check on them and to encourage them. This could be a ministry that God is calling you to. People need to know that someone is thinking about them, and cares for them. You can be Christ's representative as you pick up that telephone and dial it today. Telephone hospitality is a creative outlet for those who are called to such a ministry.

When Bill's Aunt Kay became very ill one summer in Minnesota, I was given the privilege of going back to the farm near Lowry to care for her, her husband and their home. She was suffering from heart failure, and needed careful watching and medication. What a blessing those three months were in my own life. I saw this dear woman of God at peace with her Lord, enjoying life, and with a sense of humor. At the same time, she knew that she would soon be going home. Home to be with her Saviour! Yet, what a victorious Christian she was as she awaited her "home going," always triumphant in Christ. She never spoke a cross word to me, although I knew that most of the time she was feeling very ill. I had to return to California in September; it was the next December that she went home to be with the Lord.

As I was allowed the privilege to cook, clean, wash and iron and shop for this dear couple, I was tremendously blessed. We never give out more than what God gives back to us in blessings! Sometimes we don't always see that immediately. And sometimes the elderly aren't as kind and gentle spirited as Auntie Kay was.

Auntie Kay's motto, framed and hung above the kitchen sink, was always an inspiration for me to trust God for His strength, day by day, moment by moment, as I helped her that summer. Now her picture motto hangs in my own kitchen, reminding me of Auntie Kay's triumph and peace in her last days on earth, and challenging me to trust Him daily. It reads, "Not Somehow, But Triumphantly."

I used to ponder which Scripture this motto was taken from. There are several verses from which it could have been inspired. First Corinthians 15:57 says "But thanks be to God, who gives us the victory through our Lord Jesus Christ" (*NASB*). Also, 2 Corinthians 2:14 could have been the inspiration—"But thanks be to God, who always leads us in His triumph in Christ, and manifests through us the sweet aroma of the knowledge of Him in every place" (*NASB*).

Certainly we are privileged if God calls us to be hospitable either in our own homes or in the homes of elderly or infirm people, to manifest "the sweet aroma of the knowledge of Him in every place." As we look to Jesus Christ, His life will flow through us. I realize that no one is adequate in their own strength and wisdom, but the following verses from this challenging hymn can be our prayer of commitment that the Lord will use us:

Is your life a channel of blessing?
Is the love of God flowing through you?
Are you telling the lost of the Savior?
Are you ready His service to do?

Make me a channel of blessing today,
Make me a channel of blessing, I pray;
My life possessing, my service blessing,
Make me a channel of blessing today.

—H.G. Smyth[7]

I had one other blessed experience of caring for an elderly aunt, my mother's sister, whose husband had just passed away. Not able to drive a car, she was totally helpless. So she was completely dependent upon me for her groceries, medicines, doctor visits and for the trips back and forth to the hospital to see her husband before he died of lung cancer and emphysema. I had the privilege of leading her husband to the Lord in the hospital. He had resisted the gospel message for years, but now that he knew his time was drawing near, he, like the thief on the cross, turned to Christ in faith. It was beautiful to experience such childlike, simple faith, which he expressed.

When he grew so weak that he was moved to intensive care and could no longer speak, I would take my aunt to his bedside. I would ask him if he still knew that Jesus was right there with him and caring for him; he would squeeze my hand to let me know, "Yes, I am still trusting Jesus!" I would ask him if he knew Christ had forgiven him and was right now preparing a place for him in heaven. Again, he would squeeze my hand so tight that it almost hurt me. What a joy it was to see this man, who had been an agnostic for years, and years come to faith in Jesus Christ!

After he died, I helped Aunt Lila with all of the funeral arrangements and got our pastor to preach at his service. The message was how Mack had come to know and love Christ. The family who gathered for the service, many of whom did not know the Lord, heard the "Good News" that day.

Afterwards, my aunt kept saying to me, "Where do you think Mack is now, Doris? Where do you think he is now?" What an opportunity God gave me! I opened my Bible and showed her the Scriptures I had read to Mack over and over again, and shared my faith with her as well. I asked her if she would like to come in simple faith to Christ and receive Him as her Saviour, and she responded immediately. From that day forward, Auntie Lila began to go to our Sunday School class with us, and gave her first testimony of faith shortly thereafter in that class. She attended church and Sunday School with us faithfully until she fell one day on the deck of her condominium and broke her hip.

Once again, I was privileged to care for her while she was in the hospital recovering from the broken hip. I had to arrange for 24-hour, around-the-clock nursing care for her when she came home from the hospital since I still had a family at home to care for. However, I called her each day and frequently went down to see her. I also brought the groceries and other essentials in to the nurses, as well as took this dear aunt of mine to the doctor for her return visits. We had good fellowship together, and grew even closer because of this beautiful experience. Her pain turned into a blessing for both of us. We used to sing hymns together as we drove in the car back and forth to the doctor's office, and as we took scenic drives around the area, so that she could enjoy a bit of the outdoors.

In the last few months that she lived, Auntie Lila kept saying, "Why is the Lord keeping me?" She was so very limited and was in a retirement home. She did not feel strong or well, and God had made her ready for heaven. I told her I didn't know why God was keeping her, but I knew He had a purpose, and one of the purposes was so I could enjoy her love and her sweetness a bit longer. This always pleased her, and she felt more at peace when I shared that Christ's timetable was perfect!

Auntie Lila went to be with the Lord Thanksgiving 1984. Bill and I had the privilege of conducting her funeral service, since she had no pastor in our area. We lived in Ventura, California, where we had moved three years earlier. Bill and I shared Auntie Lila's faith with the small family gathered at the graveside, just as our pastor had shared Uncle Mack's faith at his service in Glendale. Many wept gently as we shared Lila's favorite Scriptures and told of her faith in Christ. We shared how much she had longed to go home to be with Christ, and now she was in the home He had prepared for her in heaven!

Who knows how the seed of God was sown in hearts that day. The Bible tells us that some sow, others cultivate and the Lord harvests. Do not be discouraged if you have sown and see no immediate results. Remember that God is working in a life even when you can see nothing happening in the situation.

Both Mack and Lila had parents or grandparents who were praying people. Bill and I were privileged to see the harvest of their prayers. We are told to "Pray without ceasing" (1 Thess. 5:17, NASB). Never give up hope; just keep on praying for that one God has placed on your heart.

We read in John 4:34-38:

> Jesus said to them, "My food is to do the will of Him who sent Me, and to accomplish His work. Do you not say, 'There are yet four months, and *then* comes the harvest'? Behold, I say to you, lift up your eyes, and look on the fields, that they are white for harvest. Already he who reaps is receiving wages, and is gathering fruit for life eternal; that he who sows and he who reaps may rejoice together. For in this *case* the saying is true, 'One sows, and another reaps.' I sent you to reap that for which you have not labored; others have labored, and you have entered into their labor" (*NASB*).

God Is Calling You

1. Is there someone you know who tends to see his or her life from the underside of the tapestry? What steps can you take to help this person see God's beautiful plan for his or her life?

2. King David restored Mephibosheth's proper inheritance to

him, just as God has restored to us our inheritance through His Son Jesus Christ. Mephibosheth was seated at the king's table. Have you taken your rightly place at God's table? If not, what do you need to do to claim the treasures that God has in store for you? Many times all we have to do is *accept* what He has already given us. Does this apply to you?

3. Listening is an art and a most important part of conversation. How would you rate your listening skills? What could you do to improve upon those skills in order to be more open and sensitive to those around you?

4. Have you been challenged to start praying for someone or continue on in your prayers, even when the situation seems hopeless from a human view? Have you ever experiencd the joy of reaping a soul for Christ that someone else has prayed many years for?

Notes:
1. Anonymous. Source unknown.
2. Albert J. Nimeth from *I Like You Just Because: Thoughts on Friendship* (Chicago: Franciscan Herald Press, 1970). Used by permission.
3. Corrie ten Boom, *Not Good if Detached.* Copyright material—by kind permission of Christian Literature Crusade, Ft. Washington, PA, all rights reserved.
4. Ibid.
5. Albert J. Nimeth, *Tenderly I Care* (Chicago: Franciscan Herald Press, 1977).
6. From *Sitting by My Laughing Fire*, by Ruth Bell Graham, copyright © 1977. Used by permission of Word Books, Publisher, Waco, Texas.
7. H.G. Smyth, "Make Me a Channel of Blessing." © Copyright 1903. Public domain.

9

Reach Out and Touch Someone *Today*

Yes, there are many kinds of hospitality. And we can be assured that God always leads us to those opportunities He has equipped and empowered us to take hold of! He promises to give us the love to reach out and touch someone with Christ's love and compassion: "The love of God is shed abroad in our hearts by the Holy Ghost which is given unto us" (Rom. 5:5, *KJV*). Thus, we do not have to feel inadequate, nor unprepared when God sends opportunites our way for sharing His loving hospitality.

Through the years, your gifts of hospitality will change. So don't get yourself set into one pattern and say, "This is all I will ever do, because this is what I know how to do!" I have seen God change my directions, and other women's direction, in the patterns of hospitality we have practiced. Do you know that if you give just one cup of cold water to a workman who is thirsty, that is hospitality? The Lord wrote about this in Matthew, chapter 25.

We studied this passage earlier, but it bears repeating:

"Then I, the King, shall say to those at my right,

'Come, blessed of my Father, into the Kingdom prepared for you from the founding of the world. For I was hungry and you fed me; I was thirsty and you gave me water; I was a stranger and you invited me into your homes; naked and you clothed me; sick and in prison, and you visited me.'

"Then these righteous ones will reply, 'Sir, when did we ever see you hungry and feed you? Or thirsty and give you anything to drink? Or a stranger, and help you? Or naked, and clothe you? When did we ever see you sick or in prison, and visit you?'

"And I, the King, will tell them, 'When you did it to these my brothers you were doing it to me!' " (Matt. 25:34–40, *TLB*).

So you see, if we give a cup of cold water in the name of Jesus Christ, that is being hospitable, and we are doing it unto the Lord Jesus Christ.

I also picked up on the word *hungry* in this passage—this can refer to a spiritual or physical hunger. Those of us who watch today's news turn away in pain as we realize that much of our world is starving to death. But you know, we have countless opportunities to feed the hungry in our own communities and around the world. We can give of our food, serve it in our local mission kitchen or church kitchen, and that is hospitality in the name of Jesus Christ.

We can also respond in a warm way to the needs of the world by giving of our resources to mission agencies who supply food and clothing to the strangers of the world, as well as sharing the love of Jesus Christ with them.

In many places in the Old Testament, God teaches that we are to be generous and love the strangers as ourselves (see Lev. 19:34). "He gives justice to the fatherless and widows. He loves foreigners and gives them food and clothing. (You too

128

must love foreigners, for you yourselves were foreigners in the land of Egypt)" (Deut. 10:18, 19, *TLB*). God warns His people that they cannot know His blessing unless they are loving, generous and kind to the fatherless, widows and strangers. Deuteronomy 27:19 puts it this way, "Cursed is he who is unjust to the foreigner, the orphan, and the widow" (*TLB*).

God taught from the very beginning that the fields were not to be so thoroughly harvested that the poor could not glean them for their food. Leviticus 19:10 says, "And thou shalt not glean thy vineyard, neither shalt thou gather every grape of thy vineyard; thou shalt leave them for the poor and stranger: I *am* the Lord your God" (*KJV*).

This principle still stands today. If we are hospitable in the name of Jesus Christ, God will provide for our needs, as well as for the needs of strangers He calls us to minister to.

There is an organization in Ventura County, California, called *Project Understanding*, which has developed a gleaning of the fields program, their first step in meeting the food needs of people in this area.

From this first step, many other opportunities to help the poor and homeless have developed. Bakeries, grocery stores and warehouses give their excess products to this organization. This all started when God nudged one man, Virgil Nelson, and has grown since 1978 to the point where a full-time director was hired in 1985. What difference has *Project Understanding* made in Ventura County in this short span of years? Let's take a look. The following report from *Project Understanding* as found in their literature will give you a picture of the type of program they have:

> "Since 1978, Project Understanding has created or helped to establish many programs: Food Share (food bank), Brown Bag (groceries for seniors), Emergency Food Pantry (serving an average of 300 people per month), Family to Family Hot

Meals, Summer Food Program for Kids, Hunger Coalition (hunger education and sponsorship of six Crop Walks Against Hunger), Emergency Housing Task Force, Habitat for Humanity Ventura, Ventura Avenue Tutoring Station, The Coalition for the Homeless of Ventura County, and Ventura Avenue Neighborhood Improvement Program.

Since 1978, we have operated from private homes, garages and a donated city facility for Food Share in Saticoy. In 1982 and 1983, we operated out of an old fire station in Ventura, rent free. Beginning in 1984, the owners gave us a unique opportunity to purchase the old 3,600 square foot building. Sale Price: $105,000. They were excited about our work in the county, so they deducted $30,000. The Bargain Sale: We raise $75,000 plus closing costs in three years, and the sale is complete with no interest.

Our Board of Directors voted to make this purchase, which means: space for new programs, especially our focus on the homeless, without the problem of rent or continuous lease problems. Already we share offices for free counseling from other agencies, free showers, drop-in referrals for homeless, emergency food service for the hungry, and tutoring for school children."

This kind of thing can happen anywhere. If you are called by God to help care for the hungry, the homeless and those without Christ, God can use you to reach out in just such a way. You may want to cooperate with an already established program in your area, or He could use you to begin a program just as He used Virgil Nelson in Ventura County. The Lord may call you to reach out and touch someone for Him in this way.

> *If effort is organized, accomplishment follows.*

For further information write: Project Understanding, P.O. Box A.E., Ventura, CA 93002. Enclose a self-addressed, stamped envelope with your request.

The New Testament teaches that we are to store up our treasures in heaven, and some of those treasures are the thirsty, hungry, imprisoned and unclothed people whom God calls us to minister to physically and spiritually, that they may come to know Jesus Christ as their Lord and Saviour. Thus, the treasure that we lay up in heaven are those who come to know Jesus Christ through our ministry, and the ministry of other Christians. "Do not store up for yourselves treasures on earth, where moth and rust destroy, and where thieves break in and steal. But store up for yourselves treasures in heaven, where moth and rust do not destroy, and where thieves do not break in and steal. For where your treasure is, there your heart will be also" (Matt. 6:19–21, *NIV*).

I am reminded of people who say, "I can't afford to have people over for dinner," and offer other excuses for not extending hospitality in giving food and lodging to those in need. A parable of this type of thinking is told about a toddler, Emma Rivers, who got her hand stuck in a roadside grate trying to retrieve her lucky coin. It took a team of firemen to free her! Neighbors in Torquay, England, tried butter, grease and laundry detergent to no avail. The tot's hand remained inside the grate. When firemen finally freed her, they discovered the five-year-old could have easily slipped her hand through the grill if she had merely released her grip on the coin. Many a Christian

131

"vision" is impaired by money, just as this little girl's judgment was impaired by her lost coin! We need to take God's Word to heart. In Ecclesiastes 7:18 we read, "Tackle every task that comes along, and if you fear God you can expect his blessing" (*TLB*).

We are told by the Lord to visit the sick. This is a ministry that any Christian can have, although it does take some effort. We need to be willing to sacrifice our own personal time and resources if we are to minister to the sick. Hot dishes taken to the family of a sick mother are much appreciated. It helps to keep some homemade soup or casseroles and muffins in your freezer for times such as these. Caring for their children and doing simple basic housework for them until they recuperate is another way that one family can minister to another. Driving the sick to the doctor or to the hospital is another act of Christian love. Simply getting behind the wheel of your car and driving someone to the doctor or the hospital is a service of hospitality. God will give you all sorts of creative ideas! These are just a few of the things that you might do for your neighbors. Hospitality, in this way, is a two-way street. You will reap a harvest of goodwill, respect and love from your neighbors. This was one of the ministries God equipped me for. If your neighbors are like mine, they will in turn extend hospitality in a similar manner to you. It is then that you are able to build bridges to share your faith in Jesus Christ.

We need to reach out to that hurting neighbor: the widowed, the recently divorced, those out of work, those suffering the loss of a baby or child, the person experiencing physical or emotional pain. Whatever the cause, they need us there to stand by them and to pray for them.

When you are younger, you have ready-made bridge builders! Did you know that? No, bridge builders are not necessarily big diesel tractors and trucks that make lots of noise and lift dirt. If you are a young mother, your bridge builders are your children! My bridge builders are all grown, and I miss them terribly.

I have to build bridges in other ways now. But children are the most wonderful bridge builders; they provide opportunities for meeting your neighbors and finding out their needs.

I remember one day when my next-door neighbor Anna called me on the phone. My bridge builders had brought her to my yard with her child and we had become close friends as we sat around the swimming pool, lifeguarding our children. On this afternoon she called, sobbing uncontrollably; she asked me to come to her home immediately. I told her I would be right over. In this case, she couldn't even make it to my kitchen door for me to offer her a cup of coffee. I had to take my hospitality to her house this time.

Anna was 40 and had prayed to have another baby. It was her last chance, and she was now pregnant. The doctor had just informed her that the cord had wrapped around the baby's neck and she would have to carry that dead baby until natural labor came. I could never understand her doctor's decision; the emotional pain for her was almost unbearable. All I knew was that I was allowed to put my arms around my neighbor and give her a warm hug and kiss, and let her cry on my shoulder. What a privilege of hospitality it was, to minister to her in her kitchen. Although she was of an entirely different faith, Anna asked me to pray for her, and I was allowed to pray in the name of my Lord and Saviour, Jesus Christ.

Ruth Graham's poem expresses wise advise to us:

> Never turn your back
> on tears,
> do not stem the flow;
> put your arms about her
> gently,
> let her go.
> Knowing why
> is not important,

weeping
sometimes is.
Let her cry—
but kindly—
with a kiss.[1]

It was interesting to me that Anna called me and in her tears
requested I come and pray with her, rather than calling a member of the cult church to which she belonged. I thank God that I
was the first one she called and that I had taken time to build a
bridge of friendship earlier on. It would have been so easy to
plead a multitude of demands upon my time. It would have
been so easy to say in those earlier days, "I have too many
things to do; I don't have time to sit around the pool with my
neighbors." Yet, how important are these demands? Being
available means to take the initiative; to be there to listen when
the conversation is light, so that you will have the opportunity
when the crisis comes to listen and pray with that one whom
God sends your way.

Someone has written, "Oh, the comfort, the inexpressible
comfort of feeling safe with a person." May it be each Christian's prayer that those whom our lives touch will feel safe with
us at all times, so that they can open up their hearts to us, in joy
and in sadness.

Robert Lewis Stevenson said, "A friend is a present you
give yourself." I have taken friendship and made it into an
acrostic of characteristics that make one the kind of friend others want to have for a present for themselves.

> F—Fun loving; Feeling of acceptance; Faithful in all
> circumstances
> R—Risk being real; Risk being understood or mis-
> understood
> I—Interested in the welfare of others; Impartial
> E—Expect the best of others; Empathetic

134

N—Natural relationship (a wholesome acceptance of the person); Nonexclusive

D—Diplomatic; Delightful to be with; Durable in hard times

S—Sympathetic; Supportive with prayer and help; Stable and loyal

H—Helpful; Hopeful; Healing; Happy

I—Interdependent by helping each other (not a one-way friendship); Interested in the best for the person

P—Patient; Protective of reputation and confidences; Pleasant to be with; Personable (neat and clean)

As I think about friendship, I wonder if I had my life to live over, how differently I would live it. Would I have invited more friends over for dinner, even if it was just for a hamburger fry or macaroni and cheese? Would I have sat on the lawn more often with my neighbors and visited while we watched the children play? Would I have cried more often with them when appropriate, and laughed more when that was in order? Would I have said, "I'm sorry" more often?

If I were given another opportunity at life, I would seize every minute of it! I would look at it and *really* see it and live it for Jesus Christ. I realize I will never live this day again.

Someone has written these words entitled "God's Day":

There are two days in the week upon which, and about which I never worry—two carefree days kept sacredly free from fear and apprehension. One of these days is Yesterday. Yesterday, with its cares and frets and pains and aches, all its faults, its mistakes and blunders, has passed forever beyond my recall. It was mine; it is God's.

The other day that I do not worry about is Tomorrow. Tomorrow, with all its possible adversities, its burdens, its perils, its large promise and performance, its failures and mistakes, is as far beyond my mastery as its dead sister, Yesterday. Tomorrow is God's Day; it will be mine. There is left, then, for myself but one day in the week—Today. Any person can fight the battles of today. Any woman can carry the burdens of just one day; any man can resist the temptations of today. It is only when we willfully add the burdens of these two awful eternities—Yesterday and Tomorrow—such burdens as only the Mighty God can sustain—that we break down.

It isn't the experience of Today that drives people mad. It is the remorse of what happened Yesterday and fear of what Tomorrow might bring. These are God's Days—Leave them to Him.[2]

Ian Thomas put it this way, "God has plans—no problems. There is no panic in heaven." We just need to look to Jesus and pray, "Teach me thy way, O Lord" (Ps. 27:11, *KJV*).

The day is long
and all that I must do
too much for my small strength.
When at length
the day is through,
shall I find
I failed to tap
the Infinite Resources
forever open to the weak
who seek?
Shall I die

136

regretting
not getting?
Shall joy
weep
for my sake
—who would not
take?

—Ruth Bell Graham[3]

There are restless millions awaiting the coming of the light of Jesus Christ, who makes all things new. Christ also waits, but we, as His ambassadors, are slow and few. Have we done all we can? Have I? Have you? The Scriptures challenge us: "The harvest is plentiful, but the workers are few. Ask the Lord of the harvest, therefore, to send out workers into his harvest field" (Luke 10:2, *NIV*).

Ask the Lord what He would have you do on this, "His day." "Let us not become weary in doing good, for at the proper time we will reap a harvest if we do not give up" (Gal. 6:9, *NIV*). Draw upon the resources from the Spring of Life, the Lord Jesus Christ, and you will not grow weary in doing good. You will be like the person described in Psalm 1:3, "Like a tree planted by streams of water, which yields its fruit in season and whose leaf does not wither. Whatever he does prospers" (*NIV*).

So reach out and touch someone with the love of Christ today! Trust God, for His promises are true. "The Lord will guide you always; he will satisfy your needs in a sun-scorched land and will strengthen your frame. You will be like a well-watered garden, like a spring whose waters never fail . . . . You will be called Repairer of Broken Walls, Restorer of Streets with Dwellings" (Isa. 58:11,12, *NIV*).

God *will* use you to repair and restore the broken walls and streets in your neighborhood, community and world, as you trust the Lord Jesus Christ to be your guide and your strength. People will be drawn to you, seeing you as a well-watered garden, like a spring whose waters never fail, because of Christ's inner power and strength in your life in the person of the Holy Spirit. You will seem like a ministering angel to those to whom God calls you. So reach out and touch someone for Jesus today!

God Is Calling You

1. Does your area have program such as *Project Understanding?* If so, have you investigated what is being offered through this organization, and how you and your family can get involved? If not, would you care to get one started?

2. This chapter discussed youngsters as being bridge builders. Do you have ready-made bridge builders in your family? Do you have an example in your life that illustrates how through your children you were able to develop a relationship with a neighbor or parent of one of your children's school friends? Through this experience have you been able to share God's love and concern for this person?

3. When "Anna" was in serious need, she turned to her Christian friend instead of going to someone from her cult church. Have you had the privilege and great joy to be able to pray in the name of Jesus Christ for someone like Anna?

4. What kind of a friend are you? Do you have several of the qualities and characteristics named in the acrostic appearing in this chapter? Which qualities are your strong qualities and which of those do you need to make better?

Notes:
1. From *Sitting by My Laughing Fire,* by Ruth Bell Graham, copyright © 1977; used by permission of Word Books, Publisher, Waco, Texas.
2. Author unknown.
3. From *Sitting by My Laughing Fire,* by Ruth Bell Graham, copyright © 1977; used by permission of Word Books, Publisher, Waco, Texas.

10

Relaxed Availability

"Two are better than one; because they have a good reward for their labour." (Eccles. 4:9, *KJV*).

Often it is easier to be hospitable when you can share the responsibilities with someone else. We find an example of this type of hospitality when the apostle Paul left Athens and went to Corinth. Here, "He met a Jew named Aquila, a native of Pontus, who had recently come from Italy with his wife Priscilla" (Acts 18:2, *NIV*). Priscilla could have missed the blessing of having Paul stay in her home if she had said, "We can't have company; we're not settled into our new home in Corinth yet." But, both Priscilla and Aquila opened their home and their hearts to Paul the tentmaker who stayed and worked with this couple.

Every Sabbath Paul reasoned in the Synagogue trying to persuade the Jews and Greeks through his preaching that Jesus was the Christ. Thus, we see in relaxed availability the hospitable teamwork of Priscilla and Aquila to one God had sent their way. They were "enablers" allowing Paul to be a tentmaker during the week and on the Sabbath preach in the Synagogue.

One June day, we were given the opportunity to be an

enabler to Ray Netherly, with Campus Crusade for Christ. He had come to Minnesota in the early days of this organization to open the first chapter of Campus Crusade at the University of Minnesota. Bill and I invited him to stay in our home despite the fact that, as earlier stated, I was expecting a baby on July 3, and, as I was threatening to miscarry, had to be off my feet most of the time. This was the summer we had George and Dick Kraft, sons of missionaries from Taiwan, with us as well as Mary, a foster daughter who was a great help with the household chores.

The household ran amazingly smooth that summer because my husband was a tremendous help. He has continued to be my helpmate for over 35 years! We have found out that indeed, "two are better than one."

We so enjoyed hearing Ray tell how things were going at the University. The Lord was really opening doors for the new ministry, which continues to this day. We thank God that He allowed us to play an active part in His work that first summer.

We still have "a good reward" for our labor of love in opening our home to Ray. Hundreds and hundreds of students at the university have come to know Christ personally, and Christians have been encouraged in their faith as better witnesses through the Bible studies given by Ray and other Campus Crusade leaders through the years. Ray's wife Eunie came to Minnesota in the fall; they rented a home near the campus.

One funny little side note (and there will always be some when you open your hearts and homes to others) was the day I came home from the hospital with our first son, Bill Greig III. Ray and Eunie had no children. Ray, along with the Kraft boys, Mary and our nearly four-year-old daughter Kathy came rushing into the living room to see the baby.

I shall never forget Ray's first comment! He looked at my beautiful baby, my miracle child, and said, "Why, he looks just like a little red monkey."

I didn't know whether to be hurt, insulted or disappointed.

So, I chose none of the above emotions. I laughed and told Ray that when Eunie has her first baby, I might see a little red monkey too; he might not be so excited about my first impressions of his child. Ray and Eunie had four daughters in the years to come, and they were all tiny, rather red babies I thought. I managed to restrain my thoughts as I viewed them though, remembering that I thought my baby boy was one of the most beautiful babies in the nursery. They undoubtedly felt the same about their babies, so why should I say anything different.

So you see, when you make yourself available, you are opening yourself up to some little hurts, and sometimes big hurts. Yet, God still calls us to be hospitable in some way or another, and we are to respond faithfully when He calls.

We see loving and obedient availability in the home of Mary and Joseph, where the Lord Jesus Christ was welcomed and nurtured from birth. Joseph obeyed God after hearing an angel of the Lord reveal to him that, "'The virgin will be with child and will give birth to a son, and they will call Him Immanuel'—which means, 'God with us'" (Matt. 1:23, *NIV*). As we read on in chapter one, we discover that Joseph did as the Lord commanded him, and when Mary gave birth to a son, he gave Him the name Jesus. Mary, in the same way, was obedient to the Lord when the angel told her, "Do not be afraid, Mary, you have found favor with God. You will be with child and give birth to a son, and you are to give him the name Jesus. He will be great and will be called the Son of the Most High. The Lord God will give him the throne of his father David, and he will reign over the house of Jacob forever; his kingdom will never end" (Luke 1:30–33, *NIV*).

Mary's response to the angel's message was, "I am the Lord's servant . . . May it be to me as you have said" (Luke 1:38, *NIV*). Here we see the hospitality of Mary and Joseph as they opened their hearts and their home to the Lord Jesus Christ. The so-called lost years in the life of Christ as a child are

141

still not known to us today. Yet, we can imagine the loving home that Mary and Joseph provided for the Lord Jesus.

We read of Joseph's loving care when he set aside his own plans in order to escape to Egypt because the wicked King Herod plotted to kill Jesus (see Matt. 2:13). Joseph and Mary were instantly available to leave at a moment's notice for Egypt, and they stayed there until the death of King Herod.

Obedience to the Lord's leading continues, as we see in Matthew 2:20. An angel of the Lord again appeared in a dream to Joseph, instructing him to take the child and his mother and go back to the land of Israel: "For those who were trying to take the child's life are dead" (*NIV*). Again we see Mary and Joseph's availability to be obedient to God and return to the land of Israel where they settled in Galilee, in a town called Nazareth. Thus, the prophecy was fulfilled: "He shall be called a Nazarene" (Matt. 2:23, *KJV*).

Certainly Mary and Joseph exhibited "relaxed availability" to the Lord in their life responses to His call. It wasn't always easy or pleasant either. Quite the opposite is seen in the inn-keeper's life at Bethlehem where Joseph and Mary had gone to register for the census that was required by Caesar Augustus.

The innkeeper found no room for the young couple. He was too busy making money. Mary and Joseph were sent to a stable behind the inn, where the Christ child was born and laid in a manger (see Luke 2:7). What a blessing the innkeeper and his family missed that night. Somehow I feel they could have found a space for this dear, young pregnant Mary, and the Lord Jesus' stepfather Joseph. Looking at it from a human stand-point, it seems like a very heartless act to send a young woman in labor back to a stable to have her baby.

Yet, how often are we just as unavailable when God sends someone in need our way? It is so easy to rationalize, "There will come a day when I can do this and this, and this; but right now I am not able to." Or, "This is too much of a risk. I don't want to be hurt." Or, "This is too hard for me to do." We may say, "My house is too small," or we may even use the same excuse the innkeeper used: "My house is too crowded."

We are not all called to the same kind of hospitality, but I want to share this next story to show that if we keep entertaining simple it is not so threatening.

One summer, we had visited in many churches in Mexico, and everywhere we went my husband would say, "If you are ever up our way, do come and see us." Well, one summer day at about 3:30 in the afternoon, the doorbell rang. It was very hot that day, and I had been lifeguarding by the pool. I ran to the door and opened it to a group of five teachers and a pastor I vaguely remembered meeting in Mexico. Beyond them across the street I saw two buses, each packed with about 20 junior- and senior-high school students. They were on a singing tour for the Lord, and their next stop was Glendale. So, they had all come to see us!

Remember the K.I.S.S. motto, "Keep it simple, stupid!" Well, everyone came in, changed into bathing suits and went for a swim. While I got wieners and hot dog buns out of the freezer, someone went to the store for fruit and ice cream. We used paper plates and fed everyone while sitting around the pool. We all had such a good time. It was fun to watch their joy.

Now, had I known earlier about this gang coming, I would have really panicked! Looking back, I'm glad I did the meal simply, so I too could enjoy the teachers and young people. God provided the energy just when I needed it.

> If you have faith—God's got the power!
> If you make the commitment—God opens the
>   way!
> If you make the pledge—God gives you
> the winning edge![1]

How quickly time passes by. Opportunities are missed simply by putting off until tomorrow what we could do today. It is not too late! As the Lord calls us, we need to immediately follow Him with relaxed availability. This means that we do not worry about what others think of us or our homes when God calls us to minister to them. We need to put aside our pride, humble ourselves and open our hearts and homes to those whom God sends our way. We need never apologize for dust or slight clutter in our home. After all, we all belong to the same human race, and this is part of it!

One evening we had five dinner guests, and they were to stay overnight. As we were having dinner, I looked up at the dining room chandelier and saw cobwebs trailing to the ceiling! I laughed and said, "We have busy spiders in this house." I didn't let it bother me. There was a day when I would have been embarrassed to even mention the fact, and would hope that they'd never notice. I think we can put our guests more at ease by letting them know we are not perfect. This enables them to have relaxed availability in their homes also.

There is a little trick I have learned, and that is to turn the lights down low and use candlelight. Your house will look so nice and clean in this type of light. Even the dirty windows don't show up at night; that's a wonderful side benefit!

We are urged in Romans not to think too highly of ourselves. It is so easy to be conformed to this world, but Paul instructs the Christian to "Be transformed by the renewing of your mind, that you may prove what the will of God is, that which is good and acceptable and perfect" (Rom. 12:2, NASB). Certainly a relaxed availability to the will of God is good, acceptable and perfect. When we want to appear perfect to a world that tries to conform us to perfection in our homes, as well as in the way we dress and appear, through TV, newspapers and magazines, we need to remember the principles from God's Word. He has told us not to be conformed to this world: "Don't let the world around you squeeze you into its own mold, but let God remold your minds from within, so that you may prove in practice that the plan of God for you is good, meets all his demands and moves toward the goal of true maturity" (Rom. 12:2, *Phillips*).

In Romans 12:3 we are told, "Don't cherish exaggerated ideas of yourself or your importance, but try to have a sane estimate of your capacities by the light of the faith that God has given to you all" (*Phillips*).

Pride interferes with relaxed available hospitality and sound judgment. We need to keep our priorities straight! Paul expressed it in Galatians 6:14: "As for me, God forbid that I should boast about anything except the cross of our Lord Jesus Christ. Because of that cross my interest in all the attractive things of the world was killed long ago, and the world's interest in me is also long dead" (*TLB*).

What we are to do and be, and the power given to us by the Holy Spirit for that, is described in John 15:11–14: "I have told you this so that you will be filled with my joy. Yes, your cup of joy will overflow! I demand that you love each other as much as I love you. And here is how to measure it—the greatest love is shown when a person lays down his life for his friends; and you are my friends if you obey me" (*TLB*).

The Lord Jesus goes on to say, "You didn't choose me! I chose you! I appointed you to go and produce lovely fruit always, so that no matter what you ask for from the Father, using my name, he will give it to you" (John 15:16, *TLB*). Here the Lord Jesus deals with us as our friend from eternity, preparing us to be a friend to those He calls us to with His unconditional love: "The greatest love is shown when a person lays down his life for his friends" (v. 13).

The living Lord Jesus wants to give us a ministry that is relaxed and available to the "unlovely" as well as the "lovely," in order to shower His blessings on all people. When our great friend of eternity, the Lord Jesus, deals with us and empowers us with the Holy Spirit, we can be a friend, even to those who have hurt us. We can relax in the will of God, and minister His love to the people He calls us to be hospitable to.

145

Jesus Christ wants to make us the kind of friend who becomes involved in the needs of others, even when we are not invited to do so. He wants us to be willing to give ourselves away, whether people deserve it or not. Christ calls us to dare to be to people all that He has been to us. He gave His all, laid down His life for us and He asks us who are indwelled by the Holy Spirit to give ourselves in hospitable love.

The Lord has built into our nature the longing for deep, intimate associations in which we can care, and be cared for. Thus, He longs to bind us together in mutual support in a relaxed hospitable atmosphere. None of us can make it alone. We need the Lord and each other.

Some of the people whom God calls us to minister to may be some of the most difficult people in our lives. They are people who have hurt us, frustrated us and disturbed us by their actions or attitudes. There are those who have disappointed us or brought great heartache into our lives, and here is Jesus Christ speaking to us through this passage in John telling us that He has laid down His life for just these sorts of people. He challenges us to lay down our lives for such people too. It is when we minister in the name of Jesus that He comes to us and says, "Inasmuch as ye have done *it* unto one of the least of these my brethren, ye have done *it* unto me" (Matt. 25:40, *KJV*).

Christ always matches perfectly what is needed in the life of another with that which He has given to us, or has allowed us to experience. God enables us to grow through trials and tests, and this, in turn, enables us to minister to others in their trials. Thus, we are privileged to be the channel of Christ's grace to another, by the power of the Holy Spirit.

We are only asked to open our lives for His "water of life" to flow through us. We are to empty ourselves of foolish pride and selfishness so that He can fill us with the refreshing water from His springs, high in the mountains. "And if you give yourself to the hungry, and satisfy the desire of the afflicted, then your light will rise in darkness, and your gloom *will become* like midday. And the Lord will continually guide you, and satisfy your desire in scorched places, and give strength to your bones; and you will be like a watered garden, and like a spring of water whose waters do not fail" (Isa. 58:10,11, *NASB*).

We often feel inadequate and weak, but these words of the apostle Paul should encourage us: " 'My grace is sufficient for you, for power is perfected in weakness.' Most gladly, therefore, I will rather boast about my weaknesses, that the power of Christ may dwell in me" (2 Cor. 12:9, *NASB*).

Later Paul wrote, "Now unto him that is able to do exceeding abundantly above all that we ask or think, according to the power that worketh in us, unto him *be* glory in the church by Christ Jesus throughout all ages, world without end. Amen" (Eph. 3:20,21, *KJV*).

Only as we, in our weakness, rely upon the grace of God and His power that works within us can we hope to see glory brought to Christ, and see the revelation of His glory to all generations forever and ever.

This following poem by Jo Carr and Imogene Sorley seems to sum up the call of God to every Christian to relaxed availability in His service of hospitality:

Dear Lord,

My faith contains such splendid, glowing nouns:

holiness
benediction
peace
heaven.

They are words rich in meaning, and just saying them over brings an image of dimly lighted sanctu-

147

aries and stained-glass windows. And I bask in this feeling of goodwill. But somehow the verbs don't give the same comfortable warmth:

come	forgive
go	work
do	pardon
be	understand
help	love.
console	

They *require* of me.
    They require not just a feeling, but an action.
They require involvement
    and straining my mind
    and getting my hands dirty.
They require more than the self-fulfillment, the
    receiving of the nouns.
They require an *expenditure* of self for the good of
    all mankind.
They require of me.
You require of me.
I go.
        Amen.[2]

Any love that we have for another human being stems from the fact that God loved us before we loved Him (see 1 John 4:19). His commandment to love others as He loved them is impossible apart from the fact that He loved us! Thus, He calls us to be a hospitable friend to sinners, to failures and a friend to all those in spiritual, emotional or physical need.

Christ went about doing good, and He was always interruptible and available. He had eyes to see, and was always sensitive to the one in the crowd who needed Him most. He wants to give us "eyes that see" the needs of those around us. Christ was drawn like a magnet wherever people needed Him. He also wants us to open our hearts and homes that people may be drawn like magnets into the territory of God where they can come to know His grace and love. Figuratively, let us put on God's "eyeglasses" as we listen and look at the people around us today.

We are called to lay down our lives for others; this is not laying down our lives in atonement as Christ did. It is a voluntary sacrifice of self, the expenditure of self, time, energy and resources for the good of another. We do not repeat the atonement, but we claim its power! Thus, we claim the love that was exposed on Calvary, and lay down our lives for others in Christ's resurrection power. On the basis of Christ's death and resurrection, we are to lay down our schedules, lay down our time, lay down our possessions, lay down our unforgiveness, lay down our selfish attitudes, and our laziness, and reach out with the reconciling love of Jesus Christ in hospitable ways. To lay down our lives in such a manner is to become vulnerable. We dare to risk and to take the first step, regardless of what another person has said or done. The question is, "Are we willing to be a channel of God's love?" That is "relaxed availability!"

We need to remember to pray and invite the Lord to be our guide and guest whenever we open our hearts and homes. In this way, the Holy Spirit will be in charge of our hospitality and it will be warm and relaxed because of the Lord. Whether we have guests for 15 minutes, an evening, overnight or for a matter of weeks, we need to ask Christ to bring His peace into our household so that it will be evident to all. May it be our goal, as well as our prayer, to be relaxed, available and good listeners. If so, He will enable us to enjoy our guests. They in turn will know God's blessing through our relaxed, available hospitality, whatever the occasion or length of time.

Always Thinking

Thinking, always thinking . . .

Again today, dear Lord
I think of my friend
And the miserable quarrel
That shattered our friendship
After years of beautiful closeness . . .

I think of the soloist
I refuse to acknowledge
On a worshipful Sunday morning
Because of envy and pride . . .

I think of the young mother
Down the street
Deserted and divorced
Picking up bits and pieces . . .

The wrinkled old woman
Languishing in a rest home
For many faithful years
Taught me from God's Word . . .

Thinking, always thinking . . .

Lord, if suddenly You said,

"This is your last week
On the planet called Earth"
How quickly, how spontaneously
My thoughts would convert to action.

How eagerly I would do
In seven short days
What You persistently pressed upon me
For the past several months.
Lord, is it too late?

"And they immediately . . . followed Him" (Matt.
4:20).

—Ruth Harms Calkins[3]

God Is Calling You

1. Generally, how would you rate yourself in the area of
   "relaxed availability"? Are you quick to respond positively
   to opportunities to be hospitable even when the occasions
   don't seem to fit in with your plans?

2. In the past, have you let opportunities slip by thinking you
   would be better prepared at a later date to accommodate
   someone's need? Think of the times when you didn't put off
   until *tomorrow* what God was calling you to do *today* in the
   way of reaching out to others. Compare the blessings or
   lack of blessings evidenced in both cases.

3. Have you come up with any little hints along the way that
   allow you to be more relaxed about having guests in for dinner or for an evening of fellowship?

4. Oftentimes we feel inadequate and weak when it comes to opening our hearts and homes to others. God tells us His power is made perfect in our weakness. What areas of your life do you consider to be weak spots? Have you called upon God for His grace and power in these particular areas?

Notes:
1. Author unknown.
2. From *Bless This Mess and Other Prayers* by Jo Carr and Imogene Sorley. Copyright © 1969 by Abingdon Press. Used by permission.
3. Ruth Harms Calkins, *Lord It Keeps Happening and Happening* (Wheaton, IL: Tyndale, 1984).

11

Plenty of Help!

Sometimes we feel like the prophet Elijah who ran 90 miles for his life! He collapsed beneath the juniper tree; overwhelmed with self-pity, he declared, "'I've had enough . . . . Take away my life. I've got to die sometime, and it might as well be now'" (1 Kings 19:4, *TLB*).

These were truly human emotions that Elijah experienced as he sat under the broom brush and prayed to God. Then he slept!

While he was sleeping, an angel touched him and told him to get up and eat. "He looked around and saw some bread baking on hot stones, and a jar of water! So he ate and drank and lay down again. Then the angel of the Lord came again and touched him and said, 'Get up and eat some more, for there is a long journey ahead of you'" (1 Kings 19:6,7, *TLB*).

Elijah wisely chose to act in obedience to God and ate and drank the food given to him, which in turn gave him the

153

strength to travel 40 days and 40 nights to Mount Horeb, the mountain of God. Here the Lord spoke to him and asked, " 'What are you doing here, Elijah?' He replied, 'I have worked very hard for the Lord God of the heavens; but the people of Israel have broken their covenant with you and torn down your altars and killed your prophets, and only I am left; and now they are trying to kill me, too' " (vv. 9,10).

God dealt with Elijah's self-pity by telling him to go stand on the mountain and hear the Lord reveal His power to him! "The Lord passed by, and a mighty windstorm hit the mountain; it was such a terrible blast that the rocks were torn loose, but the Lord was not in the wind. After the wind, there was an earthquake, but the Lord was not in the earthquake. And after the earthquake, there was a fire, but the Lord was not in the fire. And after the fire, there was the sound of a gentle whisper. When Elijah heard it, he wrapped his face in his scarf and went out and stood at the entrance of the cave. And a voice said, 'Why are you here, Elijah?' " (1 Kings 19:11–13, *TLB*).

God proceeded to give instructions to Elijah and encouraged him by giving him Elisha to replace him as a prophet.

Thus, we see what self-pity can do to us. Elijah had such fear that, forgetting that God was in control, he only looked inward and saw many enemies. He felt unloved, deserted and trapped. He felt that there was no one else who loved God, and that only he was left as faithful. God told him, " 'And incidentally, there are 7,000 men in Israel who have never bowed to Baal [a false idol] nor kissed him," (1 Kings 19:18, *TLB*).

Haven't we all felt like this at one time or another? The smog that pollutes the air and hides the glory of the sun and all creation is a parable picture of self-pity, which is the smog that pollutes the soul and obscures the light of the Son of God. As the smog hurts our eyes and does untold damage to our bodies, so self-pity causes pain, tears in the eyes, doubt of God's power in the soul and brings about the great sting of loneliness, just as Elijah knew it.

154

God knows us because He created us. Just as He did not rebuke His prophet, Elijah, but ministered to him, He longs to minister to us. If we will just stop running long enough to listen to Him, He will supply our rest and our nourishment, both physical and spiritual, to refresh us. As He encouraged Elijah to take a long rest and to eat well, He helped Elijah, through this simple technique, to get his eyes off himself and his situation.

He gently prodded the prophet to focus anew on the Lord God who is always there, and always available to give strength to those who will trust in Him. "I can do all things through Him who strengthens me" (Phil. 4:13, *NASB*). Not only did God provide Elijah with renewed strength, but He also gave him a close friend named Elisha, with whom he might share his life and load here on earth.

We feel sorry for ourselves today, don't we? We feel trapped into hospitality, be it a meal, an overnight guest or ministering to someone over a cup of coffee. We can become as easily caught up in self-pity as Elijah was! But why not try God's remedy: a decent, well-balanced diet and plenty of rest to renew us mentally and physically.

As God called Elijah to stop and listen to Him on the mountain, He calls to us today to take a well-needed look at our Saviour through His Word, the Bible. The pattern also calls for all of this to be followed with quality time spent with a friend whom God will provide.

If we follow this perfect pattern that God has created for us, and we see illustrated in 1 Kings 19, we will be amazed at the outcome. We will discover that God has "plenty of help" available to us for any form of hospitality He calls us to.

God longs for Christians to develop spiritual insight, rather than to dwell in the realm of the obvious, the expected, the ordinary. Many refuse to go deeper, to believe God more for His strength in the possibilities that He offers to us for service to Him through hospitality. We allow ourselves to be overwhelmed with self-pity, when we should look to the Lord for

155

wisdom and strength. I have been caught in this "snare of the devil" from time to time.

Even the disciples were guilty of this "nearsightedness." We read in Mark chapter 6 of the disciples whom Jesus sent away in a boat after He had miraculously fed thousands of people with a few loaves and fish. Jesus slipped off to a quiet place on a mountain to pray, while the disciples were crossing the Sea of Galilee.

Suddenly a storm broke upon the sea, and they were filled with panic. Christ came to their rescue and calmed the sea by stilling the wind. He assured them there was no reason to be afraid. Mark later comments on this event by stating in his Gospel: "They were greatly astonished, for they had not gained any insight from the *incident of* the loaves, but their heart was hardened" (Mark 6:51,52, *NASB*). Jesus had spoken the words, " 'It's all right . . . . It is I! Don't be afraid' " (Mark 6:50, *TLB*).

> *Sometimes the Lord calms the storm; sometimes He lets the storm rage and calms the believer!*

It wasn't that the disciples were unable to understand; they just didn't want to understand. They were insensitive to God's power, even after seeing Him multiply the loaves and fish to feed the crowd. They made a choice to fear the storm.

We say, "What a tragedy! They knew the Lord, they saw Him face to face, and yet they did not believe in His power to help them." Had they applied what they had observed earlier that day, when the thousands were fed, their response to the storm would have been insightful trust in the Lord Jesus. They would have called immediately to their Saviour for help.

And yet, how many of us, when feeling overloaded and fearing the circumstances in our own lives, forget to cry out to Jesus Christ for His help? We are like the disciples described in Hebrews chapter 5. It says that some had become "dull of hearing" (v. 11, *NASB*), lazy, lacking insight and maturity. We find God challenging our hearts through these words from Hebrews 6:1, "Let us go on instead to other things and become mature in our understanding, as strong Christians ought to be" (*TLB*).

Just as Christ prepared a feast for the crowd on the shores of Galilee, He may call us to prepare in some small manner a "feast" for needy people. It may not necessarily be *food* He asks us to provide for them. It may be instead time, energy or space in our home. We need to put our trust and faith in Jesus Christ's abundant supply of resources, recognizing that He will never leave us or forsake us (see Heb. 13:5) and that by His Spirit, He will provide all that we need. "Be very careful, then, how you live—not as unwise but as wise, making the most of every opportunity, because the days are evil. Therefore do not be foolish, but understand what the Lord's will is" (Eph. 5:15–17, *NIV*).

As we ponder these things, we realize that leisure time is a rare treasure, a gift from God to restore us. It is important to read God's Word, and to seek His will for each day, treasuring it as a new gift from God.

Analyze what relaxation means to you. Then choose to spend a portion of each day relaxing in the presence of the Lord. Enjoy some form of relaxation that restores you physically as well. Your "thing" may be to read, walk, work puzzles, sew, bowl, play tennis, work in the yard, bake or something entirely different. Choose to use your leisure time wisely; do not squander it!

> *You will never find time for anything. If you want time, you must make it.*
>
> —*Charles Buxton*

Sometimes relaxation comes in big chunks, but most often I find "small breaks" in my day are times for refreshment from the Lord. Often, leisure time can come in the form of an over-due phone call to a friend, a letter to someone in need, a walk or a cup of tea with a friend or neighbor. Take time to rest and enjoy God and His wonderful creation, just as He rested and enjoyed His creation after forming the world and all that is in it.

Whether our home is a mansion, a cottage or a small room, God wants it to be a place where joy is shared and sorrow is eased. Billy Graham said, "The first essential in a happy Christian home is that love must be practiced."

Recipe for a Home

Half a cup of friendship
And a cup of thoughtfulness,
Creamed together with a pinch
Of powdered tenderness.

Very lightly beaten
In a bowl of loyalty,
With a cup of faith, and one of hope,
And one of charity.

Be sure to add a spoonful each
Of gaity-that-sings
And also the ability
To-laugh-at-little-things.

Moisten with the sudden tears
Of heart-felt sympathy;
Bake in a good-natured pan
And serve repeatedly.

—Author Unknown[1]

Another recipe for a hospitable Christian home is this one written by Pauline and Leonard Miller:

> To three cups of love and two cups of understanding add four teaspoons of courtesy and two teaspoons each of thoughtfulness and helpfulness. Sift together thoroughly, then stir in an equal amount of work and play. Add three teaspoons of responsibility. Season to taste with study and culture, then fold in a generous amount of worship. Place in a pan well greased with security and lined with respect for personality. Sprinkle lightly with a sense of humor. Allow to set in an atmosphere of democratic planning, and of mutual sharing. Bake in a moderate oven. When well done, remove and top with a thick coating of Christian teaching. Serve on a platter of friendliness garnished with smiles.[2]

The power of a hospitable home is shown through these words. It influences not only those who live in it, but those who live around it and visit within its walls. Such a home is a haven of refuge to family, friends and strangers. It makes people hungry for the Lord Jesus Christ! Home is the place where character is built, and where sacrifices contribute to the happiness of others. Thus, the love of Christ shines forth like a lighthouse, a beacon of Christ from such a place.

There is joy in sharing our homes with others. Unfortunately, having people in is one of the first things that flies out the window when we feel rushed and tired. Listed are some practical ideas on how to be hospitable and bring glory to God without feeling frazzled:

1. Accept God-given "interruptions" as a part of His plan, and rejoice in opportunities to serve Him through these interruptions.

2. To buy time for needed planning, rest, devotions, etc., make a "do not disturb" sign for your front door and bedroom door.

3. Try to keep your house "picked up" by training the whole family to put away the things they use. Many times it's the clutter that discourages us from extending hospitality to others. Find a system that works for you and other members of your family, encouraging all to pitch in.

> *Ninety percent of failure is due to lack of organization.*
>
> —*Henrietta Mears*

4. Communicate your needs to everyone you live with, so that they may realize your pressures and be encouraged to help according to their capabilities.

5. Don't compare yourself to other homemakers. Find your comfortable place in God's economy, and seek His will concerning the standards for the upkeep of your home.

6. Try to clean a couple of drawers or a cupboard each day during a few spare moments. Don't wait to do a whole room at one time! It is too discouraging.

7. As you clean drawers and closets, be sure to give unused items away either to Christian thrift shops, or sell them in a garage sale. Eliminating clutter will free your cupboards, as well as your mind!

8. Remember that perfection is unattainable, so don't be frustrated by such a goal.

9. Use separate filing boxes for addresses, guarantees, recipes, finances, health records, birthdays and other records.

10. Keep a list of major chores that need to be done in the house, and when you find time to do one, enjoy checking it off your list.

11. Buy time for mending, embroidery or some other craft while watching the news on TV or talking on the phone. You can even write letters if you use the advertising breaks for the important items you want to write in your letters!

12. Get a long extention cord for your telephone so you can accomplish a variety of chores and still talk with someone who needs you. I have managed to polish silver, mend, iron clothes, clean kitchen cupboards and refrigerator and even exercise while talking on the telephone! Be creative with such ideas in your own household.

13. Keep a record for a week of how you use your time, and analyze it. You will be amazed at some of the ways you spend your time, and you'll be able to analyze what could be done while waiting for someone, etc. Experts estimate

that we spend approximately 10 percent of our lives waiting. Use the time wisely as our Lord Jesus did. He talked to the Samaritan woman while getting a drink at the well. He took a nap while crossing the water on a boat. He went up to the mountain to pray while the disciples crossed the Sea of Galilee.

14. Establish a place for family messages in a central location where you can count on them being read.

15. If you have children, plan ahead by laying out everyone's clothes and setting the breakfast table before you go to bed. You can even prepare some of the breakfast and refrigerate it for morning.

16. Company meals can be cooked in advance and refrigerated, or frozen for a few weeks.

17. Eliminate depression by not allowing procrastination to enter your scheduled plan for the day.

18. Simplify your household as much as possible by adding good storage shelves and other conveniences as needed.

19. Buy inexpensive, plastic boxes or baskets for folded, clean laundry. Write each family member's name on a basket. Make them responsible for returning the clean laundry to their room and putting it away. Also, have an attractive covered basket in each bathroom for dirty laundry to be placed as people step into the tub.

20. Child proof your household by storing medicines in a high cupboard, so that if you have small guests who are inquisitive, you need not worry about their getting into something poisonous. The same would go for storage under the

sink and in other cupboards where children can easily reach.

21. There are many books in the library with helps for busy mothers and suggestions on how to get kids to help. If you have children in your household, go to the library and find resources on this topic. Read and make notes of helpful information for your home.

22. Remember you are the emotional pacemaker, the cellophane tape or "glue" that holds everyone together in the household. Make it a priority to pray the first thing each morning, reporting to duty to the Lord, and asking for His guidance, strength and blessing on your day. Search His Word for encouragement and direction.

Here is a list of helpful hints for those times when you are entertaining:

1. Pray before guests arrive, and ask God to bless them in your home. It is more important to pray than to worry about cleaning your house or cooking. As you pray, the Lord will prepare your heart, as well as prepare your guests for the blessing He wants to give them. Remember, most people don't come to see your home, they come to see you! It is Christ Himself who brings beauty to the home.

2. When you find a menu that is easy to prepare, and that can be done ahead, put it down on a recipe card. Keep a note of the guests you serve the menu to. Have a separate file for this type of menu planning, and your entertaining will be much simpler to plan, leaving you more relaxed.

Note: A friend of mine, Nancy Vukovich, reminded me that I had shown her that she could extend hospitality in simple ways by keeping my own entertaining simple. She said she had appreciated the fact that I had used creative, inexpensive recipes and kept my dinner parties simple. She noted that I didn't buy florist flowers for my table (I used what I had in my garden) or serve expensive nuts and mints, etc. She said this was a pattern she could manage financially as a young homemaker and this made her feel comfortable about her own dinner parties.

3. Don't apologize for how your house looks, drawing attention to problem areas. Welcome your guests with joy, and they will not see all of the flaws! Don't forget, they have come to see you.

4. This may seem a simple, logical suggestion, but a lot of people don't do it! Turn off your TV or radio when your guests arrive. Enjoy listening to them. Learn to be a good listener.

5. Concentrate on enjoying your guests. You do not need to serve a gourmet meal. Sometimes you may just want to invite people for coffee, tea and some sweets, and afterwards have a time for talking, playing games, working puzzles, etc.

6. A fire pit in the yard is easy to build and will bring a return far beyond your investment. Many good talks were shared around the flickering fire after we roasted our wieners and marshmallows. We had many a family dinner here, and the children were always free to invite their friends, for the menu was so simple: wieners, buns, potato chips, fresh fruit and milk.

7. Think of inviting families to join you at a park for a picnic breakfast or barbecue. Here is a relaxed atmosphere where the food can be kept simple, and you don't have to worry about your house. Some of my fondest family memories are

of breakfasts or barbecues with neighbors and friends in a nearby park. I'm sure our children enjoyed those relaxed times as much as we parents did!

8. If you live in a small apartment, or a single room, you can entertain by preparing a meal and taking it to the house of your friends. They will enjoy this "love gift" of hospitality to them.

9. If you do not have a home in which to entertain, you can always invite someone to a restaurant for a piece of pie and a cup of coffee, and practice hospitality in this way.

Again, remember that *you* are the emotional pacesetter in your home! You are the smoother of nerves, calmer of confusion and the keeper of schedules and sanity. Your mood sets the atmosphere. If you lose control, your entire household suffers. Most home crises that cause quarrels or chaos result from our looking too much at the circumstances, rather than to Christ. Let God begin with you, as you begin your day! Look well to the ways of your household (see Prov. 31:10–31), and God will prepare your heart and your household for loving hospitality. "Whether, then, you eat or drink or whatever you do, do all to the glory of God" (1 Cor. 10:31, *NASB*).

To build a hospitable home takes courage, planning and Christ's power. Now is the time to take your stand and let God, through the power of His Holy Spirit, work in you. He will transform you, and your home! "Except the Lord build the house, they labour in vain that build it" (Ps. 127:1, *KJV*).

There Is Nothing . . .

. . . No circumstance, no trouble, no testing—

that can ever touch me until, first of all,
it has gone past God, and past Christ right through
    me.

If it has come that far,
it has come with great purpose,
which I may not understand at the moment.

But as I refuse to become panicky—
as I lift up my eyes to Him
to accept it as coming from the throne of God
for some great purpose of blessing to my own
    heart—
no sorrow will ever disturb me,
no circumstance will cause me to fret,
for I shall rest
in the joy of what my Lord is . . .

    . . . that is the rest of victory!

—Alan Redpath[3]

So, let us look at every opportunity to be hospitable that God sends our way as coming from the heart of the Lord for some great purpose of blessing to our own hearts, as well as to others! Let us not fret over circumstances, but rather rest in the joy of victory that Christ is waiting to give us!

And remember, we have a great God who is ready and willing to give us "plenty of help"!

I am only one,
But still I am one.
I cannot do everything,
But still I can do something;
And because I cannot do everything

I will not refuse to do something that I can do.

—Edward Hale[4]

God Is Calling You

1. Have you ever felt like Elijah felt, deserted, overworked, fearful and just plain overwhelmed by a situation? Were you able to turn that situation over to the Lord and lean upon Him for His strength, power and wisdom?

2. Many times all we need to do when we are feeling out of control in certain matters is to get a good rest and proper nourishment. What steps are you taking (or should you begin to take) to ensure that you are getting the proper rest and nutrition?

3. Relaxation is an important part of our busy lives. What are some of your favorite ways to relax? Are there others you would like to pursue?

4. We have listed several practical ideas on how you can extend hospitality to others without feeling hassled. Can you think of others?

Notes:
1. Author unknown. From *Sourcebook for Mothers* by Eleanor Doan (Grand Rapids, MI: Zondervan Publishing House, 1969).
2. Pauline and Leonard Miller from *Sourcebook for Mothers* by Eleanor Doan.
3. Alan Redpath. Source unknown.
4. Edward Everett Hale, 1822-1909. Public Domain.

Epilogue

Bless me and my family forever! . . . for you, Lord God, have promised it.

When you grant a blessing, Lord, it is an eternal blessing! The Lord's blessing is our greatest wealth. All our work adds nothing to it!

I remember the words of the Lord Jesus, "It is more blessed to give than to receive." When you put on a dinner . . . invite the poor, the crippled, the lame, and the blind. Then at the resurrection of the godly, God will reward you for inviting those who can't repay you. Come, blessed of my Father, into the Kingdom prepared for you from the founding of the world. For I was hungry and you fed me; I was thirsty and you gave me water; I was a stranger and you invited me into your homes; naked and you clothed me; sick and in prison, and you visited me.

Feed the hungry! Help those in trouble! Then your light will shine out from the darkness, and the darkness around you shall be as bright as day. And the Lord will guide you continually, and satisfy you with all good things.

For Jehovah God is our Light and our protector.

(See 2 Sam. 7:29; 1 Chron. 17:27; Prov. 10:22; Acts 20:35; Luke 14:12-14; Matt. 25:34-36; Isa. 58:10,11; Ps. 84:11.)

Taken from *Living Light* (Wheaton, IL: Tyndale House Publishers, 1972).

Part 2

Greig Family Favorites

Recipes and Household Hints

The Greigs Share
Their Family Favorites

Although hospitality does not always include food, it is often an integral part of opening our hearts and our homes to the people God sends our way. Therefore, it is wise to have on hand a few basic recipes that can be used, but not over-used.

Many women like to cook and experiment with new recipes. However, generally we like to use the old standbys, the ones we can count on.

This section of the book consists of menus and foods we have collected over 35 years and have found to be easy and delicious. We have even sprinkled in some helpful household hints. The recipes have been *time-tested* by our family, and that is why they are valuable! Sunny, spotless test kitchens can make anything taste good, but when a mother of four hears her husband and children exclaim over a certain dish, she adds that recipe to her files.

The prime source for this section are some very good cooks who were graciously willing to share recipes that over the years have delighted their families and guests.

It is our hope that you will find contained in these pages some recipes that your family will like and some menus that will work for you.

Special Note to Cooks: In the recipes that follow t = teaspoon, T = tablespoon.

Super Sunday Dinners
(or for any other day!)

```
┌─────────────────────────────────────────┐
│                 Menu:                     │
│                                           │
│       Chicken and Rice Casserole          │
│                                           │
│            Layered Salad                  │
│                                           │
│          Fresh Sliced Oranges             │
│       (or other fresh fruit in season)    │
│                                           │
│     Homemade Cookies or Chocolate Cake    │
│                                           │
└─────────────────────────────────────────┘
```

Baked Chicken and Rice (Serves 4)

    1 cup of white uncooked rice
    1 can cream of chicken/mushroom, or celery soup
    1 can water or skim milk
    1 envelope Lipton's Dry Onion Soup Mix
    1 chicken, cut up
    ½ cup sliced almonds (optional)

Place uncooked rice in a 9×12 baking pan. Mix soup with water or skim milk and pour over rice. Sprinkle soup mix over rice. Place chicken, skin side up, on top of this mixture. Cover, bake at 350 degrees for 1½ hours. After cooking, sprinkle casserole with almonds, and run under the broiler until they are browned.

Layered Salad (Serves 10 to 12)

1 large head of lettuce
1 medium Spanish red onion—sliced thin
2 cups of carrots—sliced thin
2 bunches of broccoli (just the tops)
 (or substitute uncooked petite frozen green peas)
1 cup of celery—sliced thin
1 cup of sliced zucchini or cucumber—sliced thin
1 small basket whole cherry tomatoes (optional)
 Bacon bits (optional)

Layer lettuce on the bottom of a large serving bowl. Add the rest of the ingredients as listed, one layer at a time.

1 pint of mayonnaise
2 T. sugar
1/3 cup of Parmesan cheese, or about 6 oz. shredded cheddar cheese
8 slices of bacon crisply cooked and crumbled (or use 1 jar of bacon bits)

The day before serving, layer mayonnaise over the top of the salad, sealing to the edges of the bowl. Sprinkle sugar over mayonnaise evenly. Top with cheese, then bacon. Top with plastic wrap and refrigerate overnight. Fold in dressing just before serving.

Fresh Fruit Plate

Cut up or slice seasonal fresh fruit and arrange on an attractive serving dish. Cover with plastic wrap and refrigerate. Remove plastic wrap just before serving and add freshly sliced bananas and apples, if desired, to the other fruit.

Delicious One-Bowl Chocolate Cake

This is an old family "standby" that all the children learned to bake at an early age. Make this cake ahead a day or two. It stays very moist. (If you are in a hurry, simply make a cake mix!)

1½ cups hot water
 ¾ cup of oil
   3 squares (1 oz. each) unsweetened baking chocolate (4 squares if you prefer a darker chocolate cake)
   3 cups flour, lightly spooned into cup (Remove 3 T. and sift in 3 t. cornstarch. This makes a "cake flour.")
   1 t. salt
   2 t. soda
   3 large eggs, beaten
2½ cups sugar
   1 cup sour cream

Preheat oven to 350 degrees. Combine hot water and chocolate in a heavy pan and melt over low heat, or in the microwave. Set aside to cool. In a large bowl, mix with electric beater (or by hand): sugar, beaten eggs, sour cream, oil. Add chocolate and beat. Add flour, salt and soda (that has been sifted together in a separate bowl) into the chocolate mixture, 1 cup at a time, until well blended. Bake in a lightly greased 9 × 12 pan filled only half full, and one 9 × 9 pan also half full for 30 to 35 minutes until the cake pulls from the sides of the pans. (You may use the extra batter to bake as cupcakes.) *Note:* This batter will be thin. Do not overbake.

179

Frosting

3 oz. unsweetened baking chocolate
$\frac{1}{3}$ cup butter or margarine
$\frac{1}{2}$ cup sour cream
2 t. vanilla
3 cups of sifted powdered sugar
   Chopped nuts (optional)

Melt unsweetened baking chocolate and butter over low heat, or in microwave. Stir in sour cream when the chocolate mixture has cooled slightly. Add vanilla, and gradually add sifted powdered sugar. Beat to spreading consistency, and spread over the cooled cake. May be topped with chopped nuts.

Note: This is the best chocolate frosting recipe I have ever used!

or

Easy Cream Cheese Frosting

1 (8 oz.) Cream Cheese (at room temperature)
2 egg whites
1 lb. powdered sugar
1 t. vanilla

Beat egg whites and vanilla until frothy. Add cream cheese and beat until well blended. Sift 1 cup of sugar at a time into mixture, beating well after each addition, until frosting is thick enough to spread.

Greig Chocolate Chip Cookies—at their Best!

1 cup (½ lb.) butter or margarine
½ cup solid vegetable shortening
1⅓ cups granulated sugar
1 cup firmly packed brown sugar
4 large eggs
1 T. vanilla
1 t. lemon juice
3 cups all-purpose flour (unsifted)
2 t. baking soda
1½ t. salt
1 t. cinnamon
½ cup rolled oatmeal (preferably "old fashioned")
2 large packages of chocolate chips (12 oz. each)
2 cups chopped walnuts or 2 cups of raisins

Preheat oven to 350 degrees (if you desire a *softer* cookie, bake at 325 degrees). In a large bowl beat the room temperature butter and shortening with granulated sugar and brown sugar until light and fluffy. Add eggs, one at a time, beating well after each addition. Beat in vanilla and lemon juice. In another large bowl, stir together flour, baking soda, salt, cinnamon and oats. Gradually add to butter mixture, blending thoroughly. Stir in chocolate chips, walnuts or raisins if desired. Drop the dough a scant ¼ cup for each cookie (spacing about 3 inches apart on ungreased cookie sheet). Bake for 16 to 18 minutes, until brown. Immediately transfer baked cookies to racks to cool. Store in an airtight container. Makes about 3 dozen large cookies. They may be frozen after baking.

Note: Use ice cream scoop to measure out the dough.

Menu:

Sliced Baked Ham

Assorted Breads or Rolls

Potato Salad

Three Bean Salad

Lemon Cake Dessert

All of these foods can be prepared the day before and refrigerated, and the cakes can be baked the day before and kept on the counter.

Baked Ham

Bake one 3 to 5 lb. ham according to instructions at 325 degrees. The temperature should reach 160 degrees when measured with a meat thermometer. Choose a precooked boneless ham if you wish easy slicing, or let your butcher slice it in 1/4 inch slices and tie it for you. For cold ham, cook the day before, arrange on a platter, cool, cover and refrigerate. If you wish to serve the ham warm, set your oven timer for 2 and one half hours at 300 degrees while you are in church or on errands. This method works well for a 5 to 7 lb. ham. When you return home, the ham will be ready to slice.

Pineapple Basting Sauce

If you desire to baste the ham with a sauce while you are preparing your table and getting the rest of the food out, you may mix these ingredients in the blender the day before:

2 cups fresh diced pineapple
1½ cups brown sugar
1 T. dry mustard
1 t. ginger
1 cup pineapple juice (or orange juice)

Pour off all fat from the ham pan, or transfer the ham to a new baking pan. Pour the basting sauce over the ham and baste with this sauce every 10 minutes for the last 40 minutes it is in the oven. Or simmer sauce on top of stove. Put the basting sauce in a dish and serve with the ham.

Meg Alexander's Hot Mustard Sauce

1 cup dry mustard
1 cup malt vinegar
    Soak these two ingredients together overnight.
The next day: Beat 3 eggs well in top of a double boiler. Add ½ cup sugar and the vinegar mustard mixture. Stir, cooking until thick, in top of double boiler over hot water. This sauce can be stored covered in the refrigerator indefinitely. It is good with ham and also for other meat sandwiches. It can be served cold or warmed slightly if you wish a warm sauce. This is similar to Dijon Mustard.

183

Potato Salad

Make your favorite potato salad, or try this easy shortcut!
   1 quart of potato salad purchased at your local market
   8 oz. frozen petite peas—place in sieve and thaw under
   water, but do not cook. Drain thoroughly.
1½ cups chopped celery
   ½ cup (or more) of chopped green onion tops or red onion
   (onion optional)

   Mix together 1 cup plain white yogurt with 2 T. yellow mustard, and fold all of the ingredients into the purchased potato
salad. Add a bit more yogurt if the salad seems too "dry."
Allow to season in the refrigerator, covered overnight. This
salad looks very nice garnished with parsley.

Three Bean Salad (Called Calico Salad by our family)

   1 16 oz. can green beans
   1 16 oz. can kidney beans
   1 16 oz. can garbanzo beans
   ½ cup diced green pepper (optional)
   ⅓ cup chopped onion

Dressing:
   1 cup sugar blended with 1⅓ cup vinegar, ⅔ cup oil, 2 t.
   salt, and 1 t. pepper.

   This dressing is most easily mixed in the blender.
   Drain beans thoroughly. Place in a container which has a
tight cover. Add diced pepper and onion. Pour dressing over
all, and refrigerate several hours or overnight or for several
days before serving. This salad keeps well in the refrigerator for
at least a week.

184

Lydia Tamme's Lemon Cake Dessert

 1 yellow cake mix
 4 eggs
 3/4 cup water
 1 package of lemon gelatin (3 oz. size)
 3/4 cup oil
  grated rind of 3/4 orange or lemon, using fine grater (optional)

Preheat oven to 350 degrees. Place eggs and water in large bowl and beat. Add 3/4 cup oil and blend. Add cake mix, lemon gelatin and grated rind. Beat until well blended (approximately 2 to 3 minutes) at medium speed with electric mixer. Pour batter into 9 × 12 greased pan. Bake 30-35 minutes—until cake tests done. Remove from oven and place cake pan on a rack. Immediately poke holes with fork all over the cake while it is hot.

Glaze:
Prepare this while the cake is baking: Sift 2 cups of powdered sugar and mix well with 1/3 to 1/2 cup of lemon juice. The consistency of the powdered sugar lemon glaze should be like light maple syrup. Pour over the cake while it is hot, spreading evenly with rubber spatula. Cover until ready to use. Serve plain, or with a scoop of ice cream or a bit of whipped cream. *Note:* Bake this cake a day ahead. Left-over cake packs well in lunches!

```
┌─────────────────────────────────────────────┐
│                                               │
│                  **Menu:**                    │
│                                               │
│   Microwave Lasagna (or Savory Spaghetti)     │
│                                               │
│      Cole Slaw and Special Dressing           │
│                                               │
│        "The Very Best" Garlic Bread           │
│                                               │
│      Fresh Fruit and Oatmeal Cookies          │
│         (or Ice Cream with Cookies)           │
│                                               │
└─────────────────────────────────────────────┘
```

Easy Microwave Lasagna (Serves 4-6)

2 cups grated mozzarella or Jack cheese (about 8 oz.)
1 lb. ground beef
1 can (15½ oz.) spaghetti sauce—or your own homemade
   sauce
1 can (8 oz.) tomato sauce
1 T. dried parsley flakes—crumbled between fingers
1 t. dried oregano leaves or ½ t. ground oregano
1 t. dried basil leaves or ½ t. ground basil

Note: Dried flakes should always be soaked in hot water (a
   few drops) for 10 minutes before used in Italian recipes
   to release flavor

1 carton (16 oz.) creamed cottage cheese
¼ cup grated Parmesan cheese and 3 additional T. of
   Parmesan cheese to be used on top of the casserole
1 egg
8 uncooked lasagna noodles

Crumble ground beef into 1½ quart casserole dish. Cover
loosely and microwave on high (100 percent power) for three
minutes. Break up beef with a fork and stir. Cover casserole

186

again and microwave until very little pink remains (2-3 minutes longer at 100 percent power). Drain off fat and liquid. In a large bowl, mix spaghetti sauce, tomato sauce, plus the parsley, oregano and basil. Stir all of this into the casserole with the beef. Cover tightly and microwave at high (100 percent power) until it boils 3-4 minutes. Place egg in medium sized bowl and beat with egg beater thoroughly. Add cottage cheese and $\frac{1}{4}$ cup Parmesan cheese to the egg and stir with a spoon, until blended. Spread $1\frac{1}{3}$ cup of the spaghetti meat sauce in baking dish ($12 \times 7\frac{1}{2} \times 2$). Place 4 *uncooked* lasagna noodles on top of sauce. Spread 1 cup of cottage cheese filling evenly over noodles. Sprinkle 1 cup of grated mozzarella or jack cheese evenly over the cottage cheese filling. Reserve the final cup of grated mozzarella or jack cheese for the top of the casserole at the end of the cooking time.

Repeat layers in casserole as follows:
1. First $1\frac{1}{3}$ cup of meat sauce.
2. Place the last 4 uncooked lasagna noodles over the meat sauce.
3. Spoon the rest of the cottage cheese sauce evenly over the noodles.
4. Top with the remaining meat sauce.

Cover tightly and microwave on high (100 percent power) for 10 minutes on a microwave turntable, or rotate the dish by hand after five minutes. Microwave the casserole on medium (50 percent power) until noodles are tender—22 to 28 minutes longer, turning casserole on turntable, or by hand occasionally.

Note: If you do not have a medium setting on your microwave, use full power for 10 minutes and let stand for five minutes.

Sprinkle top of lasagna with remaining 1 cup of mozzarella or jack cheese, and on top of that sprinkle 3 T. Parmesan cheese. Cover and let stand 10 minutes. Cut and serve.

187

Savory Spaghetti Sauce

Make the sauce two or three days before you plan to use it and allow the flavors to blend in a tightly covered container in your refrigerator. Any leftover sauce may be frozen for future use, either in lasagna or for more spaghetti.

    1-2 lbs. ground beef or ground turkey
      4 cloves garlic (finely minced or put through garlic press)
      2 T. olive oil
      2 large carrots (chopped fine or grated)
      3 medium onions (chopped fine or grated)
     10 cups tomato juice
      6 T. tomato paste
      2 one pound cans of whole tomatoes (*not* drained)
      4 T. chopped fresh parsley (or 2 T. dried parsley)
   1½ t. ground oregano
   1½ t. ground basil
      2 bay leaves (tied in cheese cloth or placed in a tea strainer)
      2 T. butter or margarine
      1 t. chili powder

Brown meat over low heat and drain off excess fat. Add garlic, olive oil, carrots, onion and 3 T. of water to beef. Saute over low heat for 30 minutes, covered (checking to make sure there is enough liquid so the mixture does not burn). (This process could be done in a microwave in a covered casserole for 15 minutes on high). In a large pan, combine the sautéd vegetables and beef with all of the rest of the recipe ingredients and simmer for six hours at the lowest stove setting. When partially cooled, store sauce in the refrigerator in a tightly covered container. Extra sauce may be frozen at this point. When you are ready to use the sauce, heat it slowly while you boil the spaghetti.

Cole Slaw

1 medium cabbage—chopped or sliced finely
If desired, 1 or 2 medium carrots grated

Make Ahead Dressing:

1 cup sugar
1/2 cup apple cider vinegar
1 t. pepper
1/2 cup salad oil
2 t. salt

Place dressing ingredients in mixing bowl and beat with egg beater, or put all ingredients in blender and blend thoroughly. Refrigerate in covered jar. Shake well each time before using. Use as much dressing as the cabbage you have shredded requires. Add dressing to salad just before serving.
Note: Dressing keeps up to 3 months in refrigerator!

The Best Garlic Bread (Serves 3 to 4)

1/4 lb. butter or margarine
2 cloves garlic (minced through garlic press)
French or Sourdough French bread thickly sliced
Shredded American cheese or Parmesan grated cheese

On day before serving: Melt butter and combine with minced garlic. Let stand several hours (or overnight) at room temperature to blend flavors.
On serving day: Warm and strain butter or margarine and discard the garlic bits. Dip 6 to 8 fresh bread slices in melted butter

189

mixture, and then into grated cheese. Place bread slices, cheese side up, on cookie sheet. Turn on broiler unit in your oven. Place bread approximately 3 inches from broiler and broil until heated and golden brown. (This requires watching so that it will not burn!)

Alternate method: Preheat oven to 375 degrees. Place bread, dipped in garlic butter, butter side up, on ungreased cookie sheets. Omit cheese. Bake for 10 minutes, or until slightly browned.

Fresh Fruit with Oatmeal Cookies

Arrange seasonal fresh fruits on a platter, or in a bowl. Provide fruit plates for your guests. Pass the oatmeal cookies around the table!

Grandma Blanche Walters' Oatmeal Cookies (Makes about 50 cookies)

4 eggs
2 cups of sugar
1 cup shortening at room temperature (Crisco type)
1 cup margarine or butter (at room temperature)
1 t. salt
2 T. water or milk
1 t. soda
1 t. baking powder
2 cups unsifted flour
4 cups old fashioned oatmeal
1 to 2 cups of raisins
1 cup chopped nuts (optional)

Preheat oven to 350 degrees. In a large bowl, place the eggs, sugar and salt and beat until light and fluffy. Add the shortening and margarine, and again beat until thoroughly creamed. Dissolve the soda and baking powder in the 1 T. water, and add to the large bowl. Mix thoroughly. Add flour to the above mixture, stirring by hand. Gradually add 4 cups of oatmeal, stirring in by hand. Last of all, add the raisins and the nuts (optional), and stir until well blended. Drop cookie dough by teaspoon on ungreased cookie sheet. Bake 10 to 12 minutes, until brown. Remove cookies immediately from the cookie sheet and cool on rack. When cool, store in air-tight containers.

Bill Greig's Homemade Strawberry or Peach Ice Cream

This quantity makes 2 gallons of ice cream, so if you only have a 1-gallon freezer, you will want to cut this recipe in half.

    3 or 4 boxes of hulled and mashed strawberries or 12
        medium peaches peeled and mashed
    1 (2 lb.) carton of plain yogurt
    1 qt. of half and half (half cream and half whole milk)
    1 pint of whipping cream
    4 cups of sugar (or part sugar and part artificial sweetener)
        Juice of ½ medium lemon
    1 t. salt
    2 t. vanilla

    Mix all of the ingredients together, until well blended. *Note:* Ice cream will always taste too sweet before it is frozen. Read the instructions for your ice cream freezer, and follow the directions accordingly.

Homemade ice cream with an old fashioned hand-cranked freezer was always a fun project for our family of six, plus

191

numerous friends who came to help "turn the crank" and enjoy the ice cream! I am including our family recipe for this reason. However, if you do not have an ice cream freezer, you may just buy a gallon of your favorite ice cream and serve it with cookies!

Cook-Out!

Menu:

Hamburgers on the Grill and Toasted Buns

Big Mac Sauce

Potato Chips or Salad

Strawberry Gelatin Salad

April Fool Cookies

Hamburgers on the Grill (Serves 4 to 5)

1 lb. ground beef (not more than 22 percent fat)
1 T. instant minced onion
$\frac{1}{2}$ t. salt or Lawry's Seasoning Salt
$\frac{1}{4}$ t. pepper
$\frac{1}{8}$ t. garlic powder (optional)
1 T. Worcestershire sauce (optional)
$\frac{1}{4}$ cup water or skim milk

Place all ingredients in a large mixing bowl. (I find it easy to mix these ingredients by hand, wearing rubber gloves). Shape into 5 patties. This can be done easily by putting waxed paper on a saucer, 1/5 of the ground beef mixture, and another piece of waxed paper—place the second saucer on top of this and gently press to form a patty. Transfer waxed paper covered patty to pan in which you will store the patty overnight in the refrigerator for your Sunday dinner. When you return home from church, prepare your charcoal grill or light your gas grill. When coals are hot, or grill is heated, place patty on grill 4 to 6 inches from the hot coals. Cook, turning once about 9 to 12 minutes—depending on how well done you like your burger. You may use your oven broiler as an alternative in cold climates when the snow has covered your outdoor grill! To broil hamburgers in your own oven, set the oven control at broil or 550 degrees. Broil burgers 3 inches from heat for 3 to 4 minutes on each side for rare, 5 to 7 minutes for medium. The hamburger buns may be toasted on the grill, warmed or toasted in your oven in the kitchen, or heated in a microwave oven. If you wish to serve cheeseburgers (on your outdoor grill or oven/broiler) about 1 minute before the hamburgers are done top each with a cheese slice. Continue cooking until cheese is partially melted. Have the following arranged in serving dishes and covered tightly in your refrigerator:

> sliced tomatoes
> lettuce
> mustard
> catsup
> sliced onions

Hamburger Sauce Just Like Big Mac

> 1/3 cup creamy French dressing
> 1 cup mayonnaise
> 1/4 cup sweet pickle relish
> 1 T. sugar
> 1 t. dried onion
> 1/4 t. pepper

Mix all ingredients together well. Store in jar in refrigerator (stores well for 3 months). Serve with hamburgers.

Strawberry Salad (Serves 12)

  2 (3 oz.) packages of strawberry gelatin
1½ cups boiling water
  2 (10 oz.) packages frozen strawberries
  1 can (1 lb., 4 oz.) of crushed pineapple, drained
  3 medium bananas, mashed
  1 pint of sour cream, *or* 1 large package of cream cheese
    blended with ¼ cup of mayonnaise

Dissolve gelatin in 1½ cups of boiling water, stirring until completely dissolved. Fold in the frozen strawberries, which have either been cut up or broken up into small sized chunks. Continue stirring until all icy particles are melted. Add well-drained, crushed pineapple. Add the mashed bananas. After stirring all the ingredients well, put *half* of this mixture in a 12 × 8 × 2 pyrex baking dish and refrigerate until firm. Keep the other half of the gelatin mixture on the counter so that it does not solidify. After the gelatin becomes firm, remove it from the refrigerator and spread the top evenly with 1 pint of sour cream, *or* 1 large package of cream cheese (at room temperature) that has been creamed with ¼ cup of mayonnaise. Spoon carefully, a bit at a time, the remaining gelatin mixture over the sour cream or cream cheese mixture in the pyrex dish. Return to the refrigerator to solidify. Cover with waxed paper or plastic wrap after the top layer is firm.

April Fool Cookies (Makes 10 cookies)

   6 oz. milk chocolate chips, plus ¼ bar (1 oz.) of paraffin wax
   1 small jar of peanut butter (either chunky or smooth)
   20 saltine soda crackers

   Spread peanut butter between two saltines. Using tongs, dip into melted chocolate and paraffin and cover all. Set on waxed paper. To harden faster, put in refrigerator.

   This recipe sounds crazy, but it tastes good! Children love to help make these too! Make as many as you need for your crowd. Serve with French Vanilla ice cream.

This Is a Simple Sunday Dinner for a *Cold* Day!

Menu:

Split Pea Soup

Corn Bread and/or Bran Muffins

Assorted Vegetable Plate—raw carrots, celery, cherry tomatoes, broccoli heads, etc.

Pecan Pie and Whipped Cream

Split Pea Soup

2 quarts of water
1 lb. green split peas
1 carrot, diced
1 medium onion, diced
1 medium stalk of celery, diced
1 bay leaf (put in a tea strainer or piece of cheese cloth)
1/4 t. thyme
1 t. salt
1 dash of pepper
1 pinch of cayenne

If desired, a ham bone and small amount of cut up ham (1 cup, more or less) can be added to this soup.

Put all ingredients in a large soup pot. Bring to a boil, and boil 15 minutes. Simmer, covered, until the peas are soft. If you do not add ham, and wish a smooth soup, you may put small quantities in the blender and blend it to the texture you wish. Make this soup during the week. Store in the refrigerator for Sunday. It also freezes well.

197

Doris Greig's Favorite Corn Bread
(Just Like Marie Callendar's)

 3 eggs, beaten
 1 cup milk
 1 stick melted margarine (½ cup)
 2 cups Bisquick (plain or buttermilk)
 ½ cup yellow cornmeal
 ½ cup sugar
 ½ t. baking powder

Preheat oven to 350 degrees. Grease an 8 × 8 pan. Blend eggs, milk and melted margarine. Sift sugar and baking powder together into a separate bowl. Stir in cornmeal and mix well. Add the cornmeal mixture and Bisquick to the egg-milk mixture, and using a wooden spoon stir only until blended. Pour batter into greased pan and bake 30 minutes. *Note:* To make a double recipe use a 9 × 14 pan or two 8 × 8 pans. Pan sides should be approximately 2½ inches deep as this is a lovely thick corn bread that rises high just like "Marie's."

"Easiest Mix" Corn Bread

 1 (18 oz.) package yellow cake mix
 1 (15 oz.) package corn muffin mix

In a large bowl prepare yellow cake mix according to directions on package. Mix corn muffin mix in another bowl. Blend both mixes together. Preheat oven to 350 degrees. Pour batter into two 9 × 9 well-greased pans. Bake corn bread for 30 to 35 minutes, until it tests done.

This corn bread is easy to mix and pop in the oven on a Sunday morning when you get home from church. It also freezes well, and re-heats very nicely in the microwave. Or, you may split the corn bread in half, place on the broiler pan and toast under the broiler until slightly browned on the top before serving it.

Honey Butter:

Blend equal amounts of honey and room temperature butter or margarine together, beating well with an electric mixer until light in color and somewhat thickened. Serve with corn bread.

Refrigerator Bran Muffins

2 cups boiling water
1 rounded cup shortening
5 t. soda
3 t. salt
2 cups of white flour (unsifted)
3 cups whole wheat flour (unsifted)
8 cups of Bran Buds (1 lb. 2 oz. box)
1 quart of buttermilk
4 eggs
3 cups of sugar
1½ cups raw bran
3 cups of raisins (optional)

Preheat oven to 400 degrees. Put shortening and soda in a large bowl and pour boiling water over it. Stir until shortening has melted and cool down to lukewarm. Add buttermilk and eggs to the bowl and mix with hand or electric beater until blended. Add salt and sugar, and again beat well with hand or electric beater. Fold in white and whole wheat flour 2 cups at a time and beat the batter until smooth. Gradually fold in the Bran Buds and raw bran. Add raisins (if desired). Grease muffin tins (or use paper liners in them). Fill muffin cups only half full! Bake as many as you need and refrigerate the rest of the muffin batter in a covered container. Bake approximately 25 minutes, or until they test done. This recipe makes 5½ dozen muffins. They may be baked all at once and some frozen for re-heating later. Or, you may choose to store some of the batter in containers in your refrigerator. This batter will keep up to a month at a time! These muffins re-heat beautifully in the microwave, as well as in the oven.

Microwave Bran Muffins (Makes 18)

1¼ cups whole wheat flour
  1 cup bran cereal (All-Bran or Bran Buds)
  ½ cup regular wheat germ
  ¼ cup sesame seeds
  ½ t. baking soda
  ¼ t. salt
  1 cup buttermilk
  ½ cup water
  ½ cup firmly packed dark brown sugar
  ⅓ cup salad oil
  3 T. dark molasses
  1 T. grated orange peel
  1 large egg

In a large bowl, combine flour, bran cereal, wheat germ, sesame seeds, baking soda and salt. In a medium sized bowl, mix buttermilk, water, brown sugar, oil, molasses, orange peel, and beaten egg. Add liquid ingredients to dry, stirring just to blend; batter can be lumpy. Cover and refrigerate at least two hours, or up to 2½ weeks. In a microwave muffin pan place paper cups, or use custard cups to hold paper cup liners. Spoon ¼ cup batter into each baking cup. Place one or two muffins in the microwave oven at a time. Cook 2 muffins for 1 minute 10 seconds at full power. Rotate muffins halfway through if baking appears uneven. Tiny bubbles will pop on the surface, and the muffins will look dry on top when done. To test, open oven and touch top of muffin lightly; it will feel moist, but should spring back without sticking to your finger. If needed, cook on full power an additional 5 to 10 seconds at a time, until done. Let muffins stand 30 to 60 seconds before serving.

    Note: Six muffins will take about 4 minutes on high power or 6 minutes on medium power.

"The Best" Pecan Pie

Preheat oven 350 degrees. Prepare your own favorite crust and put in a very large, deep pie pan, or buy a prepared large sized crust. See Kathy Greig Rowland's Fool Proof recipe in Desserts section.

1¼ cup dark corn syrup
1 cup brown sugar
4 T. butter
4 large eggs
2½ cups whole pecans
1 t. vanilla
Ingredients for homemade pie shell (or use a deep dish frozen pie shell)
Whipping cream to top pie

Place corn syrup and brown sugar in a pan and bring to a boil while stirring. Remove from burner. Add butter and stir until melted. Cool these ingredients slightly. In a large bowl, beat the 4 eggs well. Gradually add the cooled syrup mixture to the beaten eggs. Add 2½ cups of pecans and 1 t. of vanilla to the mixture in the bowl. Pour the pecan pie filling into a prepared pie shell. (*Note* that this pie shell needs to be extra large and deep, as this is a large recipe. Pour in half of the mixture, then place the pie dish in the lower shelf of the oven and put in the rest of the pie filling). Bake at 350 degrees for approximately 45 minutes, or until done.

```
┌─────────────────────────────────────────┐
│                                           │
│              **Menu:**                    │
│                                           │
│  Chicken Salad and/or Corned Beef Mold   │
│                                           │
│              Pasta Salad                  │
│                                           │
│           Pacific Fruit Salad             │
│                                           │
│    Carrot Sticks and Cherry Tomatoes     │
│                                           │
│             Buttered Rolls                │
│                                           │
│              Carrot Cake                  │
│                                           │
└─────────────────────────────────────────┘
```

This menu is for a cold Sunday dinner, which could be served in the backyard, at a park, or at the buffet table in your dining room.

"Old Standby" Cold Chicken Salad (Serves 10 to 12)

- 2 cups of cooked chicken, cut into bite sized pieces
- 2 cans of water chestnuts (small sized cans), drained and cut up
- 2 lb. seedless grapes, washed, drained and removed from stems (or Mandarin oranges if grapes are not available)
- 2 cups of sliced celery
- 1 (16 oz.) can of pineapple tidbits, drained well
- 1 T. curry powder (optional)
- 2 T. soy sauce
- 1¾ cup mayonnaise
- 1 cup of slivered almonds—toasted in the oven or microwave if you prefer them toasted.

Mix all of the ingredients except the last two. Chill ingredients in the refrigerator at least three hours, or overnight in a covered container. *Note:* Turkey may be used instead of chicken. Mix in mayonnaise and almonds just before serving. Serve on greens, with a garnish of half an orange slice and parsley.

Curried Chicken Salad (Serves 6)

½ to 1 cup of golden raisins
1 cup of plain yogurt
3 T. to a full (11 oz.) jar of Major Grey's mango chutney
1 t. curry powder
1 t. ground coriander
¾ t. garlic salt
½ t. dry mustard
    dash cayenne pepper
3 cups of diced, cold chicken
1 green pepper, chopped
1 (11 oz.) can mandarin oranges, drained
¼ cup thinly sliced green onion
1 unpeeled apple, diced
2 stalks of celery, chopped

Soak raisins in hot water to barely cover, and let stand 30 minutes. Combine yogurt, mango chutney, curry powder, coriander, garlic salt, mustard, and cayenne in bowl and blend well. Combine chicken, green pepper, oranges, drained raisins, green onions, apple and celery. *Note:* The yogurt mixture can be tightly covered when prepared on the day before, and stored in the refrigerator. The chicken mixture except for the apple can also be tightly covered and stored.

Doris Greig's "Lo-Cal" Chicken Pasta Salad Supreme
(Serves 6)

2 cups corkskrew macaroni
2 whole chicken breasts
1 T. salad oil
1/4 t. paprika
1 cup water
1/2 bunch broccoli (cut into 1-inch pieces)
2 medium oranges
1/2 cup orange juice
3 T. cider vinegar (more if you like)
3/4 t. ground ginger
1/4 t. pepper
lettuce leaves

Prepare the macaroni as label directs; drain in colander and run cold water over the macaroni to cool it, and so that it will not stick together. Discard skin and excess fat, and cut bones from chicken breasts. Cut chicken into 3/4-inch pieces. Cook over medium heat in hot salad oil, until the chicken loses its pink color (about 5 minutes, stirring often). Add paprika and cook 1 minute. Remove chicken to a shallow 12×8 baking dish. In skillet, over high heat, heat water to boiling and add broccoli. Return to boiling; then reduce heat to low. Cover and simmer 5 minutes (or until broccoli is tender-crisp). Drain, rinse under cold water to stop cooking. Peel and section oranges, and cut the sections in half. To the chicken in the dish, add oranges, orange juice, cider vinegar, ginger, pepper, macaroni, broccoli, salt to taste—toss to coat. Cover and refrigerate at least six hours to blend flavors, tossing occasionally. To serve, arrange lettuce leaves on platter. Spoon chicken mixture on top of lettuce leaves. Parsley makes a nice garnish.

The Easiest Pasta Salad Ever!

1 small box of linguini
1 bottle Kraft zesty Italian dressing
½ bottle Salad Supreme (optional)
   Assorted vegetables cut to bite sized pieces—radishes, carrots, mushrooms, cucumbers, celery, green pepper, broccoli and onions
1 to 2 cups of ham or chicken cut into bite sized pieces (optional)

Cook pasta according to the directions on the box. Rinse under cold water. Cut up the assorted vegetables to total 2 to 3 cups. Place well drained pasta in a bowl. Fold in vegetables, Salad Supreme, and ham or chicken if desired. Add dressing. Marinate, stirring 2 or 3 times. Cover and refrigerate overnight. Stir occasionally to blend the flavors well. This salad will store well in the refrigerator. Use a covered bowl.

Anne's Corned Beef Salad (Serves 8 to 10)

1 (6 oz.) package of lime gelatin
1½ cups of boiling water
   Juice of ½ lemon or 2 T. vinegar
1 cup mayonnaise
1 t. salt
3 T. grated onion
½ cup chopped green onion tops (optional)
1 can of corned beef (broken up)
1 cup of finely cut cabbage
2 cups of finely cut celery
1 green pepper, finely chopped (optional)
1 cup grated cheddar cheese (optional)
1 T. horseradish (optional)

Add gelatin to boiling water and stir until completely dissolved. Add 1½ cups of cold water (or ice cubes to equal that amount). Refrigerate until it thickens and is like a thin custard in consistency. Stir in the juice of the lemon, salt, salad dressing, grated onion, cabbage, celery and green pepper. Break up the corned beef into fine pieces and fold in. If desired, one cup of grated cheddar cheese may also be added to this salad. Place in a mold, or a serving bowl. Cover and refrigerate overnight. Serve right from the serving bowl, or unmold onto greens.

Pacific Fruit Salad (Serves 8 to 10)

2 (3 oz.) packages or (one 6 oz.) package orange gelatin
2 cups hot water
1 (6 oz.) can frozen orange juice concentrate
1 (10 oz.) can mandarin oranges, drained (save juice) or 1
   cup fresh oranges, cut up and drained
1 cup canned pineapple cubes, drained (save juice)
2 cups grated carrots

Dissolve gelatin in hot water. Stir in orange juice concentrate undiluted. Add 1 cup of either mandarin orange or canned pineapple juice. Place in a bowl and chill in refrigerator until gelatin is like a thin custard. Fold in all other ingredients. Pour into a 1½ quart mold, or into a nice serving bowl. Cover and chill in refrigerator 6 hours or overnight.

Elegant Carrot Cake

1½ cups corn oil
2 cups sugar
3 eggs
2 cups of flour
2 t. ground cinnamon
2 t. baking soda
2 t. vanilla
1 t. salt
2 cups grated carrots
1 cup chopped walnuts
½ cup crushed pineapple, drained

Preheat oven to 350 degrees. Mix all ingredients but flour, carrots and pineapple with an electric beater. Beat in the flour. Hand stir in carrots, walnuts and pineapple. Mix until blended. Pour into greased 13 × 9 pan. Bake for 1 hour. Cool and frost with Cream Cheese Frosting.

Cream Cheese Frosting

1 three oz. package of cream cheese
1¼ cups sifted powdered sugar
½ cup butter or margarine
⅛ cup well-drained crushed pineapple
¼ cup chopped walnuts

Mix cream cheese (at room temperature) with powdered sugar and margarine until fluffy. Add pineapple and walnuts. Mix well. Spread over cooled cake in cake pan.

```
┌─────────────────────────────┐
│           Menu:             │
│                             │
│       Acapulco Delight      │
│      Assorted Fruit Plate   │
│           Mud Pie           │
│                             │
└─────────────────────────────┘
```

Acapulco Delight (Serves 6)

   2 lb. lean ground beef
   1 package taco seasoning mix
   2 (7 oz.) cans green chili salsa
   6 corn tortillas
   2 cups shredded cheddar cheese
   1 (17 oz.) can refried beans
   2 cups sour cream
   ½ cup chopped green onions
   1 (2.2 oz.) can of black olives, sliced
   ¼ cup grated Parmesan cheese
      Chopped lettuce and tomatoes

   Brown beef in skillet and drain excess fat. Stir in taco seasoning mix and water, according to package directions. Add
green chili salsa. Simmer for 5 to 10 minutes. Place 2 tortillas in
bottom of 13 × 9 baking dish. Spread ½ of meat mixture over
tortillas. Sprinkle with ½ cup cheddar cheese. Top with 2 more
tortillas. Spread with refried beans. Cover with about ⅔ of sour
cream. Sprinkle with green onions and sliced olives. Place
remaining two tortillas over mixture. Cover with remaining
meat mixture and cheddar cheese. Sprinkle with Parmesan
cheese. If you have an oven timer, set it at 350 degrees for 45
to 50 minutes before you want to serve this dish. Put your cas-

serole in the oven, and when you get home from church it should be bubbly. It may continue to cook while you make a few other preparations for your dinner, if it is not quite as hot as it should be. Serve it with chopped lettuce, tomatoes and remaining sour cream.

Note: This dish can be prepared the day before, covered and refrigerated. Remove casserole from refrigerator 2 hours before placing in preheated 350 degree oven.

Assorted Fruit Plate

Arrange fruits in season on a plate and cover tightly, the day before. Any fruits that will turn brown because of the air should be cut up at the last moment and arranged alongside the other fruits. You may want to use some canned fruits also.

Sweet Fruit Dressing—"The Best!"

1½ cups sugar
1½ t. salt
1½ t. paprika
1½ t. onion (small chunks)
 ½ cup catsup
 ½ cup cider vinegar
1½ cups oil
1½ t. celery seeds

Put all ingredients in blender and blend until smooth. Store in jar in the refrigerator.

Mud Pie (Serves 8)

½ -⅔ package Nabisco Chocolate Wafers (about 8½ oz.)
½ stick butter or margarine, melted (¼ cup)
½ gallon coffee ice cream
¾ cup fudge sauce (recipe follows)

Crush wafers and add butter or margarine. Mix well. Press into 9-inch pie plate. Cover with soft coffee ice cream. Put into freezer until ice cream is firm. Top with chocolate fudge sauce that has been placed in the freezer for a time to make spreading easier. Store in freezer approximately 10 hours. Remove from freezer 15 to 20 minutes before serving. Slice and serve on chilled dessert plate with a chilled fork. Top with whipped cream and slivered almonds.

Chocolate Fudge Sauce

5 squares unsweetened Swiss Chocolate
½ cup butter or margarine
1 (5.3 oz.) can evaporated milk
3 cups powdered sugar
1¼ t. vanilla

Melt chocolate and butter in small saucepan or in the microwave. Mix in milk alternately with powdered sugar. Bring to a boil over medium heat, stirring constantly. Cook and stir 8 minutes or until thickened and creamy. Remove from heat and stir in vanilla. Store in refrigerator and use as needed. Makes three cups. May be served over ice cream.

```
┌─────────────────────────────┐
│                             │
│          Menu:              │
│                             │
│   Peg's Chicken Casserole   │
│    Temple Treasure Salad    │
│     Coconut Fruit Bowl      │
│        Bread Sticks         │
│      Frosted Brownies       │
│                             │
└─────────────────────────────┘
```

Peg Nelson's Chicken Casserole (Serves 8)

    4 whole chicken breasts
    3 cups coarsely chopped celery
 1/2 package petite frozen peas (thawed, but not cooked)
    2 cups Best Foods Mayonnaise
    1 can cream of mushroom soup
 1/2 can cream of chicken soup
    2 T. lemon juice
 1/4 cup chopped (or grated) onion
    1 cup grated cheddar cheese
    1 cup toasted slivered almonds
      Buttered bread crumbs

Simmer chicken breasts in water with a bit of onion and celery. When tender, cool in broth; drain and then cut up into bite-sized pieces. Grease 9 × 13 casserole. Evenly distribute the chicken on the bottom of casserole. Layer celery and peas over the chicken. Mix together mayonnaise, cream of mushroom soup, cream of chicken soup, 2 T. lemon juice, 1/4 cup chopped (or grated) onion. Pour this over the celery, peas and chicken in the casserole. Sprinkle grated cheddar cheese evenly over the casserole. Top with 1 cup of toasted, slivered almonds. Top with buttered bread crumbs and cover with plastic wrap. Refrigerate for one or two days. Remove from refrigerator 2 hours before baking, uncover and bake 35 to 45 minutes in 375 degree oven.

212

Temple Treasure Salad (Serves 8)

1 head of cauliflower
1 bunch of broccoli
4 oz. fresh mushrooms
   Green salad olives
2 bunches of green onions
3 or 4 stalks of celery
1 green pepper
1 cucumber
   Cherry tomatoes

Wash vegetables well, and drain. Cut flowerets of broccoli and cauliflower in bite-size pieces. Also cut celery, green pepper, mushrooms, cucumber and onions into uniform size pieces. Leave cherry tomatoes whole. Place in a large salad bowl.

Salad Dressing

¾ cup apple cider vinegar
½ cup sugar
½ cup salad oil
1 t. salt
½ t. dried dill weed, crushed
⅛ t. pepper

Combine vinegar, sugar, salt, pepper, dill weed and oil. Mix and heat just below boiling temperature. Pour over vegetables while hot and refrigerate for at least 24 hours, or 2 or 3 days, stirring occasionally to re-distribute the dressing. Before serving, drain off the salad dressing and line a salad bowl with lettuce leaves. Spoon vegetables into serving bowl.

Coconut Fruit Bowl (Serves 8)

1 (no. 2) can of pineapple tidbits or chunks, thoroughly
   drained
1 (11 oz.) can of mandarin oranges, thoroughly drained
1 to 2 cups seedless grapes
1 cup tiny marshmallows
1 (3½ oz.) can of flaked coconut (optional)
2 cups dairy sour cream (or substitute Imo, a soybean product)
¼ t. salt

Combine fruits, marshmallows and coconut. Stir in sour cream and salt. Place in a pretty serving bowl and cover with plastic wrap or aluminum foil. Chill overnight.

Chewy Brownies (Makes 30)

½ cup butter or margarine
4 oz. baking chocolate
4 eggs, at room temperature
½ t. salt
2 cups sugar
1 cup flour
1 cup pecans or walnuts, optional

Preheat oven to 350 degrees. Melt butter and chocolate in microwave or double broiler. Cool this mixture. (If you don't cool, brownies will be heavy and dry.) Beat eggs and salt together until light and foamy. Gradually beat sugar into the egg mixture. With a few quick strokes with your wooden spoon, combine the cooled chocolate mixture into the eggs and sugar. Before the mixture becomes uniformly colored and well blended, fold in flour. Before flour is fully blended in, fold in nuts. Pour batter into a greased 9 × 13 pan. Bake 25 minutes. Cool.

Chocolate Frosting

    3 T. shortening
    3 oz. baking chocolate
    2 cups sifted confectioner sugar
    1/8 t. salt
    1/2 cup milk
    1 t. vanilla

   Melt shortening and chocolate in saucepan over low heat. Stir in remaining ingredients and beat until smooth. Place pan of frosting in bowl of ice water and continue beating until it is of spreading consistency. If desired, stir in 1/2 cup finely chopped nuts. Frost brownies and serve with vanilla ice cream, if desired.

Easy Dips and Appetizers

Zesty Spinach Dip (Makes 2 cups)

1 (10 oz.) package frozen chopped spinach, thawed
1/3 cup coarsely chopped green onion
1/2 cup chopped fresh parsley
1 T. lemon juice
1 cup sour cream
1 1/2 t. pepper
2 cloves of garlic (pressed through garlic press or minced finely)
1/2 t. salt
About 6 cups of raw vegetables—such as strips of carrots, celery, red bell pepper, turnips, zucchini, or whole cherry tomatoes

Drain spinach, then squeeze out as much liquid as possible. Place in a blender or food processor and blend green onions, parsley, lemon juice, sour cream, pepper and garlic. If you do not have a blender or food processor, blend all ingredients together by hand after chopping spinach, green onion and parsley fine. Place in covered container for at least 6 to 8 hours, or overnight. Serve in a bowl and arrange raw vegetables around dip.

Good and Easy Spinach Dip

   1 package frozen chopped spinach—thaw and squeeze out
     the juice
   1 small package Knorr Vegetable soup mix, or Lipton's Veg-
     etable soup mix
   1 cup mayonnaise
   1 cup sour cream
½ to 1 whole can of water chestnuts, drained and cut up
   1 large, round loaf of crusty bread—or 1 long loaf of crusty
     bread

Prepare the mix the night before by blending all ingredients
well. Cover and store in the refrigerator. The day you wish to
serve the dip, hollow out the loaf of bread and fill with the dip.
Surround the bread with the cut away bread pieces and extra
crackers. Provide a spoon or spreader to put dip on bread (you
don't need it for crackers).

Hot Crab Dip

¼ cup sliced almonds
  1 (8 oz.) package cream cheese at room temperature
  1 T. lemon juice
  1 (6½ to 7¾ oz.) can crabmeat, undrained
½ t. curry powder

Preheat oven to 350 degrees. Spread almonds in shallow
pan and bake four minutes, or until golden brown. Turn out of
pan into a bowl. Beat cream cheese, lemon juice, undrained
crab and curry powder until well blended. Mix in half of the
toasted almonds. Turn dip into 2 cup baking dish or oven-proof
bowl. Bake 20 to 30 minutes, depending on shape of the dish

(deeper dish takes longer). Dip is done when pick inserted in center comes out fairly dry and the center is hot. Top with remaining almonds and serve hot with chips, crackers, or raw vegetables.

Barbara Buckbee's Clam Dip (Serves 12 or more)

    3 (7 oz.) cans of minced clams (pour off the juice)
    2 (8 oz.) cream cheese, at room temperature
    2 T. onion, chopped fine
    2 T. chopped parsley
    1/2 t. salt
    2 T. lemon juice
    2 T. Worcestershire sauce
    6 drops Tabasco (optional)
    1 loaf of unsliced round bread or long unsliced French bread

Slice off the top of the bread and scoop out the center, leaving 1/2 to 3/4 inch of bread inside crust. Mix the dip together well and place inside the bread crust. Replace top crust. Wrap bread in foil. Bake at 300 degrees for 1 1/2 hours. Serve with crackers.

Microwave Quick Crab Dip (Makes 2 cups)

1 (8 oz.) package cream cheese, softened
1 (7 oz.) can crabmeat rinsed and drained well (or 7 oz. arti-
    ficial crab made from fish, and cut up like crab)
2 T. light cream or half and half
2 T. minced green onion
1 T. minced parsley
1 T. lemon juice
1/2 t. Worcestershire sauce
1/4 cup slivered toasted almonds

Oven setting: high (100 percent power). Combine all ingredients except almonds in a one quart microwave casserole.
Cover with a lid or plastic wrap. Microwave 2 minutes; stir well
to blend. Then microwave 2 to 3 minutes longer, until heated
through. Garnish with toasted slivered almonds and serve hot
with crackers or fresh vegetables.

Easiest Appetizers Ever!

Number One
    Stuff seeded dates with cream cheese. Wrap 1/3 slice bacon
    around each date and fasten with a toothpick. Place under
    broiler and broil until bacon is crispy.

Number Two
    Combine one bottle of grape jelly and one bottle of chili
    sauce. Heat on top of stove or in a microwave. Place wiener
    chunks on toothpicks in this barbeque sauce and simmer in
    a small pan for 30 to 35 minutes. If making a large recipe,
    this may be simmered in an electric frying pan and served
    from the frying pan.

Number Three

Stuffed mushrooms—use only mushroom caps. Stuff with a mixture of half mashed potatoes and half cream cheese (at room temperature), blended together with garlic salt to taste. (I use instant mashed potatoes). Place stuffed mushroom caps on broiler pan—3 inches from broiling unit—and broil until potatoes and cream cheese mixture is puffy and brown. Garnish with parsley.

Hot Bean Dip

   2 large cans refried beans
   6 or 8 green onions, chopped (chop whole onions finely)
   2 T. Worcestershire sauce
  1/4 lb. tillamook or cheddar cheese, grated
  1/2 cup tomato sauce
   2 (12 oz.) packages of corn chips

Preheat oven to 350 degrees. Mix all ingredients together except cheese. Bake 1 hour in attractive casserole. Fold in the 1/4 lb. grated cheese and bake half hour more. Serve dip directly from casserole. *Note:* If you are in a hurry, this dip can be heated on top of the stove. Then stir in the cheese and continue to stir until it melts. The dip should always be served hot.

Cheese Balls from Ann Simertz

½ lb. butter or margarine
½ lb. New York sharp cheese (at room temperature), grated
   or crumbled
⅛ t. salt
14 drops Tabasco sauce
 2 cups flour

Preheat oven to 400 degrees. Place room temperature margarine and cheese in a bowl. Work with a fork and your hands (I wear rubber gloves) to mix the two together until very creamy. Add salt and Tabasco sauce and mix well. Gradually add flour and work by hand into the cheese/margarine mixture. Form into balls about the size of a walnut. Put in refrigerator for several hours before baking (or freeze on cookie sheets until solid and then place in plastic bags for storage in the freezer—up to 3 months). Bake cheeseballs about 15 minutes, or until done.

Note: If using frozen cheeseballs, let stand at room temperature at least 30 minutes after you have removed them from the freezer before putting in the hot oven.

Serve these cheeseballs hot. They are delicious. Serve with cold tomato or V8 Juice.

Liz Anderson's Barbecued Chicken Wings
(Serves 8 to 10)

20 to 25 chicken wings, or Drumettes
   If you get the whole chicken wing, cut off the tip end and
   discard. Cut the meatier two pieces of the wing in half.

Make marinade:

   1/2 cup catsup
   1/2 cup cider vinegar
   1/2 cup soy sauce
   3/4 cup sugar
   1/4 cup pineapple *or* orange juice
   1/4 cup oil
     1 t. garlic powder
     1 t. ginger

   Preheat oven to 350 degrees. Arrange the chicken wings in
the bottom half of a broiler pan, in a roaster, or for smaller
quantities use a cake pan or casserole dish. Stir the barbecue
marinade until all of the sugar is dissolved and all of the ingredients are well blended. Pour over the chicken wings and let
stand covered in the refrigerator overnight until ready to bake.
Place single layer of chicken wings in pans and pour some of
the sauce over them to bake. Bake for 1 to 1 1/2 hours, or until
done. Can be held at 200 degrees until serving time.

Robin Johnson's Best Cheeseball Ever!

1 (16 oz.) package of cream cheese
4 oz. of blue cheese
1 green pepper, chopped fine
$\frac{1}{2}$ cup to $\frac{3}{4}$ cup chopped pimento
   Crushed walnuts or pecans to roll the cheeseball in
   (approximately 1 cup)

Two hours before making the cheeseball, remove the cream cheese and blue cheese from the refrigerator. Unwrap both cheeses and break them up into small pieces in a large mixing bowl. When the cheese is at room temperature, beat the two cheeses together with a fork until well blended. Add the chopped green pepper and well drained chopped pimento into the cheese bowl and mix in. Place the crushed nuts on a piece of waxed paper. Spoon the cheese out in a ball onto the nuts, and gently roll across the nuts to cover all of the outside of the ball. Place on an attractive serving plate and chill until ready to serve. Serve with several kinds of crackers around the cheeseball. This recipe may be doubled, but if you wish to make more cheeseballs, I would recommend that you only mix double batches at one time. It would be too hard to handle any more mixing of the cream cheese and the blue cheese than two batches at a time. Nice for a Christmas buffet.

Fantastic Meatballs (Makes 500)

5 lb. ground beef
3 lb. bulk hot pork sausage meat
3 lb. regular pork sausage meat
10 eggs
3⅓ cups whole bran flake cereal (fine dry bread crumbs or
    crushed saltines may be substituted)
4½ to 5 t. ground sage
7½ cups of catsup
2½ cups brown sugar, packed
    1 cup vinegar
    1 cup soy sauce

Preheat oven to 325 degrees. Mix ground beef, pork sausages, beaten eggs, cereal flakes and sage. *Note:* A good idea is to use rubber gloves for mixing these ingredients well. Form into bite-size balls (if you have a small size scoop or watermelon ball scoop, try this. It speeds up the process.) Brown in batches in the skillet, or broil in the oven until the meatballs are brown on top. Drain all fat off meatballs by placing them on paper towels. Combine catsup, brown sugar, vinegar and soy sauce, and blend well. Place meatballs in sauce and bake for 30 to 40 minutes (your broiler pans are nice sized pans to use for this. Remove the rack and use the lower part of the pan). This recipe makes 500 small appetizer meatballs! You will want to cut the size of this recipe if you are serving only a small group, or freeze the meatballs in the sauce and store in your freezer. Do not bake them until you want to serve them. When ready to serve, remove the meatballs 3 hours before baking to thaw, and bake at 325 degrees for 40 minutes.

Salads and Salad Dressings

Doris Greig's Favorite Pasta (Serves 4 to 6)
Make this the day ahead and refrigerate in container.

1/2 cup white vinegar
6 T. lemon juice
1/4 cup honey (or 1/4 cup sugar)
3 T. fresh ginger (peeled with potato peeler and grated) *or*
1 t. dry ground ginger
  Note: The fresh ginger is far better, if available.
2 T. soy sauce
1/8 t. cayenne pepper
12 oz. dry fettuccine
1 T. oil (preferably sesame oil)
1/2 cup chopped green onion tops
1 1/2 cups finely sliced carrots, *or* broccoli flowerets
  Note: To the above, add *one* of these ingredients:
        1 1/2 lb. large or medium cooked shrimp
        1 1/2 lb. imitation crabmeat (*or* crabmeat)
        1 1/2 cup albacore fish (canned-drained well)
        1 can salmon, drained well

In a 3 qt. pan, stir together lemon juice, vinegar, soy sauce, honey, ginger and cayenne. Bring to a boil and simmer one minute. Remove dressing from heat and let stand 10 minutes or longer. Bring 3 quarts of water to a boil in a 5 to 6 quart pan. Add fettuccine and cook uncovered over high heat, until tender to the bite, about 15 to 18 minutes.

After fettucine is cooked: Pour into a large colander and rinse under cold running water until cool. Drain well. In a large bowl, mix fettuccine, dressing, sesame oil and onions. Cover and refrigerate 5 hours or overnight. Before serving, carefully blend in fish or shrimp if you want to have it in your pasta salad. Also, before serving, add sliced carrots or broccoli flowerets to pasta.

231

Shirley Prothero's Cantonese Salad (Serves 8 to 10)

2 cans tuna or albacore
1 (6 to 8 oz.) can of water chestnuts, drained and sliced
1 (20 oz.) can pineapple, either crushed or tidbits
½ cup finely sliced green onion
½ cup chopped celery
1 can of Chinese noodles (the tall can)
4 T. pickle relish
1 cup sour cream
¼ t. curry powder

In a small bowl mix together sour cream, pickle relish and curry powder. In a large bowl, place drained tuna, drained chestnuts, well-drained pineapple, celery, and sliced green onions. Mix well. Add the dressing to the large bowl and mix in well. Cover and refrigerate. Just before serving, fold in the Chinese noodles and serve on lettuce leaves.

Barbara Sheffield's Oriental Salad (Serves 6 as a main course or 10 as a side dish)

¾ cup sesame seeds
4 cups shredded cabbage (or 2 bunches of spinach, washed and broken up, or leaf lettuce)
2 cups (or more) of cut up cooked chicken or turkey
2 packages chicken flavored Ramen Soup Mix
½ cup sliced or slivered almonds
¼ cup butter or sesame oil
1 bunch green onions, cut up, tops and all

Dressing:

½ cup oil
½ cup vinegar
4 T. soy sauce
2 chicken Ramen flavoring packets from the soup mix
½ cup sugar
½ t. pepper

Stir until all ingredients are blended and dissolved. Store in covered container in the refrigerator. Use only as much dressing as desired. Stores well. Brown crumbled Ramen (crumbled by hand while still in its packet) with sesame seeds and almonds with butter or sesame oil. Use a heavy fry pan or kettle, and stir constantly until brown. Remove from heat immediately. Set aside in an ovenproof dish. Cover when cool with waxed paper. Cook chicken, or cut up already cooked chicken, and chill. Cut up cabbage and other greens and store in a plastic bag. Cut up onions, tops and all, and store in plastic bag.

Note: All of these steps can be done the day before.

Twenty minutes before serving, spread the noodle mixture in a 9 × 12 cake pan and warm in a 350 degree oven 4 or 5 minutes, *or* in the microwave to "re-crisp" it if you wish. Watch carefully! Just before serving, put all of the ingredients in a large bowl. Stir dressing and add gradually until salad ingredients are well coated. Refrigerate any extra dressing to use later.

Macaroni Salad for Janie Greig

    1 lb. salad macaroni
    2 cups chopped celery
    6 to 8 hard cooked eggs
    1 large jar of green salad olives
    ¾ cup chopped sweet pickles, or ½ cup of well drained
       sweet pickle relish
    1 small onion, grated
    1 green pepper, chopped (optional)
    ½ cup sweet pickle juice (or enough to thin mayonnaise
       down so it can be blended well into the salad ingredients)
    1 cup mayonnaise

   Cook macaroni according to package directions. Rinse
under cold water in colander, and drain thoroughly. Put macaroni in a bowl with celery, eggs, salad olives, sweet pickles,
green pepper and onion. Mix mayonnaise with sweet pickle
juice to thin down. You may add celery seed if you wish. Fold
dressing into salad and refrigerate for 3 to 4 hours, covered,
before serving. (You may let this refrigerate overnight.)

Note: You may substitute 2 cans of tuna, well drained, in place
       of the eggs in this salad. Or you may use 4 eggs and 1
       can of tuna (large size) which has been well drained.

Joy of Living—Newhall Bible Class Taco Salad

    1 (6-7 oz.) package of corn chips
    ½ large red onion, thinly sliced and diced
    2 large (or 4 medium) tomatoes, sliced thin
    1 can Mexican style (Ranch) beans, rinsed and drained well
    1 lb. cheddar cheese, grated
    1 large head of lettuce, broken in pieces
    4 oz. creamy French dressing

Layer ingredients, starting with the tomatoes. Next, layer the beans, onions, broken pieces of lettuce and ending with the cheese on top. Cover and chill at least 4 hours, or overnight. One hour before serving, toss with the French dressing, and return to chill in refrigerator for 1 hour. When ready to serve, top with corn chips and garnish wtih tomato slices. *Optional:* 1 lb. ground beef browned in a frying pan with 1 clove of garlic (minced), or ½ t. garlic salt. Drain off excess fat. Cool. As you layer ingredients, use the ground beef as your first layer.

Betty Minnick's Stuffed Tomato Chicken Salad
(Serves 6)

> 6 large tomatoes
> 2 cups diced, cooked chicken (chicken breasts can be cooked quickly and easily in the microwave)
> 2 cups diced celery
> 2 diced, hard cooked eggs
> 1 t. salt
> ¼ cup slivered almonds, toasted to a golden brown at 350 degrees—4 to 5 minutes.
> ¾ cup sour cream, or Imo Sour Cream substitute
> ½ t. salt
> ½ t. dry mustard
> ¼ t. sugar
> ¼ t. paprika
> ¼ cup lemon juice

Scoop pulp from centers of tomatoes and chill. Combine chicken, celery, eggs, salt and almonds. Combine remaining ingredients and add to sour cream to make dressing. Mix dressing with the chicken mixture. Fill tomato shells and serve on salad greens.

Mound Luncheon Chicken Salad

3 cups diced cooked chicken or turkey
1 cup celery
1 cup nuts—walnuts or toasted slivered almonds
1 cup mandarin oranges, drained well (or 1 cup of fresh,
 chopped orange that has been drained well on paper
 towels)
1 cup pineapple tidbits, drained well
2 T. orange juice
2 T. vinegar
2 T. salad oil
1 t. salt
½ cup whipping cream
½ cup Miracle Whip

> *Note:* Save mandarin orange and pineapple juice for a
> fruit punch.

Mix orange juice, vinegar, salad oil and salt together. Pour
over the chicken, celery, mandarin oranges and pineapple tidbits in a bowl. Mix and let stand 1 to 2 hours, or overnight in
the refrigerator. Before serving, add the nuts. Beat cream until
it holds peaks. Fold in Miracle Whip. Gently fold this dressing
into the chicken salad. Serve on a lettuce leaf and garnish with
parsley and more slivered almonds, if desired.

Ever Ready Slaw (Serves 8 to 10)

1 cup cider vinegar
1 cup sugar
1 t. salt
1 t. dry mustard
1 t. celery seeds
1 medium head cabbage
1 green pepper (optional)
1 small onion
1 carrot

Combine vinegar, sugar, salt, mustard and celery seeds. Microwave on high until boiling for 4½ to 5 minutes, stirring once. Can be cooked on top of stove also. Cool. Finely shred cabbage, green pepper, onion and carrot. Combine in covered container with cooled dressing. Cover tightly and refrigerate 12 hours before serving, turning container over occasionally to distribute dressing. Slaw will keep up to a week.

Carol Bartel's Cinnamon Apple Salad (Serves 4 to 6)

1 (3 oz.) box of cherry gelatin
1½ cups of boiling water
¼ cup cinnamon candies
¼ cup cold water
1 cup chopped apple, unpeeled
1 cup finely chopped celery
½ cup chopped walnuts

Stir 1 cup of boiling water into the cherry gelatin until dissolved. Stir ½ cup of boiling water with the cinnamon candies over medium heat until dissolved (or use your microwave).

Add ¼ cup cold water to all of the above combined ingredients, and put in the refrigerator until partially set (watch carefully as this is a small recipe). When the gelatin begins to set up, add the apple, celery and walnuts. Pour into a small mold and chill until ready to serve.

Mary Jo McCurry's Quick Fruit Salad (Serves 12 to 16)

- 1 (32 oz.) carton of cottage cheese
- 1 (30 oz.) can pineapple chunks or fruit cocktail, drained well
- 2 to 3 cups of well drained mandarin oranges, or fresh oranges cut up and drained well
- 1 (6 oz.) package of a red gelatin
- 1 (12 oz.) Cool Whip

Mix dry gelatin with cottage cheese in a large bowl. Fold in pineapple (*or* fruit cocktail) and oranges. This much of the salad may be prepared as much as 24 hours in advance of serving time, and kept in the refrigerator. One to 2 hours before serving time, fold in the Cool Whip. Place the fruit salad in an attractive serving bowl and refrigerate until time to serve.

Grandma Rick's 24 Hour Salad (Serves 8 to 10)

3 eggs
1/4 cup white vinegar and 3 T. lemon juice
1/4 cup sugar
2 T. butter or margarine
1 cup whipping cream
1 (1 lb. 13 oz.) can of peaches, well drained.
1 (1 lb. 4 oz.) can of pineapple chunks or tidbits, well drained
2 cups seedless grapes (washed, removed from stems, drained)
4 bananas, peeled and sliced
4 oranges, peeled and diced and well drained in a colander
2 cups of miniature marshmallows (may be omitted and add 2 cups more of one of the fruits listed above)

Beat eggs in top of double boiler. Add vinegar and lemon juice, sugar and butter or margarine. Put top of double boiler over boiling water, cook and stir until thick. Remove upper part of double boiler, and set on rack on counter to cool, stirring the thickened mixture occasionally, or cool in freezer in covered container, stirring frequently until cool.

In the meantime—open canned fruit and drain well, cut up peaches and pineapple chunks into "tidbit" size, dice oranges and drain well separately. Prepare grapes, and measure marshmallows.

Whip the cream until it holds peak well. Fold cooled dressing and whipped cream together in a large bowl. Add all of the fruit, sliced bananas and marshmallows and fold gently together. Place in a serving bowl and chill, covered, for 24 hours. This salad may be served in lettuce cups, or may be used on a buffet in an attractive serving bowl in which it has been chilled.

Mary Jo McCurry's "Not Too Sweet" Cranberry Orange Mold (Serves 12)

- 1 envelope unflavored gelatin
- 2 (6 oz.) packages of wild strawberry gelatin (or plain strawberry)
- 3 medium oranges, chopped
- 1 (13 to 16 oz.) package of fresh or frozen cranberries
- 2 cups of apples and/or celery may also be added to this mold if desired
- ½ cup sugar

In a 4 qt. saucepan with 2 cups of water, sprinkle unflavored gelatin. Stir over medium heat until gelatin dissolves and mixture is boiling. Remove pan from heat and stir in dry gelatin and ½ cup sugar until totally dissolved. Add 1 cup of cold water to this. In blender, place 2 cups of cold water and the fresh or partially thawed cranberries. Blend until chopped well. Add this mixture to the pan of gelatin. Place in refrigerator to thicken; meanwhile chop oranges, (and celery and/or apple, if you wish). When mixture is syrupy and thick, fold in the rest of the fruit. Pour into a 3 qt. mold or a serving bowl and refrigerate for at least 3 hours or overnight.

Old Stand-by Red French Dressing

  1 can tomato soup
$\frac{1}{2}$ cup vinegar and $\frac{1}{2}$ cup wine vinegar
$\frac{1}{2}$ cup oil
$\frac{1}{2}$ cup sugar
$\frac{1}{2}$ t. garlic powder
$\frac{1}{2}$ t. paprika (if desired)
  1 small onion (cut into small pieces for blender)
$2\frac{1}{2}$ t. salt
$1\frac{1}{2}$ t. pepper

Place all ingredients in a blender and blend thoroughly. Place in covered container in the refrigerator and chill. This dressing keeps up to 3 months (but never lasts that long because it is so good!)

Note: Apple cider vinegar may be substituted for wine vinegar.

Clara Johnson's French Dressing

  1 cup of Mazola oil, or safflower oil
$\frac{1}{2}$ cup sugar
$\frac{1}{4}$ cup vinegar
$\frac{1}{3}$ cup chili sauce or catsup
  1 t. paprika
  1 t. salt
    Juice of 1 lemon
  1 small onion, cut into small pieces

Place all ingredients in blender and blend well. Place in jar and store in refrigerator up to 3 months. This makes an excellent red french dressing for any tossed salad. It is also delicious served with avocado and orange salad.

Marie Callender "Type" Hot Bacon Dressing for Spinach Salad

    Wash and thoroughly drain spinach
½ lb. bacon or bacon bits
3 T. cornstarch
1¼ cup pineapple juice
1 T. soy sauce
¼ cup + 2 T. white or apple cider vinegar
⅓ cup water
½ cup brown sugar
2 t. salt
½ t. pepper
1 small grated onion

If you are using bacon, fry it crispy and drain, saving the bacon fat for use in the dressing. Place cornstarch in a sauce pan and slowly blend in pineapple juice. Stir in the soy sauce, vinegar, water, brown sugar, salt and pepper. Simmer until thick, stirring. Add 2 to 3 T. of bacon fat or cooking oil. Just before serving add bacon or bacon bits, and as much grated onion as you wish. Toss with the spinach and enjoy! This recipe makes approximately 2 cups of dressing, which should be enough to serve 4 people a spinach salad. The salad may be garnished with sliced, hard-cooked eggs and/or baby shrimp.

Note: To drain spinach, place in a clean pillowship, take outside and whirl it around several times. Works well!

Low-Calorie Vinegrette Dressing
30 Calories per Tablespoon

¼ cup oil
¼ cup wine vinegar
¼ cup lemon juice
¼ cup tomato juice or water
1 clove finely minced garlic put through a press
⅛ t. pepper
¼ t. thyme (optional)
¼ t. salt
1 or 2 packages Equal, to sweeten (optional)

Mix in blender or in a bottle, and store in covered container in refrigerator up to 3 months.

Main Dishes

The following are foods that I have enjoyed preparing through the years because they are simple and delicious.

Esther Shackelford's Tortilla Casserole (Serves 8)

    4 chicken breasts—cut up (or leftover chicken or turkey)
    1 dozen corn tortillas
    1 can cream of mushroom soup
    1 can cream of chicken soup (or the equivalent of 1 can
        sour cream)
    1 medium size grated onion
    ½ cup milk
    2 T. chicken broth (or water)
    1 can green chili salsa (8 oz.)
    ½ lb. sharp to medium grated cheddar cheese

Preheat oven to 325 degrees. Mix the chicken with the 2 cans of soup (or 1 can of sour cream and 1 can of soup), grated onion, milk, 2 T. of liquid, and green chili salsa. Grease a 2-quart casserole, and alternate layers of tortillas and the mixture listed in the first step. Top casserole with cheese and bake for 1½ hours. This casserole can be prepared ahead of time and kept in the refrigerator. Remove at least 2 hours before placing in oven.

Lil Ash Hammond's Layered Enchilada Pie
(Serves 4 to 5)

1 lb. ground beef, or ground turkey
1 chopped onion, medium size
1 minced clove of garlic
1 t. salt
1/4 t. pepper
1 to 2 t. chili powder (according to how hot you like your food!)
1 (4 1/2 oz.) can chopped olives (optional)
1 (8 oz.) can tomato sauce
6 corn tortillas
1/2 lb. grated cheddar cheese (reserve 1/2 cup for top of casserole)
2/3 cup water

Preheat oven to 400 degrees. Brown ground beef, onion and garlic together. Drain off excess fat and liquid. Add seasoning, olives and tomato sauce to the beef, and stir until well blended. In a greased, 2-quart casserole, preferably round, start with a tortilla and alternate layers of tortillas, meat sauce and cheese. Repeat until all 6 tortillas, sauce and cheese are in the casserole. Pour the water evenly over the casserole ingredients and cover. Bake for 20 minutes. Sprinkle remaining 1/2 cup of cheese on top. Cover and continue to bake for 10 minutes or prepare the night before and refrigerate. Remove 2 hours before baking. You may microwave approximately 10 minutes on high on a turntable instead of baking in oven.

Microwave Mexican Casserole (Serves 6)

1½ lb. ground beef
  4 green onions, chopped
  1 t. garlic salt
  2 (8 oz.) cans of tomato sauce
  ¼ cup water
  1 8 oz. can of sliced, black olives (drained)
  1 cup sour cream
  1 cup small curd cottage cheese
  1 can (4 oz.) Ortega chopped chilies
  ¾ lb. jack cheese (grated)
6¾ oz. package of tortilla corn chips

Place ground beef in covered casserole in microwave. Cook at high speed (100 percent) for 6 minutes, stirring once, breaking up the meat halfway through. Drain off fat. Add onions, garlic salt, tomato sauce, water and olives. Cook on high in microwave 2 minutes, stirring after 1 minute. In a separate bowl, mix cottage cheese, sour cream and green chilies. In a 3-quart, greased casserole, place ½ of the crumbled tortillas. Layer ½ of the meat mixture, ½ of the cottage cheese mixture, then ½ of the jack cheese. Repeat layers with corn chips first,

249

meat mixture, cottage cheese mixture, and jack cheese on top of this. Cover casserole with plastic wrap and microwave on high (100 percent power) for 10 minutes. When the casserole has cooked 5 minutes, turn it around in the oven, or use a turntable. Continue cooking the last 5 minutes.

Chili Rellenos—Casserole Style (Serves 6)

1 lb. 4 oz. can refried beans
1 (4 oz.) can whole green chilies or a 4 oz. can chopped chilies, drained well
¼ lb. jack cheese (cubed or grated)
4 eggs, separated (and at room temperature—if you think far enough ahead!)
4 T. flour and ½ t. salt stirred into the flour
Taco sauce or salsa to serve with this dish

Preheat oven to 350 degrees. Spoon beans into greased, 1½ quart casserole, spreading out evenly to cover bottom of casserole. Remove seeds from chilies and cut in half, or quarter lengthwise. Wrap chilies around cubes of cheese, or toss chopped chilies with grated cheese, and place on top of the beans. Separate egg yolks from egg whites, and beat egg whites until stiff. In a separate bowl, beat egg yolks slightly and fold into the beaten egg whites, also sprinkling flour, salt mixture over the whites and folding in at the same time. Spoon egg mixture evenly over beans, chilies and cheese in casserole, and spread evenly to sides of pan. Bake uncovered for 25 to 30 minutes, until egg whites are set.

A Missionary's Enchilada Stack Up (Serves 6)

1 to 1½ lbs. lean ground beef
1 onion chopped
¼ t. garlic powder
1 t. salt
1 (4 oz.) can green chili salsa (more if you like it hot!)
8 corn tortillas
1 cup dairy sour cream
About ½ lb. shredded cheddar cheese (or jack cheese)

Preheat oven to 400 degrees. Cook beef and onion until meat loses red color, breaking up meat with fork to keep crumbly. Drain off fat. Add salt, garlic powder, tomato sauce, onion and chili salsa to beef and cover and simmer 5 minutes. In a round, covered casserole (this shape is preferable because of the tortillas, but another type of casserole can be used). Alternate layers of tortillas, meat salsa mixture, sour cream and cheese—starting with a tortilla. End with cheese. Bake, covered for 30 minutes—until cheese melts.

Betty Adcock's El Dorado Beef Casserole (Serves 6)

1 lb. lean ground beef
1 T. instant minced onion
½ t. garlic salt
2 (8 oz.) cans tomato sauce
1 cup sliced, ripe olives, drained
1 cup sour cream
1 cup small curd cottage cheese
3 or 4 canned chilies, seeded and chopped—or One 4 oz. can drained, chopped green chilies
1 package (6½ oz. size) corn tortilla chips
½ lb. jack cheese, grated

251

Preheat oven to 350 degrees. Brown meat, breaking up with fork. Drain off excess fat. Add onion, garlic salt, tomato sauce and olives to beef. In a bowl, combine sour cream, cottage cheese and green chilies. Blend well. Crush tortilla chips slightly, reserving a few for garnish. Place half of the crushed chips in the bottom of a well-greased 2½ qt. casserole. Add half the meat mixture evenly over the chips. Cover with half the sour cream mixture. Sprinkle with half the grated cheese. Repeat layers. Bake, uncovered for 35 to 40 minutes, or until hot and bubbly. Garnish top with reserved whole tortilla chips.

Homemade Salsa

   4 large, firm tomatoes (chopped)
   1 medium sized sweet, red onion (chopped)
   3 green onions, thinly sliced
   1 (1 lb.) can stewed tomatoes, drained and cut up
   1 (4 oz.) can chopped green chilies, drained
   1 clove garlic (minced in garlic press)
   4 drops of hot pepper sauce
   ¾ t. salt (or to taste)
   ¼ cup red wine vinegar, or cider vinegar

Combine all ingredients and blend well. Season to taste with salt. Refrigerate at least an hour before serving. This recipe makes approximately 7 cups, so you may want to cut the recipe in half for a small family. This does not freeze, but keeps in the refrigerator for 2 weeks.

Dwan Walter's Four Bean Casserole (Serves 10 to 12)
   1 (1 lb.) can pork and beans
   1 (1 lb.) can kidney beans
   1 (1 lb.) can butter beans (drained)
   1 (1 lb.) can lima beans (drained)
   1/2 lb. bacon
   1/2 lb. ground beef or ground turkey
   1 T. prepared mustard
   2 medium onions, chopped (about 1 cup)
   1/2 cup catsup
   1/2 cup brown sugar, firmly packed
   1/4 cup molasses
   2 T. vinegar
      Dash of Worcestershire sauce
   1/2 t. salt
   1 (18 oz.) can crushed pineapple, drained well (optional)

   Preheat oven to 350 degrees. Brown bacon and beef or turkey and drain off fat. Mix all ingredients well. Bake for 1 hour,
or until hot and bubbly.

Mildred Dalton's Chuck Wagon Beans
(Serves 12, 1 cup each)

   1/2 lb. bacon
   3 lbs. ground beef
   2 cups finely chopped onion
   1 cup finely chopped celery
   2 beef bouillon cubes, dissolved in 2/3 cup boiling water
   1 1/2 cups catsup
   3 T. prepared mustard
   1 1/2 t. salt
   1 1/2 cloves garlic, minced or put through garlic press
   1/2 t. pepper
   2 (29 oz.) cans of molasses style baked beans

253

Preheat oven to 350 degrees. In a dutch oven, or a frying pan, fry bacon until crisp. Drain and crumble. Set bacon aside and drain fat from your pan. In the same pan, brown ground beef. Drain fat from beef. Add onion and celery to the beef, and cook until onion and celery are tender. Dissolve boullion cubes in water. Add this to the meat mixture with catsup, mustard, salt, garlic and pepper. Add baked beans. Mix well. Bake 1 hour in the dutch oven or a large casserole dish until hot and bubbly. Sprinkle crumbled bacon over the beans just before serving. You may wish to divide the recipe in half for smaller family use.

Betty Adcock's Stayabed Stew (Serves 6)

    3 lbs. beef stew meat, cut in pieces
1½ cup carrots, sliced at an angle
    2 chopped onions (more if desired)
       Salt and pepper to taste
    2 small cans of tomato sauce (4 oz.)
1¼ cups water
   ¼ cup wine vinegar or red burgundy wine
    2 or 3 large potatoes sliced diagonally (peeled or unpeeled)
       A piece of bay leaf
       A sprinkle of mixed herbs if you like

Preheat oven to 275 degrees. Place stew meat and vegetables in a heavy dutch oven with a tight lid. Mix tomato sauce with water and wine vinegar. Pour over meat and vegetables. Sprinkle salt and pepper on meat and vegetables, as well as mixed herbs. Add bay leaf. Place lid on dutch oven and bake for five hours. No peeking! This is a fun meal for children to prepare. Note: Alcohol bakes out, but wine vinegar is good.

Catherine Berg Greig's Oven Stew (Serves 12)

   4 lbs. stew beef (or 2 lbs. of beef plus 2 large cans of gar-
      banzo beans)
   4 cups sliced carrots
   2 cups sliced celery
   4 medium onions, sliced (approximately 3 cups)
   2 (5 oz.) cans water chestnuts (optional)
   2 (6 oz.) cans mushrooms or 1 lb. fresh mushrooms, sliced
      and added the last 30 minutes of cooking
 1/4 cup, plus 2 T. flour
   2 T. sugar
   2 T. salt
   2 (16 oz.) cans tomatoes (do *not* drain)
1 1/2 cups water and 1/2 cup wine vinegar or 2 cups of bur-
      gundy wine (alcohol cooks out)
   8 garlic buds (leave whole and remove before serving stew)
      or 4 minced garlic cloves
      Optional Spices: I use 1 bay leaf finely crumbled, 1 t.
      ground thyme, 1/2 t. ground rosemary, 1 T. Worcester-
      shire. Just before serving, you can sprinkle 3 cups of
      chopped parsley over the stew, if desired.

Preheat oven to 325 degrees. Place beef, carrots, celery,
onions, drained water chestnuts and drained mushrooms in
roaster or dutch oven. Pour canned tomatoes with juice over
this, and sprinkle garlic evenly over contents. Mix sugar, flour
and salt in a bowl. Gradually add water and vinegar, blending
well to make a smooth mixture. Pour evenly over all of the rest
of the ingredients. Cover dutch oven or roaster, and bake 4
hours, or put the dutch oven on top of the stove and simmer
for 4 hours. Can be prepared a day in advance. Flavor is
enhanced by re-heating. During the last half hour of cooking, I
like to add 1 package of frozen petite peas that have been
thawed. They add a nice color to this stew.

Mushroom Beef Bake—A Busy Day Dish (Serves 6 to 8)

1 (4 lb.) chuck beef roast (about 1½ inch thick)
1 can mushroom soup
1 envelope dry onion soup mix
1 large sheet heavy aluminum foil

Preheat oven to 350 degrees. Put onion soup mix on foil and roll roast in it to coat well. Place foil and meat in a 9 × 12 pan. Spoon mushroom soup over the top of the roast. This makes a delicious gravy. Wrap meat loosely sealing edges of foil well. Bake for 3 hours. About 1 hour and 20 minutes before serving, add baking potatoes to oven.

California Rice (Serves 6 to 8)

1 cup rice, raw
1 cup chopped celery
1 cup chopped onion
1 cup diced, cooked chicken or turkey
1 lb. bulk seasoned pork sausage (browned and drained)
½ t. salt and ¼ t. pepper
½ cup slivered almonds
1 can cream of chicken soup
1 can water or chicken stock

Preheat oven to 325 degrees. Combine ingredients and place in 11 × 7 greased baking casserole. Cover. Bake about 2 hours. It may be necessary to add a small amount of water during baking.

Chicken and Broccoli Hot Dish (Serves 10 to 12)

3 packages frozen chopped broccoli
6 cups diced cooked chicken or left over turkey
1 lb. to 24 oz. of fresh mushrooms
2 cups of grated Parmesan cheese
6 T. butter or margarine
6 T. flour
3/4 t. salt
1/4 t. nutmeg
1 1/2 t. Worcestershire sauce
3 cups of milk
2/3 cup mayonnaise
1/4 t. pepper
2/3 cup whipping cream

Preheat oven to 350 degrees. Place chicken in a greased 9 × 13 pan. Cook broccoli until "tender crisp" in microwave or on top of stove. Cool with cold water, drain well and place over chicken. Sprinkle 1 cup of cheese over the broccoli. Top with mushrooms and set aside.

Prepare the sauce by melting butter in a saucepan and add flour, salt, nutmeg, Worcestershire. Blend in milk and cook slowly until thick. When thickened, cook approximately 1 minute more. Remove from heat. Fold mayonnaise and pepper into slightly cooled cream sauce. Whip 2/3 cup of whipping cream in a separate bowl until stiff. Fold into the cooled, cooked sauce and mayonnaise mixture. Pour this sauce over the broccoli and then sprinkle on the last cup of Parmesan cheese. Bake 45 minutes, until bubbly.

Easiest Hamburger Cheese Bake (Serves 6)

1 (4 oz.) package of noodles
1 lb. ground beef
3/4 t. salt
1/8 t. pepper
1 small onion, chopped
1 T. chopped green pepper
1/4 t. garlic salt
1 (8 oz.) can of tomato sauce
1/2 t. ground oregano
1 (3 oz.) package of cream cheese, at room temperature
1/4 cup sour cream
3/4 cup cottage cheese

Preheat oven to 350 degrees. Cook noodles by package directions, and drain. Brown beef with salt, pepper, onion, green pepper and garlic salt. Drain off excess fat. Stir into the beef mixture, tomato sauce and oregano. Set aside. Using cream cheese softened to room temperature, blend with sour cream; add cottage cheese, mixing well. Place half of the noodles in a greased 8 × 8 × 2 pan. Cover with the cheese mixture. Spread remaining noodles over top of the cheese mixture. Pour the beef mixture over all and spread evenly. Bake approximately 25 to 30 minutes, until hot.

San Remo Casserole (Serves 6 to 8)

1 cup ripe olives, quartered
3 cups of cubed, lean ham
1 (4 oz.) can sliced mushrooms
1 T. instant minced onion
2 eggs, slightly beaten
1 cup cottage cheese
1 cup sour cream
2 cups fine noodles

258

Combine olives, ham, mushrooms, onion, eggs, cottage cheese and sour cream. Boil noodles in salted water until cooked tender. Drain noodles well, and add to olive mixture. Turn ingredients into a greased, 2-quart casserole. Bake, covered, at 350 degrees for 45 minutes, or until thoroughly heated.

Company Meatloaf (Serves 6 to 8)

It is a good idea to keep a meatloaf frozen in your freezer for unexpected guests, so why not make two? Double this recipe for two meatloaves.

  3/4 cup grated onion
  3/4 cup finely chopped green onions
  1/2 cup finely chopped celery
  1/2 cup grated carrot
  1/4 cup minced green pepper (optional)
   2 cloves of garlic, minced
   3 T. margarine
   1 t. salt
   1 t. black pepper (1 1/2 t. if you like pepper)
  1/2 t. ground cumin
  1/2 t. ground nutmeg
  1/2 cup half and half (or milk)
  1/2 cup catsup
1 1/2 lbs. lean ground beef
  1/2 lb. lean ground pork
   3 eggs, beaten
  3/4 cup dry bread crumbs (dry bread slices in 350 degree oven)

Preheat oven to 350 degrees. Sauté onion, green onion, celery, carrot, green pepper and garlic in margarine until vegetables are soft and liquid is absorbed. Cool and reserve. Combine salt, pepper, cumin and nutmeg and add to vegetable mixture. Stir in half and half and catsup to vegetable mixture. In a large bowl, place beef, pork and eggs. Mix thoroughly. I use rubber gloves and do this step with my hands. Add vegetable mixture and mix well. Add bread crumbs and mix well. Form into a loaf and place in a greased baking pan or in a waxed paper lined 9 × 5 loaf pan. Bake 45 to 50 minutes. Let stand 10 minutes before slicing. Pour off excess fat, then slice. If in a loaf pan, use a knife to loosen sides and remove by turning pan upside down on cutting board. Peel waxed paper off the top of the meatloaf. Serve garnished with parsley. This is good with baked potatoes, a green vegetable and gelatin salad.

Greig Family Meatloaf (Serves 6 to 8)

    1 cup soft bread crumbs or oatmeal
    2 beaten eggs
    ¾ cup minced onion
    1 t. salt
    ¼ t. pepper
    1 T. chopped parsley (optional)
    ½ cup grated carrots
    ½ t. dry mustard
    1½ cups of tomato juice
    2 lbs. lean ground beef
    2 strips of bacon

Preheat oven to 350 degrees. Mix the beaten eggs with beef. I use rubber gloves and mix this by hand. Stir in salt, pepper, dry mustard, carrots, onion and parsley and mix well. Mix in crumbs or oatmeal. Gradually add 1 cup tomato juice. Shape into a loaf and place in a well-greased baking pan. Pour remaining tomato juice on top of loaf. Lay bacon on top. Bake for approximately 1 hour. Cool 10 minutes before slicing.

Dwan Walter's Frickidillar Danish Meat Balls
(Serves 4, making 10 or 12 meatballs)

1 lb. ground beef
1/4 lb. pork sausage
1 heaping T. flour
1/2 t. salt
1/4 t. pepper
1 egg
1/2 large onion, or 1 medium onion (grated)
1/4 cup milk

In a large bowl place egg, milk, salt and pepper. Beat well with whisk or egg beater. Add all of the rest of the ingredients to the bowl and mix well with a wooden spoon. If mixture seems dry, add 1 or 2 T. more milk. Shape balls about the size of golf balls. Brown the meatballs in a large frying pan. Add 1/2 cup water to frying pan, cover and simmer for about 1 hour. Remove meatballs to heated platter. Using flour and milk, make a gravy in the frying pan to pour over the meatballs. Serve with mashed potatoes and a green vegetable, plus applesauce.

Doris Greig's Easy Oven Meatballs (Serves 6 to 10)

2 lbs. ground round
1/2 cup instant cream of wheat
1 (10 oz.) can cream of mushroom soup
4 T. minced onion
3 large eggs

Preheat oven to 350 degrees. Place all ingredients in a large bowl. Put on rubber gloves and mix until well blended. Spray Pam in a large baking pan. Use a 1/4 cup measure or ice cream scoop to form meatballs. Place balls side by side in the pan. Bake for 30 minutes uncovered. Remove from baking pan with a slotted spoon and place in a large casserole. Spoon a sauce over the meatballs, such as meatless spaghetti sauce or barbecue sauce. Bake 20 more minutes, covered. Serve with noodles, rice or spaghetti.

Tangy Barbecue Sauce (Makes 3 cups)

1 T. cooking oil
1 onion, chopped
1 green pepper, seeded and chopped (optional)
1 (16 oz.) can tomato sauce
¼ cup cider vinegar
¼ cup honey (or ⅓ cup brown sugar)
2 T. lemon juice
1 T. dry mustard
2 t. paprika
⅛ t. cayenne pepper

Mix all ingredients together and simmer in a heavy saucepan for 20 minutes, stirring occasionally. Marinate meat in sauce for 4 hours at room temperature, turning occasionally, or for 12 hours, covered in the refrigerator. Also use the sauce to baste the beef or chicken while grilling. (Use a small paintbrush to baste, wash well, then store in kitchen.)

Note: This sauce keeps well in the refrigerator, so double or triple your recipe and simmer about 15 minutes longer.

Store in a covered jar.

Barbecued Steak

    1 chuck, round or flank steak (2 to 3 lbs. of meat)
      Meat tenderizer
 $\frac{1}{3}$ cup catsup
 $\frac{1}{4}$ cup vinegar
    3 T. brown sugar
    2 t. dry mustard
 $\frac{1}{4}$ t. garlic *powder* (not salt)

Sprinkle the meat with tenderizer on both sides according to directions, and prick with fork evenly on both sides. Mix the marinade in a flat *glass* baking dish. Place the tenderized meat in the glass pan. Turn the meat over to coat both sides with marinade. Let stand at room temperature about 5 to 6 hours, turning meat occasionally. Preheat grill to high. Cook approximately 7 to 10 minutes on each side, or until steak is done to your liking. Slice very thinly across the grain with a sharp knife and serve immediately. Best served rare or medium rare.

Note: This is very good served with baked potatoes, green beans and a tossed salad or fruit salad.

Glazed Baked Ham (Serves 10 to 12)

    6 to 7 lb. ham, bone in

Preheat oven to 325 degrees. Remove skin and excess fat from ham, leaving $\frac{1}{4}$ inch of fat. Score ham $\frac{1}{4}$ inch deep in 1 inch diamonds, if desired. Place fat side up in roasting pan or casserole. Insert a meat thermometer in the thickest part of the ham, making sure it does not touch the bone. Place ham in the oven and bake 1 to 1$\frac{1}{4}$ hours, or until the thermometer registers 130 degrees.

Orange Glaze Ham Sauce

2 t. sugar
2 t. cornstarch
2 t. Dijon mustard
½ t. pepper, ground
½ cup marmalade
½ cup orange juice (fresh if possible)
½ cup lemon juice (fresh if possible)
8 whole cloves

In a ½ quart sauce pan, or large microwave measuring cup, combine the sugar and cornstarch and stir together. Gradually blend the rest of the ingredients (except the cloves) with a whisk or electric mixer. Add the whole cloves. If cooking on top of stove, bring to a boil over medium heat, stirring constantly. If cooking in microwave, cook 2 minutes, stir, then cook 2 to 4 more minutes until mixture boils and thickens. Remove ham from the oven. Brush on glaze (I use a paintbrush set aside for this purpose!) Bake ham 20 to 30 minutes longer, until the meat thermometer reaches 140 degrees, brushing twice more with glaze. Remove the whole cloves. Serve the warm orange sauce in a side dish beside the ham.

Note: I triple this recipe because it is so good and everyone always wants more.

Alternate Ham Sauce

1 cup raisins
1¾ cups of apple juice
1 T. cornstarch
1 t. dry mustard
⅓ cup brown sugar

¼ t. salt
¼ t. ground cloves
2 T. lemon juice
2 T. vinegar
Red food coloring, if desired

Stir together the cornstarch, mustard, brown sugar, salt and cloves. Blend with vinegar and lemon juice. Stir this into the apple juice and raisins. Use the same cooking method as for orange sauce given following the Baked Ham recipe. Add food coloring to give a nice pink color. Serve warm with sliced ham.

Doris Greig's Chicken Curry

    1 chicken, cut up
    1 pint (2 cups) yogurt
    2 t. ground coriander
    1 t. ground tumeric
    $^{1}/_{2}$ t. ground cumin seed
    $^{1}/_{2}$ t. chili powder
    1 small onion, chopped
    1 clove garlic, minced
    1 t. oil
    $^{1}/_{8}$ t. ground cloves
    $^{1}/_{8}$ t. ground cardamon
    $^{1}/_{8}$ t. ground cinnamon
    $^{3}/_{4}$ t. salt
        Juice of $^{1}/_{2}$ medium sized lemon

Sauté onion and garlic in oil until tender. Mix onion, garlic and all of the spices with the yogurt. Place chicken in a flat glass casserole and cover with marinade. Marinate on kitchen counter for 2 hours before placing in the oven. Turn chicken once or twice in the marinade to coat it well (or marinate chicken overnight in the refrigerator, remove from the refrigerator 2 hours before you want to place it in the oven to cook it). Bake at 350 degrees for approximately 1 to 1½ hours, until tender. (Can also be simmered on top of the stove, or in an electric frying pan.) Remove chicken to hot serving platter. Add the juice of ½ lemon to the gravy. If the gravy seems too thick, thin it with milk. Serve this curry with rice. I use the oven baked recipe in this book. It is nice to accompany this dish with side dishes of:

Chutney
Coconut (flaked)
Chopped pineapple (fresh if possible)
Peanuts, chopped
Tomatoes, chopped
Mild onions, chopped

Note: This is a great "crowd pleaser" which is easily prepared in the oven. Borrow your neighbor's oven to bake the rice in, or cook on top of the stove.

For 45 people, use: 10 chickens
5 quarts yogurt
20 t. ground coriander
10 t. ground tumeric
5 t. ground cumin seed
5 t. chili powder
10 medium sized onions
10 cloves of garlic
1¼ t. ground cloves
1¼ t. ground cardamon
1¼ t. ground cinnamon
Juice of 5 medium sized lemons

Liz Anderson's Chicken Baked in Cream

     6 chicken breasts, coated in flour
     6 T. butter, melted
     1 t. paprika
     1 t. salt
     ½ t. ground oregano
     ½ t. ground pepper
     1 t. celery salt
     ¾ cup slivered almonds (optional)
  1½ cups of light cream (not whipping cream)
     ½ cup sour cream

     Preheat oven to 350 degrees. Roll coated chicken in melted butter. Place single layer in a 9 × 12 pan. Mix paprika, salt, oregano, pepper and celery salt and sprinkle evenly over the chicken. Pour 1½ cups cream around the chicken pieces. Bake covered for 60 minutes. Remove ½ cup of drippings from the pan and mix with sour cream (use electric beater, hand beater or whisk). Spread this mixture over the chicken. Sprinkle with the almonds and bake uncovered 15 minutes longer.

Grilled Chicken Breasts in Red Wine (Serves 6 to 8)

     4 whole chicken breasts boned, skinned and split
     1 cup red wine or ¾ cup water and ¼ cup wine vinegar
     ½ cup oil
     ¼ cup soy sauce
     2 t. powdered ginger
     1 t. crushed oregano or ½ t. ground oregano

Mix all ingredients except chicken. Place chicken in a deep dish and pour marinade over it, or place chicken and marinate in a Zip-lock bag. Place bag in a pan. Marinate in refrigerator, covered, for 2 to 3 hours. Turn 2 to 3 times to redistribute marinade. Charcoal broil for 5 to 6 minutes on each side (depending on their size) or until "fork tender." Or use your oven broiler. Place on a greased broiling pan and broil 6 inches below heat 20 minutes. Turn once after 10 minutes. Delicious served with baked potatoes and green salad.

Lemony Barbecued Chicken

6 chicken breasts, split (or any other parts of the chicken)
1/2 cup lemon juice (2 large lemons)
1/4 cup water
3 T. soy sauce
1/4 t. powdered ginger
1 t. garlic powder (or 1 clove crushed)

Mix marinade. Pour over chicken in a deep bowl or place in a Zip-lock bag. Marinate 2 to 3 hours, covered in the refrigerator. Turn 2 or 3 times to redistribute the marinade. Barbecue or oven broil, basting frequently with marinade until tender (20 to 30 minutes). Good with baked rice, corn on the cob and a green leaf salad.

Crispy Oven Fried Chicken (Serves 4)

      1 cup sour cream or yogurt
      1 T. lemon juice
      1 t. Worcestershire sauce
      1 t. celery salt
    ½ t. paprika
      2 cloves garlic, minced
      1 t. salt
         Dash of pepper
    2½ lbs. chicken pieces
      1 cup bread, cracker or corn flake crumbs

   Preheat oven to 350 degrees. Combine first 8 ingredients. Rinse chicken in cold water; shake off excess water. Spread sour cream over chicken, then roll in crumbs. Arrange pieces on greased 9 × 13 baking pan. Bake uncovered for 45 minutes to 1 hour, until chicken is tender and browned.

Colonel Sanders-like Chicken

      3 cups self-rising flour
      1 T. paprika
      2 envelopes (Lipton-type) dry tomato soup mix
      2 packages dry Good Seasons Italian Dressing mix
      1 t. seasoned salt (Lawrys is good)

   Preheat oven to 350 degrees. Dip chicken pieces in melted margarine and then in the above mixture of ingredients. For extra crispy chicken dip chicken in margarine and flour mixture again. Bake in greased pan for 1 hour, drizzling chicken with 1 t. oil and 1 t. water every 15 minutes of baking time. *Note:* I put

269

4 t. oil and 4 t. water in a small sprayer and spray the chicken 4 times during baking. For those watching calories, rinse the chicken in cold water instead of dipping in margarine. For the extreme calorie counter, remove the skin from the chicken before dipping into margarine. Do not use the water method if you remove skin. The above mixture is good for 32 pieces of chicken.

> *Note:* To make self-rising flour, sift together 3 cups flour with 1½ t. salt and 3¾ t. baking power.

Roast Chicken

One 3 lb. chicken makes 4 to 6 servings.

Preheat the oven to 400 degrees. Wash the chicken and pat it dry. Salt lightly in cavity and on outside skin. Place chickens in roasting pan on a rack. (I roast my chickens breast side down as I do my turkeys. It makes the white meat so moist!) Roast at 400 degrees for 20 minutes. Reduce heat to 325 degrees and roast for 1 to 1¼ hours, or until drumsticks move easily. You do not have to baste unless you choose to roast the chicken breast side up. Baste several times if you roast them breast side up. This is an easy meal and good with potatoes baked in the oven with the chicken, and a tossed green salad.

> *Note:* I buy larger fryers on sale and roast two at a time. I makes such a good meal and leftovers can be used in soup, sandwiches, casseroles or salads, or frozen for later use.

The Best Turkey Ever!

20 lb. or more—bake at 275 degrees at 23 minutes per pound
16 lb. and under—bake at 325 degrees at 23 minutes per pound

Always cook your turkey breast side down on the rack. It bastes itself this way. I have never had more moist white meat! You carve it in the kitchen usually, so looks don't count. It's the taste that counts! Always let your turkey stand 20 to 30 minutes before carving. It is easier to carve. Cover it with foil and a towel to keep it warm while it "stands."

Our Family's Favorite Dressing Is So Easy!

2 boxes (12 to 16 oz. size) dressing mix. I generally use Mrs. Cubbison's.

Melt 1 lb. margarine in a large pan and sauté in it 2 cups of celery leaves and tops chopped fine, and 2 large onions chopped fine. Cook until the vegetables are tender. Toss in the dressing and mix well. *Do not* add any liquid to this dressing. Stuff cavity and neck of bird with dressing. Boil giblets in water. Then cut up into gravy, if desired. Put any extra dressing in an ungreased crock pot and cook on low for 3 hours. Add ¾ cup of juice from the giblet pan which has cooled somewhat. Beat two eggs and slowly add the giblet juice to the eggs. Mix this into the dressing that remains after stuffing the turkey. Then spoon it into the Crockpot. Do not pack down!

Note: If you do not have a Crockpot, cook extra dressing in a casserole in the oven at 275 to 325 degrees for about 35 to 45 minutes.

Cranberry Sauce That Always Thickens!

4 cups cranberries
2 cups sugar
1 cup water

Boil 4 to 5 minutes, covered, until all cranberries are cooked through. Stir occasionally so berries don't burn. Chill.

Barbara Buckbee's Orange Cranberry Relish

 2 cups of cranberries
 2 apples
 2 oranges
  Grated rind of ½ orange
1¾ cup sugar

If you have a food processor, chop the ingredients and add sugar. Otherwise, use a food grinder or a blender. Chop the cranberries with approximately ½ cup orange juice in your blender and cut the apples and oranges up into as small pieces as you can. Refrigerate 2 hours or longer.

Greig's Easiest Baked Spaghetti (Serves 6 to 8)
(You don't have to cook the spaghetti!)

 2 medium onions, chopped fine
 1 clove of garlic, minced or put through garlic press
 ½ lb. lean hamburger
1½ t. salt
 ⅛ t. pepper
 1 (#2½) can tomatoes (do *not* drain)
 1 cup water
 ½ lb. spaghetti
 1 cup Velveeta processed cheese (cut up fine) (¼ lb. of
  cheese makes approximately 1 cup)
 ½ t. chili powder
 1 t. ground oregano
  Parmesan cheese

Brown onions and garlic with beef. Drain off fat. Stir in all spices and tomatoes with juice (break up tomatoes into smaller pieces as you add them). Simmer for about 15 minutes over medium heat. Add 1 cup hot water to the pan. Set oven temperature to 325 degrees. Break half of the uncooked spaghetti into the well-greased 2-quart casserole. Pour on half of the sauce. Sprinkle half of the cheese over that. Top with the rest of the uncooked spaghetti, sprinkled evenly over the casserole contents. Add the last half of the sauce. Sprinkle cheese evenly over the top of this. Bake 35 minutes in covered casserole. Uncover and stir contents well. Bake 15 minutes longer, or until hot and spaghetti is tender. Serve with Parmesan cheese.

Barbara Sheffield's Easiest Lasagna (Serves 8 to 10)
(You don't have to cook the noodles!)

    1 lb. ground beef or turkey (you can't tell the difference!)
    1 cup chopped onion
    3 cloves garlic, minced
    4 cups tomato juice
    1 (6 oz.) can tomato paste
    ½ lb. fresh mushrooms, sliced
    1 T. Worcestershire sauce
    1 t. salt
    ¼ t. pepper
    1 t. parsley flakes
    1 t. ground oregano
    1 pkg. lasagna noodles (½ lb.)
    1 lb. Ricotta cheese (or partially creamed cottage cheese)
    ¾ cup Romano cheese
    ¾ cups grated Parmesan cheese
    2 cups shredded mozzarella or jack chesse

Preheat oven to 350 degrees. Brown meat, onion and garlic together. Drain off fat. Stir in tomato juice, paste, mushrooms and seasonings. Simmer for 30 minutes. Arrange ½ of *uncooked* noodles over the bottom of a 9 × 13 pan. Do not overlap! Top noodles evenly with ½ hot meat sauce. Top meat sauce with ½ of the cheeses. Use the other half of noodles on top of the cheese. Add the last half of hot meat sauce evenly. Sprinkle the last half of the cheeses over the sauce. Cover with foil and bake 40 minutes. Remove foil and bake 15 minutes, uncovered. Remove from the oven when noodles are tender and let stand covered 20 minutes before cutting and serving.

Doris Greig's Easy and Quick Spaghetti Sauce
(Serves 4)

  2 T. oil or olive oil
  2 cloves garlic, minced
  1 large onion, chopped
  ½ lb. lean ground beef *or* ground turkey
  1 (1 lb. 13 oz.) can tomato sauce
  1 T. Worcestershire sauce
  ¼ to ½ t. ground oregano
  1 t. sugar
  ½ t. salt (or to taste)
  ¼ t. pepper
  1 cup beef or chicken stock (or just plain water)

Sauté in a heavy saucepan until tender oil, minced garlic and chopped onion. Add ½ lb. ground meat (more if desired), and sauté until brown. Drain off any excess fat. Add tomato sauce with sauce spices, salt, pepper, sugar, water (or stock). Simmer for 1 hour over low heat. Stir occasionally. Double or triple recipe for more people, or to freeze.

Greig's Favorite Chicago Deep Dish Pizza

1 loaf frozen bread dough, thawed

1½ lbs. mild Italian sausage (casings removed) or 1 lb. ground beef or turkey plus ½ lb. sausage

2½ cups sliced fresh mushrooms

1½ cups very thickly sliced onions (optional)

1 cup coarsely chopped green pepper (optional)

2 large cloves of garlic, crushed

2¼ cups canned pizza sauce or use homemade sauce

¼ t. pepper

1¼ t. Italian seasoning (oregano, thyme and basil)

1½ cups shredded mozzarella cheese or jack cheese

1½ cups shredded provolone or cheddar cheese

1 cup chopped Italian plum tomatoes or canned tomatoes, drained and chopped

Let dough rise at room temperature in a greased bowl covered with waxed paper and a towel on top of the paper for about 1½ hours or until double in volume. Meanwhile, cook meat, mushrooms, onions, green pepper and garlic in a large skillet until meat is browned and crumbly. Drain off all excess fat. Stir in pizza sauce and seasonings. Simmer uncovered 15 minutes. Cool. Press dough into a 12-inch pizza pan (deep dish style) or a 9×12 or 10×16 cake pan that has been lightly dusted with cornmeal. Spoon in cooled filling and sprinkle with combined cheeses. Let stand 15 minutes on counter. Bake pizza 25 minutes in a preheated 425 degree oven. Then garnish with chopped tomatoes and return to oven for 5 to 10 minutes until crust is golden. Let stand 5 minutes before cutting and serving. Serves 8.

Barbara Sheffield's Tahoe Brunch or Breakfast Dish
(Serves 8 to 10)

  12 slices of bread (French, or a firm white or wheat)
       Softened butter or margarine to spread on the bread
  ½ lb. fresh mushrooms, sliced
   2 cups thinly sliced yellow onions
  1½ lbs. Italian sausage (or ham) *Note:* if you use *sausage,*
       brown it and drain off the fat.
  ¾ lb. cheddar cheese, grated
   5 eggs, beaten
2½ cups milk
   3 t. grated nutmeg (optional)
   2 T. chopped parsley (optional)
   3 T. butter
   1 t. dry mustard
   3 t. Dijon mustard

Preheat oven to 350 degrees. Use a 9 × 13 pan. Grease it or spray with Pam. Remove crusts from the bread (optional), and spread lightly with butter or margarine. Mix beaten eggs, milk, nutmeg, dry mustard and Dijon mustard until well blended. Line the bottom of the pan with bread to cover. Sauté mushrooms in 3 T. butter. Add ½ of the onions, mushrooms, sausage, cheese and parsley. Then add another layer of bread. Repeat layers as before. Pour milk and egg mix over the casserole and refrigerate covered overnight. Remove from refrigerator at least 1 to 2 hours before baking. Bake for 1 hour or until firmly set. Let stand for 10 minutes before cutting. Can be made 2 or 3 days ahead and refrigerated, or can be frozen up to about a month. Bake just before serving. Remove from freezer, thaw and let come to room temperature before baking.

Peg Nelson's "Do Day Before" Monterey Fondue
(Serves 8 to 10)

- 12 slices of *regular* firm white bread spread lightly with butter and cut in half
- 1 (12 oz.) can of whole kernel corn, drained well
- 1 (7 oz.) can of chopped Ortega green chilies
- 2 cups grated jack cheese
- 4 eggs, slightly beaten
- 3 cups of milk
- 1 small onion, grated
- 1 t. salt

Preheat oven to 350 degrees. Arrange half of the bread in a greased casserole (approximately 9 × 12 size). Cover with ½ corn, chilies and sprinkle with half the cheese. Put the rest of the buttered bread on top of the cheese and repeat layers as listed. Combine eggs, milk, grated onion and salt in a bowl, and beat until well blended. Pour over the casserole ingredients. Cover casserole with lid or aluminum foil and refrigerate 4 hours or overnight. Can be prepared 2 days ahead of time. Remove casserole from refrigerator at least 2 hours before baking. Bake covered for 1 hour.

Williamsburg Soufflé

  8 slices of day-old egg bread, or other such as French
  ¼ cup butter or margarine
  2 cups sliced fresh mushrooms
  1 cup minced onion
  2 cups diced, cooked ham
  4 cups shredded cheddar cheese
  2 T. flour
  8 eggs
  2 T. prepared mustard
  2 cups half and half
  1 T. garlic salt
  1 t. salt

Preheat oven to 325 degrees. Trim crust off bread, if desired. Cut into bite-size pieces. Arrange in a well-buttered 13 × 9 baking dish. Heat butter in skillet and sauté sliced mushrooms and onion for about 5 minutes. Spoon evenly over bread cubes. Top with ham. Combine cheese with flour and sprinkle over ham. Beat eggs with mustard, half and half, garlic salt and salt. Pour into dish, cover and refrigerate at least 4 hours, or overnight. Remove from refrigerator 2 hours before baking. Bake uncovered for one hour, or until puffy and lightly browned. Makes 8 to 10 servings.

Barbara Sheffield's Cheese Soufflé (Serves 6)

8 slices French bread (cut off crust if you want to be fancy!)
Butter the bread and cube it.
(Plain firm white bread may be used, but it is not quite as good as using French bread)
3/4 lb. medium sharp cheddar cheese, grated coarsely
1 small onion, sliced thin
3 eggs, slightly beaten
2 1/2 cups milk
1/2 t. dry mustard
1/2 t. salt
1/8 t. paprika
1/2 t. Worcestershire sauce

Preheat oven to 350 degrees. Butter a 7 1/2 × 11 × 3/4 casserole, and layer French bread, cheese and onion. Repeat layers of bread, cheese and onion. In a bowl, beat eggs and add milk and all spices. Beat well and pour over the layers of bread, cheese and onion. Refrigerate for at least 8 hours, or overnight. (May be done 2 days ahead of time.) Remove the casserole from the refrigerator at least 2 hours before baking. Bake for one hour. After 1/2 hour, stir once.

Note: This is a good accompaniment to ham, freshly cooked green beans and a gelatin salad. If you double this recipe and place in a larger pan, allow a little longer cooking time for it.

Doris Greig's Eggs (Serves 12)

12 eggs
2 cans of cream-style corn
4 cups grated, sharp cheddar cheese
2 (4 oz.) cans chopped green chilies
1 T. Worcestershire
1 T. salt
½ t. pepper

Preheat oven to 325 degrees. Put 12 eggs in a large bowl and beat well. Add Worcestershire, salt and pepper. Blend thoroughly. Add remaining ingredients and stir with large spoon until well blended. Pour into a 9 × 13 well-greased baking dish. Bake 1 hour and 15 minutes, or until firm to the touch. Cut in squares to serve.

Note: This dish may be prepared ahead of time, covered and refrigerated. Remove from the refrigerator at least 2 hours before baking and remove the covering of the casserole. Place in pre-heated oven and bake 1 hour and 15 minutes, or until firm to the touch. Serve with fresh fruit and bran muffins, and baked ham slices (if desired).

Greig's Impossible Quiche (Serves 6)

   1 cup of any vegetable (mushrooms, cooked peas, cooked
      broccoli or asparagus)
  1/2 cup finely chopped green onions
  1/2 cup finely chopped green peppers (optional)
   8 slices of bacon (or 1/2 to 3/4 cups of cooked ham), chopped
      fine
   1 cup of grated cheese
12/3 cups of milk
  3/4 cup of biscuit baking mix (such as Bisquick)
   4 eggs
   1 t. salt
  1/4 t. pepper

Preheat oven 400 degrees. Lightly grease a large 10 1/2 inch pie pan which should be at least 1 1/2 inches deep. Layer any of the vegetables named above in the bottom of the pie plate, using about 1 cup of a variety or 1 cup of one of them. Sprinkle the chopped green onions (and optional green peppers) over the vegetables. Brown bacon, drain, cut up and sprinkle over the vegetables (or use the cut up cooked ham). Grate 1 cup of cheese and sprinkle evenly over the pie plate ingredients (or you may grate it in your blender with the milk/egg mixture). In a blender, put milk and biscuit baking mix. Add the eggs, salt and pepper. Blend the filling only until blended well. Pour over the ingredients in the pie plate. Place in the oven. When the mixture is partially cooked and firm enough, top the pie with thinly sliced tomatoes around the outside as a garnish, and continue baking. Bake until golden brown and knife inserted at center comes out clean (about 40 to 50 minutes). Let stand 10 minutes before cutting and serving.

Quick Meal in a Dish (Serves 6)

1 (24 oz.) package frozen hash browns
⅓ cup and 1 T. butter or margarine
½ cup diced green onions
1½ cups sliced zucchini
2 medium fresh (or canned) tomatoes, chopped
1 t. basil flakes or ½ t. ground basil
1 t. parsley flakes
1 garlic clove, minced
2 cups cheddar cheese, grated
⅔ cup cut up, left-over ham, chicken, turkey or bacon
4 eggs, beaten
½ cup milk

Preheat oven to 425 degrees. Thaw the hash browns and squeeze out any excess moisture. Press them into a 10½ × 1½ inch pie plate. Melt ⅓ cup butter or margarine and drizzle it over the potatoes. Bake for 20 minutes and then lower the temperature to 350 degrees. Melt 1 T. butter or margarine into a large frying pan. Add the green onion, zucchini, tomatoes, basil, parsley flakes and minced garlic clove. Sauté these ingredients, stirring until the vegetables are softened. Remove the potatoes from the oven. While they are hot, sprinkle meat and half of the cheese evenly over them. Spoon the vegetables evenly over the cheese. Beat milk and eggs together until well blended. Pour the eggs and milk over the vegetables. Sprinkle the other cup of grated cheese on last. Return filled pie plate to the 350 degree oven. Bake 30 to 40 minutes, until firm in the middle of the dish. Cool on a rack for 10 minutes before cutting and serving.

Doris Greig's Broiled Fish Au Gratin (Serves 4)

1 lb. fish fillets
4 T. mayonnaise
2 green onions, (tops and all) finely cut
1/4 cup Parmesan cheese
1 T. lemon juice
2 T. melted butter or margarine
3 to 4 drops of Tabasco

Combine mayonnaise, onions, cheese, butter, and Tabasco in a bowl. Wash fillets and pat dry with a paper towel. Place fish on oiled broiler rack. Broil 4 inches from heat for 8 to 12 minutes. If the fish is thick, turn over with a spatula after 6 minutes and cook 5 to 6 more minutes. Fish should flake easily with a fork. Spread mayonnaise/cheese mixture evenly over the fish. Again place under the broiler and broil until puffy and golden. Watch carefully. This is good served with a mixed vegetable casserole, wild rice with mushrooms and fresh orange and grapefruit salad with celery.

Note: You may make extra fish topping. It will keep well in the refrigerator for two weeks. People who don't like fish will like this!

Crafty Cockney Fish Batter (Serves 8 to 10)

4 lbs. fish fillets
2 cups of flour
1 T. MSG (optional)
3 T. baking powder
2 cups water

Combine batter ingredients and mix until smooth with electric mixer. Make 24 hours in advance and refrigerate for best results. Dust fish fillet in flour and shake off excess. Dip fish fillet one at a time in batter. Deep fat fry several fillets together at 375 degrees. Place deep fat fried fish on paper towels to drain. Line a jelly roll pan or large cake pan with paper towels and place the fillets on it. Set oven temperature at 200 degrees and as you cook the fish fillets, put them in the oven to keep warm, if you are preparing a quantity for your family to eat. This recipe is good with cold slaw, carrot sticks and hot rolls.

**Linda Stegman and Jayne Payne's
Tuna or Turkey Crepes**

10 oz. tuna, albacore or left-over turkey, cut up
1 can mushroom soup
1 cup of milk
  About 2½ cups of fresh broccoli, cut into 1 inch pieces
1 cup cheddar cheese (grated)
1 small can Durkee French Fried Onions or ¼ cup finely chopped onions
1 or 2 tomatoes chopped into small pieces
6 flour tortillas

Preheat oven to 350 degrees. Combine soup and milk, and set aside. Cook broccoli crispy tender by parboiling, or in the microwave for 2 to 3 minutes. Combine broccoli, tuna (or turkey), ½ cup grated cheese and ½ can of onions. Stir into this ¾ cup of soup and milk mixture. Put a sixth of this recipe on each tortilla and roll up. Place seam-side down in a 9×9 greased pan. Stir chopped tomatoes into the remaining soup/milk mixture, and pour over the tortillas. Bake approximately 35 to 40 minutes. Top with remaining cheese and onions, and bake 5 more minutes.

Note: This will re-heat well in the microwave oven. One tortilla takes approximately 3 minutes.

Vegetables and Rice

Nadine Nuehaus' Buffet Potato Casserole
(Serves 12 to 15)

1 (2 lb.) package of frozen shredded hash brown potatoes
1 cup butter or margarine, melted and divided in half
1 can cream of chicken soup
1 pint (1 cup) sour cream
1/2 cup grated or finely chopped onion
2 cups finely shredded mild cheddar cheese
1 t. salt
1/2 t. pepper
2 cups corn flakes

Preheat oven to 350 degrees. Combine 1/2 cup melted butter, chicken soup, sour cream, onion, cheese, salt and pepper in a large bowl. Mix well. Add thawed potatoes and mix thoroughly. Place in greased 13 × 9 × 2 baking dish. Cover with foil and bake for 25 minutes. Meanwhile, mix corn flakes and last 1/2 cup melted butter or margarine. After 25 minutes, uncover casserole, sprinkle with buttered corn flakes evenly. Bake uncovered for 20 more minutes.

Note: You may want to divide into smaller casseroles to freeze. This freezes beautifully (leave off the corn flakes). Thaw well before cooking. Add corn flakes as directed. Can be held at "low" temperature (200 degrees) until serving time too.

Doris Greig's Baked Stuffed Potatoes (Makes 12 halves)

6 large russet potatoes
1 cup melted butter or margarine
¼ to ½ cup cream, warmed
1 cup sour cream, at room temperature
2 t. salt
¼ cup chopped chives or green onion, if desired
  Grated or sliced cheese for topping
  Paprika (optional)

Bake the potatoes and cut in half lengthwise. Scoop out the pulp and put it in a bowl. Leave about ¼ inch of potato in the skins. Mash it and add the butter, cream as needed, sour cream and salt. If desired, add the chives or green onions. Stuff this evenly into the potato skins. Top with grated or sliced cheese and paprika. Bake 20 to 25 minutes at 350 degrees.

Note: These potatoes may be frozen, then thawed to room temperature when you want to bake them. It is nice to prepare a quantity ahead of time. Never add cold cream or milk to potatoes when mashing. It turns their starch to glue.

No Waste Mashed Potatoes and Potato Skins

Next time you want to serve mashed potatoes, you can prepare potato skins at the same time. Scrub the potatoes and then pierce in serveral places to let the steam escape. Bake directly on oven racks at 400 degrees for 45 or 50 minutes, or until soft when pinched with mitted hands. Half the potatoes lengthwise. Scoop out the pulp, leaving ¼ inch of white pulp in potato skins. For mashed potatoes, mash them in a bowl with butter or margarine and warm milk to bring them to the texture your family likes, and serve. To make the potato skin snacks or appetizers, brush the skins with oil and season to taste with your favorite seasonings. I like garlic powder and Lawry's Seasoning Salt. Place on a cookie sheet, or in a baking pan. Bake at 475 degrees for 15 to 20 minutes, until crisp and browned around the edges. You may want to cut the potato skins in half or thirds before baking them. Have some of the following toppings in bowls to serve with these good snacks:

Sour cream or yogurt
Refried beans
Bacon, crumbled up or Bacon Bits
Chili Salsa (there is the Greig family favorite recipe in this book)
Chopped green onions
Grated cheese

Doris Greig's Mashed Potato Casserole (Serves 6)

8 potatoes, peeled and boiled until tender
1 cube butter or margarine, melted
1 cup sour cream, at room temperature
1 (8 oz.) pkg. cream cheese, at room temperature
1-2 T. finely chopped chives or parsley
1/8 t. garlic powder
1 t. salt (more if needed)

Drain and mash potatoes with melted butter, sour cream, cream cheese, chives and spices. Spoon into buttered casserole. Bake in preheated 350 degree oven for 40 to 50 minutes, until hot. Top with chopped parsley or chives before serving. This can be prepared the day before and refrigerated. Remove 2 hours before baking and place in preheated 350 degree oven.

Easy Baked Rice (Serves 4)

   1 cup uncooked Uncle Ben's Converted Rice
   2 cans of chicken or beef bouillon
   1 stick of butter or margarine
 $\frac{1}{2}$ cup finely chopped onions
 $\frac{1}{2}$ lb. fresh mushrooms, sliced
 $\frac{1}{2}$ cup pine nuts (optional)
 $\frac{1}{2}$ cup dried apricots, snipped fine (optional)

Preheat oven to 350 degrees. Sauté the mushrooms in 4 T. butter. Melt the balance of the stick of butter. Heat the bouillon to boiling. Combine all of the ingredients and place in a covered casserole. Bake for 1 hour.

Easy Rice Pilaf—Baked (Serves 4)

   1 cup rice
$2\frac{1}{2}$ cups of boiling water
   1 t. salt
   1 T. margarine

Preheat oven to 350 degrees. Combine the ingredients in a $1\frac{1}{2}$ qt. casserole. Cover and bake for 45 minutes to 1 hour (or until water is absorbed).

Note: If you double or triple your recipe, allow a bit longer cooking time.

Good Wild Rice—Oven Baked (Serves 4)

- 1/4 cup wild rice (uncooked), washed and drained (use a sieve)
- 3 T. butter or margarine
- 1 small onion, chopped fine or grated
- 1/2 cup finely chopped celery
- 2 1/2 cups chicken broth (can be made with chicken bouillon cubes)
- 1 T. parsley flakes
- 1/2 t. salt
- 1/4 t. sage
- 1/4 t. basil
- 1 (4 oz.) can drained sliced mushrooms or 1/4 to 1/2 lb. fresh mushrooms sautéed in 1 T. butter or margarine
- 3/4 cup uncooked white or brown rice

Preheat oven to 350 degrees. Melt butter in a small frying pan. Add onion, celery and wild rice, and cook and stir until vegetables are tender. Pour this mixture into an ungreased 1 1/2 qt. casserole. Heat chicken broth to boiling and pour over the rice in the casserole. Stir in all of the spices, mixing well. Add mushrooms. Bake for 45 minutes, covered. Stir in 3/4 cup uncooked regular rice. Cover again and bake approximately 45 minutes, until all rice is done.

Muriel Larsen's Chestnuts and Broccoli

1 (10 oz.) packages of chopped frozen broccoli
1 cup chopped onion
1 (4 oz.) can drained mushrooms
½ stick butter or margarine
1 small jar of Kraft Garlic Cheese
1 (4 oz.) can drained chopped water chestnuts
   Buttered crumbs

Preheat oven to 350 degrees. Cook the broccoli until "crispy tender," drain well and rinse with cold water in a colander. While cooking the broccoli, sauté the onion, mushrooms in butter. Mix the Kraft Garlic Cheese into the onion mixture. Cook on top of stove, stirring until cheese melts. Remove at once from burner. Add water chestnuts and broccoli. Place in a greased casserole. Top with buttered crumbs. Bake uncovered for 35 minutes.

Note: Substitute approximately 2½ cups fresh broccoli for even better flavor.

Janet Nelson's Mushrooms and Green Beans

1 lb. fresh mushrooms, or use 2 (8 oz.) cans, drained
5 T. butter or margarine
2 T. flour
1 cup milk
1½ cups shredded cheddar cheese
4 drops Tabasco
1 (10 oz.) package of frozen green beans
½ cup (or more) of toasted slivered almonds for topping

Preheat oven to 350 degrees. Sauté the mushrooms in 3 T. butter for 5 minutes. Melt 2 T. butter and add 2 T. flour in a separate, medium size sauce pan. Cook, stirring constantly, for about 1 minute over medium heat. Gradually add milk to flour/butter mixture, stirring, and bring to a boil. Remove pan from heat and add 1 cup of shredded cheddar cheese and Tabasco. Continue to stir over medium heat until cheese melts and blends into the white sauce. Cook the frozen green beans just until "crispy tender," drain well and rinse with cold water in colander. Add beans to the mushrooms and toss gently with creamed milk and cheese mixture. Place vegetables in a 1½ qt. greased baking dish. Bake for 35 minutes, or until hot. Top with ½ cup grated cheese and toasted slivered almonds. Run topping under the broiler for a minute to brown before serving.

Dianne Rietveld's Broccoli Casserole (Serves 6 to 8)

    2 (10 oz.) packages of frozen chopped broccoli (mixed vegetables may be substituted for variety)
    ¼ lb. (1 stick) butter or margarine, melted
    ¼ lb. Velveeta Cheese, cubed
    1 stack pack of Ritz Crackers

    Preheat oven to 350 degrees. Cook broccoli (or vegetables) until "tender crisp." Drain and rinse with cold water in colander. Add ½ of the butter, melted, and the cubed cheese to the broccoli in a 2 to 2½ quart casserole. Roll out crackers between waxed paper, making fine crumbs. Place crumbs in a small bowl and mix in last ½ of the melted butter. Sprinkle over the top of the broccoli. Bake 20 to 25 minutes, or microwave for 8 minutes, turning twice.

Note: Be sure your casserole is at room temperature if you have made it ahead and refrigerated it. Otherwise it will not cook properly.

Soups and Sandwiches

Doris Greig's Gazpacho (Serves 12)

  1 (1 lb. 12 oz.) can tomatoes, undrained
  1 large red onion, finely chopped
  3 to 4 cloves of garlic
  4 cups tomato juice
  3 T. olive or salad oil
  3 T. red wine or wine vinegar (to taste)
  3 T. lemon juice
1½ t. Tabasco
  1 T. salt
 ½ t. pepper (to taste)
 ½ t. dried oregano leaves, finely crumbled
 ½ t. ground basil (optional)
  3 to 4 medium cucumbers, seeded and chopped (peeled or unpeeled)
  2 cups finely diced celery
  1 green pepper, finely diced
 ¼ cup parsley, finely chopped (optional)

Place canned tomatoes in the blender with garlic cloves. Blend until all mixture is fine. Pour into large container. I use a large gallon pickle jar to place all of the ingredients in. Do not use an aluminum or tin container. Stainless steel or enamel is fine. Add remaining ingredients and stir until well blended. Refrigerate, covered, until chilled. Keeps up to a week in refrigerator. Enjoy with crackers or whole wheat rolls and cheese. This makes a good summer meal. P.S. It's very low in calories.

Easy and Good Soup from the Blender
(Serves 2 large or 4 smaller portions)

2½ cups of milk
   1 T. flour
  ½ t. salt
     Dash of pepper
   1 cup coarsely chopped raw or cooked vegetables (any kind)
   1 T. minced onion
   1 to 2 T. butter or margarine

Put all ingredients in the blender except the butter or margarine. Blend well. Pour into a saucepan. Add butter or margarine. Stir and heat until slightly thickened and hot.

Turkey Soup

   1 turkey carcass
   1 large onion, grated
   4 celery stalks, cut up
    Pinch of thyme

To be added later:

     1 cup raw rice or barley
     1 to 2 onions, chopped medium fine
   1½ cups each of carrots, canned or fresh tomatoes and celery
     Diced or shredded turkey meat
    ¼ cup lemon juice
     Dash of Tabasco sauce
     Dash of salt and pepper to taste
     1 small package petite peas, thawed

Place in a large soup kettle or roaster: turkey carcass, onion and celery. Cover with cold water. Bring to a boil. Lower temperature and simmer 4 hours, or all day. Cool stock. Remove hardened fat. The next day, or the same evening—about 1 hour before dinner—add rice to stock, bring to boil and simmer for 1 hour. Meanwhile, cut up the onion, carrots, tomatoes, and celery. Add these to the broth. Also add diced or shredded turkey meat, lemon juice, Tabasco and salt and pepper to taste. Cook until vegetables are tender crisp and rice or barley is done. Thawed petite peas can be added 10 minutes before serving. Butter split rolls and lightly toast them under the broiler and enjoy with the soup!

Homemade Crockpot Potato Soup (Serves 6 to 8)

    6 potatoes, peeled and cut into bite-size pieces
    2 leeks, washed and cut into bite-size pieces
    2 medium size onions, chopped
    1 carrot, peeled and sliced thin
    1 stalk celery, sliced thin
    4 chicken bouillon cubes (crumbled but not dissolved
        before adding to crockpot)
    1 T. parsley flakes
    5 cups of water
    1 T. salt
    1 t. pepper (or less)
    ½ cup butter or margarine
    1 can evaporated milk
        Fresh chopped chives or green onion

    Put all ingredients except chives in Crockpot. Cover and cook on low for 10 to 12 hours. *Note:* Start at 8 A.M. for a 6 P.M. dinner, or cook and refrigerate and reheat the next day on top of the stove. If desired, mash potatoes with a masher. We like them chunky. Serve topped with chives.

Note: If your Crockpot is only the 2 qt. size, cut this recipe in half.

Easy Meat Vegetable Soup (Serves 6 to 8)

    2 cans beef bouillon (or use 3 bouillon cubes and 2½ cups water)
    1 large can tomato juice
    2 lbs. lean ground beef
    2 medium to large onions
  ½ t. salt
    1 t. Lawry's Seasoned Salt
    2 t. sugar
1½ bunches of carrots, peeled and sliced thin
    1 bunch of celery, cut up
    4 cans (bouillon can size) of water (about 5 cups)
  ¾ cup alphabet macaroni
    2 cups petite frozen peas, thawed

Brown the ground round with two onions. Drain fat off. Season with regular and Lawry's salt and sugar. Add bouillon, tomato juice and water. Add all of the other ingredients together and simmer 45 minutes. Add peas 10 minutes before serving. Good when reheated too!

Note: Add 2 more cans of bouillon after you have simmered the soup for 45 minutes if you desire.

Reuben Sandwich Casserole (Serves 10)

  1 (32 oz.) jar Bavarian-style saurkraut (found in refrigerator
     section of supermarket)
 ½ cup finely grated onion
  2 cans corned beef
  1 cup (8 oz.) sour cream
1½ lbs. Swiss cheese (or part jack cheese)
 ½ loaf of Jewish medium-dark rye bread
 ¾ cup Thousand Island Dressing (optional)
  1 stick soft butter or margarine

Preheat oven to 350 degrees. Grease a 9 × 12 glass casserole. Grate cheese and reserve in a separate bowl. Place saurkraut in a sieve and rinse with water. Break up corned beef into bite-size pieces and place in a separate bowl. Butter the rye bread slices (10 to 12 slices usually), and stacking approximately 4 slices of bread together, cut into bite-size pieces. Repeat until all bread has been cut up. Place bread in a separate bowl to the side also. Squeeze the excess fluid off the saurkraut and distribute evenly in the bottom of the casserole. Mix the onion, sour cream and Thousand Island Dressing. Spread evenly over the kraut. Sprinkle corned beef evenly over the sour cream mixture. Then sprinkle grated cheese evenly over the corned beef. Arrange bread pieces evenly over the top of the casserole. Bake for approximately 35 to 40 minutes, until the bread becomes browned a bit and the cheese is bubbly. This casserole can be held at 200 degrees for 10 to 15 minutes if necessary.

Lindy Elrod Cooper's Barbecued Pork and Beef Sandwiches

In a Crockpot, combine the following:

1½ lb. lean stew beef
1½ lb. lean pork cubes
  1 cup finely chopped onion
  2 cups finely chopped green pepper

Combine the following ingredients:

  1 (6 oz.) can tomato paste
  ½ cup brown sugar
  ¼ cup cider vinegar
  1 T. chili powder
  1 t. salt
  2 t. Worcestershire sauce
  1 t. dry mustard

Blend all of these ingredients well, and add to the Crockpot. Stir into the meat, onion and pepper mixture. Cover and cook on high for 8 hours. Stir to shred meat before serving on buttered rolls or pita bread. Have side dishes of lettuce and tomatoes for those who wish to add these to their sandwich.

Note: You can also simmer this mixture on top of the stove, if you do not have a Crockpot. Choose a heavy dutch oven with a tight fitting lid for this purpose.

This barbecued meat may be served over rice rather than using buttered rolls, if desired. Leftovers freeze great!

Juanita Nixon's Stuffed Egg Rolls (Serves 4)

    4 hard cooked eggs, chopped
    1 (4½ oz.) can chopped ripe olives, drained
    2 T. minced green onion
    2 T. grated cheddar cheese
    2 T. grated onion (optional)
    2 T. each of catsup and salad oil
    ⅛ t. salt, or more to taste
    8 French rolls or hot dog buns
    ⅓ cup shredded cheddar (to add last)

Preheat oven to 375 degrees. Mix all ingredients with chopped eggs. Cut off top of French rolls and scoop out the centers with a fork. If using hot dog buns, scoop out some of the center from both halves. Fill rolls with egg mixture and sprinkle a little of the ⅓ cup grated cheese on top of each. Replace roll tops and wrap each stuffed roll in foil.

Note: These rolls may be prepared 3 to 6 hours ahead if you wish, and refrigerated until 15 minutes before you plan to heat them.

Place rolls on a baking sheet and bake for 25 to 30 minutes. Serve immediately.

Greig's Good Sloppy Joes (Serves 20)

  3 lbs. ground beef
1½ t. salt
  ½ t. pepper
1½ cups onion, finely chopped
  ½ cup green pepper, finely chopped
  ½ cup celery, finely chopped
  1 (15 oz.) can of tomato sauce
  1 cup water
  ½ cup catsup
  2 T. Worcestershire
  1 T. prepared mustard
  2 T. brown sugar, packed
20 hamburger buns

Cook beef in a large skillet or Dutch oven until it loses redness. Drain fat. Add salt, pepper, onion, green pepper and celery. Cook, stirring occasionally for 5 to 7 minutes to soften vegetables. Stir in remaining ingredients. Simmer 15 minutes, stirring occasionally. Serve between buns. A fun backyard picnic dish!

Breads and Rolls

Liz Anderson's Banana Bread

   $1/2$ cup margarine
   1 cup sugar
   2 eggs, beaten
$1\,1/2$ cups bananas
   2 cups flour
   1 t. soda
   $1/2$ t. salt
   $1/2$ cup chopped nuts
   3 T. sour milk (sour the milk with a $1/2$ t. vinegar)

   Preheat oven to 350 degrees. Cream sugar and shortening together. Add mashed bananas, beaten eggs and milk to the creamed mixture, beating at medium speed with electric mixer until well blended. Stir flour, salt and baking soda together in a bowl. Add to the creamed mixture, beating well until blended. Stir in nuts. Grease 1 large loaf pan and line the bottom with waxed paper. Bake 55 minutes or until done. Remove from oven, slide knife around the sides of the pan. Cool 10 minutes and turn bread out on a rack. Remove the waxed paper from the hot loaf and turn the loaf over to cool on a wire rack.

Note: A double recipe makes 5 small loaves, or 2 large loaf
      pans. Freezes well.

Greig's Pumpkin Bread

4½ cups sugar
1½ t. nutmeg
2¾ t. cinnamon
5¼ cups of flour
  3 t. soda
2¼ t. salt
  6 eggs
1½ cups salad oil
  1 cup water
  1 (# 2½) can of pumpkin
1½ cups nuts (optional)
1½ cups raisins (optional)

Preheat oven to 350 degrees. Mix first 6 ingredients in a large bowl. Beat eggs in a large kettle or bowl. Add salad oil and water to beaten eggs and beat at medium speed until blended. Add the pumpkin and beat in at medium speed. Blend the dry ingredients into the wet ingredients. Add nuts and raisins, if you wish, and stir until well blended. Grease 4 large bread pans well. Line bottom of pans with waxed paper. Divide the dough evenly in the 4 pans. Bake approximately 1 to 1½ hours (or until the bread tests done). Cool 10 minutes in pan. Remove and peel off waxed paper. Then turn loaves right side up on cooling rack.

Note: This bread is delicious served with cream cheese between slices.

Delicious Zucchini Bread (Makes 1 loaf)

 3 eggs
 2 cups sugar
 2 t. vanilla
 1 cup vegetable oil
 3 cups of grated zucchini, drained if moist. (You may peel
   zucchini if the skin is tough.)
 3 cups of flour
 1 t. baking powder
 1 t. baking soda
 1 t. salt
 1 t. cinnamon
 ½ cup raisins (optional)
 1 cup pecans or walnuts
 1 cup of drained, crushed pineapple

   Preheat oven to 350 degrees. Beat the eggs, sugar, vanilla
and oil together in a large bowl. Add zucchini. In a separate
bowl, stir flour, baking powder, baking soda, salt and cinnamon
together. Add raisins and nuts to this flour mixture and stir. Add
the dry ingredients to the zucchini mixture gradually, stirring
until well blended. Add pineapple and mix well. Pour into
greased 9×5 loaf pan that has the bottom lined with waxed
paper. Bake 55 to 60 minutes. Cool 10 minutes. Remove from
pan and peel off waxed paper. Turn loaf over and cool on rack.

Liz Anderson's Date-Orange Bread

    2 oranges
    2 cups of dates, cut up
    2 cups of sugar
    4 T. butter or margarine, melted
    2 eggs, beaten
    4 cups flour
    2 t. baking powder
    2 t. soda
 1/2 t. salt
    1 cup chopped pecans

Preheat oven to 350 degrees. Grate orange rind (about 2 t.) and squeeze juice from oranges. Add water to make 2 cups of liquid. Combine with dates, sugar, butter and eggs, and beat until well blended. Sift dry ingredients and blend into the liquid mixture thoroughly. Add nuts and stir in. Grease baking pans. Line bottom of large pans with waxed paper. Bake for 50 to 60 minutes. Cool 10 minutes in pan, and then turn upside down. Remove the waxed paper. Immediately turn over the loaf and cool on a wire rack. Makes 4 small loaves, or 2 large loaves.

Jane O'Neil's Carrot Bread

    1 cup sugar
 1/2 cup cooking oil
    2 eggs
 1 1/2 cups grated, raw carrots
 1/4 cup chopped walnuts
 1 1/2 cups flour
 1/2 t. salt
    1 t. soda
    1 t. cinnamon

Preheat oven to 350 degrees. Mix sugar and oil together in a large bowl. Beat eggs and add, blending with mixer into the sugar, oil mixture. Put flour, salt, soda and cinnamon in a bowl and stir well together. Alternately add grated carrots and dry ingredients to the sugar/oil mixture, mixing well after each addition. Add nuts and stir in with a spoon. Grease and flour a large loaf pan. Line the bottom of the loaf pan with waxed paper. Bake for 1 hour approximately, until edges of loaf pull from side of pan. Cool 10 minutes. Remove from pan and remove waxed paper. Turn right side up immediately and cool on a rack.

Angel Biscuits (Makes 20 to 24)

Note: One nice thing about these is that you can mix the dough ahead of time and it will keep in the refrigerator for up to 3 days. Mix dough and store covered.

    2 T. sugar
    ¼ cup warm water
    1 package dry yeast
  2½ cups flour
    ½ t. baking soda
    1 t. baking powder
    1 t. salt
    ½ cup shortening
    1 cup buttermilk (or 1 cup milk plus 1 T. vinegar or lemon juice)

Preheat oven to 400 degrees. Put the warm water and 1 T. sugar in a small bowl. Add the yeast, mix well and set aside until foamy. Mix the dry ingredients (flour, baking soda, baking powder, salt and 1 T. sugar). Cut in the shortening using a fork or pastry blender. Heat the buttermilk until lukewarm, then stir the yeast mixture into the buttermilk. (Be sure buttermilk is not hot, as it will kill the yeast and your biscuits won't rise!) Add this liquid to the dry ingredients and mix well. Turn the dough out on a floured board. Knead lightly for 3 minutes. Roll the dough out about ¾ inch thick, and cut with a biscuit cutter. Place on a greased pan or cookie sheet. Let the dough rise slightly before baking. Bake 10 to 15 minutes, until lightly browned.

Note: If you are making *dumplings,* follow the usual procedure after mixing the dough. This will make a delicious dumpling also!

Knott's Biscuits (Makes 16 to 18)

    2 cups flour
    2 T. baking powder
   ½ t. salt
    1 t. salad oil
    1 cup plus 2 T. buttermilk (or milk plus 1 T and ⅛ t. vinegar)
   ⅛ t. baking soda
   ½ cup vegetable oil or butter

Preheat oven to 400 degrees. Sift flour, baking powder and salt. Add baking soda and salad oil to buttermilk. Pour into flour mixture, and stir by hand until well mixed. Put on floured board and sprinkle with additional flour. Roll ½ inch thick. Cut into biscuit size and dip in oil on all sides (I prefer to dip these biscuits in butter). Bake 8 to 10 minutes, watching carefully so that they do not burn.

Quick Sour Cream Biscuits (Makes about 2 doz.)

    3 cups flour
    1 t. baking soda
    2 t. cream of tartar
    1 t. salt
    2 T. sugar
    1 egg, beaten
 1½ cups sour cream

  Preheat oven to 400 degrees. Place the flour, baking soda, cream of tartar, salt and sugar in a large bowl and stir well. Beat egg in a separate bowl, add the sour cream and stir until blended. Add sour cream/egg mixture to flour and stir by hand until a soft dough is formed. You may need to add a little more sour cream to moisten if dough is too stiff. Roll out on a floured surface to about ½ inch thickness. Bake on greased sheet 8 to 10 minutes, until golden brown.

Lisa Herman's Streamlined Batter Bread

    1 package active dry yeast
 1¼ cups warm water
    2 T. shortening, melted
    2 T. sugar
    1 t. salt
 2⅔ cups all-purpose flour

  In a large bowl, dissolve yeast in warm water. Add melted shortening, sugar, salt and 2 cups of flour. Blend ½ minute at low speed, scraping bowl constantly. Beat for 2 minutes at medium speed, scraping bowl occasionally. Stir in remaining flour until smooth. Cover and let rise in a warm place until double in bulk (about 30 minutes). Stir down batter by beating about 25 strokes. Spread evenly in a greased (waxed paper lined) loaf pan (9 × 5 × 3). Smooth out top of batter by patting with floured hand. Cover and let rise until double (about 40 minutes) in a warm spot, such as a gas oven where the pilot light gives off a little heat. When the dough has almost doubled, remove pan and preheat oven to 375 degrees. Baking 45 minutes, or until the loaf sounds hollow when tapped. Brush top of bread with butter. Slide knife around the edges of the bread pan, and remove the bread to cool on a wire rack. Peel off waxed paper while loaf is hot. Serve for dinner, or toasted the next day.

Some variations:

Garlic Bread—add ½ t. of garlic powder when you add the shortening, sugar and salt.
Onion Bread—add 3 T. of instant onion to the yeast/water mix.
Cheese Bread—add 1 cup shredded sharp cheddar to yeast/water mixture.

Peg Nelson's Refrigerator Dough

    1 cup boiling water
    1 cup shortening
    1 cup sugar
1½ t. salt
    2 eggs
    1 cup cold water
    2 packages of dry yeast
    6 cups of flour

Pour boiling water over the shortening, sugar and salt. Stir until the shortening is melted, and the sugar and salt dissolved. Beat eggs and add to the above mixture. Dissolve the dry yeast in cold water and let stand for 5 minutes. Add this to the shortening, egg mixture. Stir in 6 cups of flour, 1 at a time, until well blended. Place in the refrigerator, covered with a damp cloth. It must remain in the refrigerator for 4 hours before it can be used, and can be kept up to a week in the refrigerator. Shape into any type of roll you wish (cloverleaf, cinnamon, parker house, etc.). After shaping by hand, or rolling out and cutting, place rolls on a greased cookie sheet. Allow dough to rise for approximately 3 hours in a warm room or until double in bulk. Preheat oven to 375 degrees. Bake for 10 minutes. Store unused dough in the refrigerator in a covered container.

Doris Greig's Kolace (Bohemian Sweet Rolls)

Use Peg Nelson's Refrigerator Dough recipe. After dough has been in the refrigerator overnight or longer, remove the bowl. Flour a board lightly and roll dough to ½ inch thickness. Cut with a large biscuit cutter, or doughnut cutter with hole cutter removed. Place rolls on well-greased cookie or jelly roll sheets. Let rise in a warm place until light (about double). In the center of each roll make a small indentation with your fingers. Fill each roll with 1 to 1½ T. of your favorite filling (*recipes* follow). Return to a warm place and let rise again for about 15 minutes. Bake at 375 degrees for 10 to 12 minutes, just until the rolls are *lightly* browned. Remove from pan and cool. Frost with powdered sugar frosting around edges, if desired. (See following pages.)

Fillings for Bohemian Sweet Rolls

Apricot Filling

   ½ lb. dried apricots (barely cover with water)
   ½ cup sugar
   1 t. lemon juice (optional)

   Cook apricots until tender. Drain and mash. Add sugar and cook until it is dissolved. Add lemon juice. Cool before filling sweet rolls. Can be made and stored in the refrigerator until time to use.

Prune Filling

   ½ lb. pitted prunes (barely cover with water)
   ½ cup sugar
      Dash of cinnamon

   Cook prunes until tender. Drain and mash. Add sugar and cook until sugar is dissolved. Add cinnamon. Can be made and stored in the refrigerator until time to use.

Cottage Cheese Filling

   1 egg yolk, beaten
   1 cup cottage cheese
      Sugar to taste (about ¼ cup)
   ½ t. vanilla
   ¼ cup seedless raisins

   Add egg yolk to cottage cheese and mix thoroughly. Add sugar, vanilla and raisins.

Note: I make triple recipes of these fillings and store in the refrigerator up to a month or a bit longer. The cottage cheese filling should only be kept 1 week.

Powdered Sugar Frosting

1/4 cup butter
1/4 t. salt
1/2 t. vanilla
1 1/2 cups of powdered sugar
    Milk for making spreading consistency

Melt the butter. Add salt and vanilla. Sift the powdered sugar and stir into butter mixture. Add milk to this until spreading consistency.

100 Percent Whole Wheat Refrigerator Bread
(Makes 2 loaves)

6 to 7 cups whole wheat flour
2 packages dry yeast
2 t. salt
1/3 cup honey
3 T. margarine (at room temperature)
2 1/2 cups hot water (not boiling but from the faucet)
    Vegetable oil (to brush surface of dough later)

In a large mixing bowl, stir together 2 cups of flour, dry yeast and salt. Add honey and margarine. Pour hot water over all and beat with electric mixer 2 minutes at medium speed. Add 1 1/2 cups more flour and continue beating until thick and elastic (about 1 minute). With a wooden spoon, stir in 2 more cups of flour. Gradually add remaining flour until a soft dough is formed. Turn out on lightly floured board and knead 5 to 10 minutes with floured hands, until the dough is smooth. Cover with a towel and let rest 20 minutes. Punch dough down and divide in two. Shape into smooth loaves and place in well-greased bread pans. Brush surface of dough with oil and cover pans with towel and refrigerate. You can bake the bread after 2 hours. It is even better to wait 5 to 6 hours, but be sure to bake within 24 hours. Preheat the oven to 400 degrees. Take bread out of the refrigerator and let stand uncovered for 10 minutes. Bake 35 to 40 minutes, or until done. It will sound hollow. Remove from pans immediately and brush tops of loaves with butter. Cool slightly before slicing.

Sticky "Do Ahead" Breakfast Rolls (Makes 24 rolls)

$5\frac{1}{2}$ to 6 cups of all purpose flour
$\frac{3}{4}$ cup granulated sugar
$1\frac{1}{2}$ t. salt
2 packages of active dry yeast
1 cup milk
$\frac{2}{3}$ cup water
$\frac{3}{4}$ cup butter or margarine
2 large eggs, beaten
2 T. ground cinnamon
$\frac{3}{4}$ cup brown sugar, firmly packed

In a large bowl, stir together 5 cups of flour, $\frac{1}{2}$ cup granulated sugar, salt and yeast. In a 1 to 2 qt. pan, combine milk, water and $\frac{1}{4}$ cup butter (cut up). Place over low heat and cook until warm (120 degrees). Butter does not need to melt completely. Gradually add liquid mixture and beaten eggs to dry mixture, mixing to blend. Beat in $\frac{1}{2}$ cup more flour until dough is stretchy. Add another $\frac{1}{4}$ cup flour if dough is still sticky. Turn dough out on a floured board and knead until smooth and elastic, 8 to 12 min. Add more flour if required to prevent sticking as you knead. Place dough in a well-greased bowl, turning over to grease top and cover with plastic wrap. Let rise in a warm place until double in bulk, about 45 minutes to 1 hour. Punch dough down and divide in half. On a floured board, roll each half in a 9 × 18 rectangle. Melt remaining ½ cup butter. Brush 2 T. butter over each piece of dough, and set aside the remaining butter. Mix together ¼ cup granulated sugar, ¼ cup brown sugar, and 2 T. cinnamon. Sprinkle half of the mixture on each rectangle of dough. From the long side, roll each portion into a log. Pinch edges to seal. Cut each log crosswise into 12 equal pieces. Use 4 round cake pans, each 8 inches across, or 3 round cake pans, each 9 inches across. Brush each pan with 1 T. reserved melted butter. Sprinkle with 2 T. brown sugar. Set rolls cut side up in the pan, placing 6 in each 8-inch pan, or 8 in each 9-inch pan. Cover lightly and chill in the refrigerator at least 2 hours, or up to 24 hours. Before baking, let rolls stand at room temperature for 20 minutes. Uncover and bake in 350 degree oven until golden brown (25 to 35 minutes). Immediately invert on serving tray.

Sticky Orange Roll

2 dozen Brown and Serve rolls
1 small can of frozen orange juice, thawed
¾ cup sugar
¼ cup margarine

Preheat oven to 425 degrees. Boil undiluted, thawed orange juice with sugar and margarine for 5 minutes. Pour half of this syrup in a 9 × 13 pan or 3 round pans, and put rolls in pan. Pour sauce over the top of the rolls as well. Bake for about 18 to 20 minutes. The last 10 minutes, turn the rolls over in the sauce. I use tongs to turn the rolls and to coat them with the orange sauce. There is enough sauce for 2 dozen rolls. They are "Oh, so sticky and Oh, so good!"

Charlotte Shackelford's "Overnight" Pull-Apart Cinnamon Rolls

  2 packages of frozen, unbaked Parker House Rolls (I use Bridgeford)
  1 T. cinnamon
  ½ cup sugar
  ½ cup raisins
  ½ cup walnuts or pecans, chopped
  1 (3½ oz.) package of butterscotch regular pudding mix (not instant)
  1 cube of melted butter or margarine

Grease a 9 × 12 pan. Dip individual frozen rolls in melted butter or margarine, and place side by side in the pan. Pour the rest of the cube of butter or margarine over the top of the rolls in the pan. Sprinkle a mixture of the cinnamon, sugar, raisins and nuts evenly over the top of the rolls. Spoon the butterscotch pudding mix over the top of the cinnamon, sugar, nut mixture. Let roll rise overnight on the kitchen counter, covered with waxed paper. Preheat oven to 350 degrees. Bake 25 to 35 minutes, depending on size of pan. Unmold hot rolls on a serving plate or tray.

Meg Kraft's Chili-Cheese Cornbread

½ lb. margarine (at room temperature)
½ cup sugar
3 eggs
¼ t. salt
1 cup of flour
1 cup of yellow cornmeal
1 (4 oz.) can of diced green chilies, well drained
1 (16 oz.) can cream styled corn
½ cup shredded jack cheese
½ cup shredded cheddar cheese
4 t. baking powder

Preheat oven to 300 degrees. Cream margarine and sugar together. Add eggs, 1 at a time, and beat until well blended. Stir in drained chilies and corn. Stir in cheeses and set aside. Sift flour, salt, cornmeal and baking powder together. Add to the cheese mixture and stir until well blended. Pour into greased 12 × 9 or 12 × 7 baking dish. Bake 1 hour. Cut in pan and serve.

Pancakes and Cereal

Buttermilk Pancakes—Light as Air! (Serves 4)

3 eggs
2 cups buttermilk (2 cups of milk mixed with 2 T. vinegar
  or lemon juice may be substituted)
3 T. melted butter or margarine
1½ cups flour
1 t. baking powder
1 T. sugar
½ t. salt

In mixing bowl, beat eggs with a whisk until frothy. Add buttermilk and melted butter and mix well. Sift the dry ingredients together in a separate bowl. Blend dry ingredients with above mixture lightly but thoroughly using a whisk. (Add a splash or two of regular milk if you wish for an even thinner pancake.) Ladle onto lightly greased, hot griddle and brown, turning only once.

Note: This batter keeps well in the refrigerator for several days.
    Stir before using.

"Melt in the Mouth" Pancakes (Serves 4)

4 eggs, separated
1 cup small curd cottage cheese
1 cup sour cream
¾ cup flour (lightly spooned into cup)
¾ t. baking powder
½ t. salt
2 T. sugar
  Salad or peanut oil for griddle

Beat yolks until thick and creamy in a large bowl. Blend in cottage cheese and sour cream. Place flour, baking powder, sugar and salt in a medium size bowl and blend together with a whisk. Fold the flour mixture into the egg yolk mixture. Heat electric griddle to 350 degrees, or use a cast iron frying pan over medium heat. In a separate bowl, beat egg whites until they form stiff, shiny peaks. Gently fold beaten egg whites into the egg yolk mixture in the large bowl. Use about ½ cup of batter for each pancake. This makes 20 four inch pancakes. Use a big pancake turner as they are "fragile," but oh so good!

Note: These cook slowly, so if you are serving more than 4 people, use 2 griddles or fry pans.

Pancakes or Waffles Without Milk!

   2 cups biscuit or pancake mix
   1 egg, beaten
  ½ cup cooking oil
   1 cup club soda or gingerale

  Blend egg and oil in medium bowl. Pour in club soda or gingerale. Fold in biscuit mix. It should be a slightly lumpy batter. Heat griddle to 425 degrees, or use a heavy frying pan over medium heat. Make small or large pancakes, depending on your mood. Batter can also be used on a heated waffle iron to make waffles.

Note: This batter will not store well, so use it all and freeze the leftovers for another day. They are good reheated in the microwave or oven (350 degrees). This is a life saver if you are out of milk!

German Egg Pancakes (Makes 10 to 12)

½ cup all purpose flour
¾ t. baking powder
¼ t. baking soda
½ cup buttermilk (or ½ cup milk plus 1½ t. vinegar)
6 large eggs, separated
1 t. vanilla
½ t. cream of tartar
1 T. sugar
Melted butter or margarine
About 1 cup sweetened whipping cream or sour cream (or equal parts of both folded together)
Fresh berries (blackberries, blueberries or strawberries), hot applesauce, or maple syrup
Powdered sugar, if desired

In a large bowl, mix flour, baking powder and baking soda. Add buttermilk, egg yolks and vanilla. Whisk until smooth. In another bowl, beat egg whites and cream of tartar until foamy. Gradually beat in sugar until whites form stiff, moist peaks. Heat an electric griddle to 350 degrees, place a griddle over medium heat or use a heavy frying pan. (I heat 2 as these cook slower than most.) Carefully fold whites into egg mixture. When the griddle is hot, brush well with butter or cooking oil. For each pancake, spoon about ½ cup batter on griddle. Turn cake over when the bottom turns golden brown. Butter griddle *again* as you turn each cake. Cook second side until golden on the second side and edges feel dry (about 4 minutes for each side). Serve at once with whipping cream, sour cream, fruit and powdered sugar. These can be held to warm in the oven at 200 degrees until ready to serve. Do not stack.

329

German Oven Pancakes (Serves 4 to 6)

1½ cups milk
  1 cup flour
  1 t. sugar
  6 eggs
    pinch of salt
  4 oz. butter (melted)

    Preheat oven to 450 degrees. In a large bowl, blend milk into flour and sugar with a whisk. Lightly beat eggs with salt and whisk into milk and flour, blending well. Pour in butter into 2 (8 inch square) baking dishes. Divide batter between dishes. Bake 15 minutes or until it rises into big golden brown puffs. (If pancakes brown too fast, lower temperature to 400 degrees.) Serve immediately with all or any of the following: Fresh berries, peaches, fruit jam, sour cream, brown sugar or cinnamon, sugar and applesauce.

My German Apple Pancakes (Serves 4)

  4 large tart apples
  1 T. sugar
  6 eggs, well beaten
1½ cups of flour
  4 T. butter or margarine (*and* ¼ cup for later)
  ¼ t. salt
  2 cups milk
    cinnamon and sugar mixture

    Preheat oven to 400 degrees Peel, core and slice apples. Melt 4 T. butter in a 12-inch cast iron frying pan. Cook apple slices over moderate heat for 5 minutes, or until tender, turning with a spatula. Mix together eggs, salt and milk. Add flour and beat just until smooth with an electric mixer. Pour batter over hot apples and bake in oven for 20 minutes. Melt ¼ cup butter and pour over the hot pancake. Sprinkle about 4 T. of cinnamon/sugar mixture over pancake and butter. Lower oven temperature to 350 degrees and return cast iron skillet with pancake to oven for 15 to 20 more minutes. Serve warm.

Oven French Toast (Serves 4 to 6)

    3 eggs, lightly beaten
    ½ t. salt
    ½ t. almond extract
    2 T. sugar
    ¾ cup milk
    12 slices of white or raisin bread
        Butter and syrup or jam

Preheat oven to 450 degrees. Grease baking sheet heavily. In a shallow dish, beat eggs, salt, almond extract and sugar. Add milk and blend well. Dip bread into egg mixture, coating both sides. Arrange on baking sheet. Bake 7 minutes. Turn over and bake 7 minutes more, or until golden. Serve at once with butter, syrup or jam.

Good Syrup for Pancakes

    2 cups sugar
    2 cups water
    ¼ t. salt
    1 t. maple flavoring

Boil sugar and water for 5 minutes. Add salt and maple flavoring. This syrup does not crystalize when stored in the refrigerator. Reheat as needed.

Cakes and Pies,
Plus Other Desserts!

Barbara Sheffield's Sour Cream Coffee Cake

(Serves 12 or more)

    2 cups flour, spooned lightly into cup
    1 t. baking powder
 1/4 t. salt
    1 cup butter (at room temperature)
    2 cups sugar
    2 egg yolks
 1/2 t. vanilla
 1/4 t. almond extract
    1 cup sour cream
    2 egg whites
    3 T. poppy seeds (optional)

Preheat oven to 350 degrees. Grease and flour a Bundt cake pan or 10-inch tube pan, or 9 × 13 cake pan. Stir together the flour, baking powder and salt. Set aside. Cream the sugar gradually into butter until light and fluffy. Beat egg yolks together with vanilla and almond extract. Slowly add to the creamed mixture. Add alternately the flour mixture and the sour cream to the creamed sugar/butter mixture. Add the poppy seeds. Beat the egg whites until they hold stiff peaks; fold them into the cake batter just until blended. Pour into pan evenly and bake for 50 to 60 minutes (until cake pulls slightly away from the edge of the pan). Cool in pan right side up for 15 minutes (on a rack). Then turn out on a wire rack or serving plate. This may be served plain or with a sprinkling of powdered sugar over the top.

> *Note:* If you use tube pan, line the bottom with waxed paper. If you use a 9 × 13 pan, bake cake only 35 to 40 minutes. Cool slightly. Cut in squares and serve from pan.

Yummy Coffee Cake (Serves 12 to 16)

$1/2$ cup shortening or butter
$3/4$ cup sugar
1 t. vanilla extract
3 eggs
2 cups sifted flour
1 t. baking powder
1 t. baking soda
1 cup sour cream
6 t. butter or margarine, softened
$1/2$ t. salt
1 cup firmly packed brown sugar
2 t. cinnamon
1 cup chopped nuts

Preheat oven to 350 degrees. Cream shortening, sugar, and vanilla thoroughly. Add eggs, 1 at a time, beating well after each addition. Sift flour, baking soda, baking powder, and salt together and add to creamed mixture alternately with sour cream, blending after each addition. Spread half of batter in 10-inch tube pan that has been greased and lined on the bottom with waxed paper. Cream butter, brown sugar and cinnamon together. Add nuts and mix well. Sprinkle half of the nut and sugar mixture evenly over the batter in the pan. Cover with remaining cake batter and sprinkle with remaining cinnamon sugar and nut mixture. Bake about 50 minutes, and then cool the cake for 10 minutes. Remove from pan.

Note: If you wish, you can bake this in a well-greased 9×13 cake pan, placing all of the batter on the bottom and the cinnamon/sugar and butter mixture on the top layer. This will take 35 to 40 minutes to bake. Cut in squares.

Shortcake for Berries (Makes 14 medium sized cakes)

3 cups flour
4 t. baking powder
3/4 t. salt
1/2 cup sugar
1/2 cup oil
1 egg
1/2 cup milk

Preheat oven to 450 degrees. Combine dry ingredients in a large bowl and stir well with a whisk or spoon. In a smaller bowl, beat together the oil, egg and milk until thoroughly blended. Add this gradually to the large bowl of dry ingredients and mix well. Knead by hand in the bowl until the dough forms a ball and sticks together. Measure about 1/3 cup of dough. Roll in hands and pat down to about 1/2 inch thickness on an ungreased cookie sheet, spacing cakes at least 2 inches apart. Bake 12 to 15 minutes until lightly browned. Cool thoroughly if you plan to freeze these shortcakes. Then package in plastic bags. These freeze well. Reheat before serving. To serve, cut shortcake in half, crosswise. Put bottom half on a dessert plate. Cover with at least 3/4 cup sweetened berries. Put upper half of shortcake on top of the berries. Place about 1/4 cup (or more) whipped cream on top of the shortcake. Garnish top with one fresh berry, if desired.

"Year-Round" Pudding Cake

    1 (30 oz.) can fruit cocktail, well drained
    1 egg
    ½ cup granulated sugar
    ½ cup brown sugar, packed
1⅔ cups flour
    1 t. baking soda
    1 t. salt
    ½ t. allspice
    ½ t. cloves
    ½ cup raisins
    1 cup chopped nuts
      Whipping cream

Preheat oven to 350 degrees. Drain fruit cocktail well, saving the juice to use in punch or gelatin. Juice may be frozen until needed. Beat egg and sugar until thickened, and add the fruit cocktail to this mixture. In another bowl, combine flour, baking soda, salt, allspice and cloves. Stir dry ingredients together thoroughly and add the egg, sugars and fruit cocktail mixture to the flour mixture. Blend just until moistened. Fold in raisins and nuts. Turn into 6-cup well-greased and floured mold and bake for about 50 minutes, or until cake tests done. May be baked in a 9 × 12 cake pan if desired. Takes a bit less time to bake. Cool 25 to 30 minutes in pan and then turn out on a plate. Slice and serve plain, with whipped cream or with ice cream.

Fruit Salad Cake by Marilyn Layfield

    2 cups flour
    2 t. soda
1½ cups sugar
    1 t. salt
    1 (1 lb.) can fruit cocktail and juice
    1 beaten egg
    1 small can (⅔ cup) evaporated milk
    ½ cup packed brown sugar
    ½ cup white sugar
    ½ cup margarine or butter
1⅓ cups coconut (optional)
    1 t. vanilla
    1 cup chopped nuts (optional)

Preheat oven 350 degrees. Grease a 9 × 13 cake pan. Mix in a large bowl: flour, soda, sugar and salt. Add fruit cocktail—juice and all—to the bowl. Add 1 beaten egg. Stir with a spoon just until well blended. Pour batter evenly into the 9 × 13 pan. Bake for 25 to 30 minutes—(325 degrees in a glass dish)

While the cake is baking, prepare the topping by placing in a cooking pan:

    1 small can evaporated milk (⅔ cup)
½ cup packed brown sugar
½ cup white sugar
½ cup margarine or butter

Boil these ingredients over low heat 10 minutes, stirring as they cook. Add 1⅓ cups coconut, 1 t. vanilla and 1 cup chopped nuts. When cake tests done, remove from oven and place on rack. Pour this frosting over the cake while the cake is still hot, and gently spread.

Gary Greig's Yogurt Cake

  ½ cup sugar
  1 t. cinnamon
  ¾ cup salad oil
  1 cup sugar
  2 eggs
  1 cup plain yogurt
  1 t. vanilla
  ½ t. soda
1½ t. baking powder
  ¼ t. salt
  2 cups of flour (unsifted all-purpose), lightly spooned into
    cup

Preheat oven to 350 degrees. Grease and flour one 10-inch tube cake pan and line bottom with waxed paper—or grease and flour a 9×13 cake pan. Mix ½ cup sugar and the cinnamon in a bowl—reserve for later. Put the following ingredients in a large mixing bowl: salad oil, sugar, yogurt, vanilla, soda, baking powder, salt. Mix altogether with an electric beater until well blended. Add 2 cups of flour. Blend just until batter is smooth. *For the tube pan*—pour half of the batter in the pan and sprinkle half of the cinnamon sugar mixture over this batter. Then cover with the other half of batter, and sprinkle the remaining cinnamon sugar. Bake 55 minutes. Cool 7 to 10 minutes and turn out on a plate. *If the cake is baked in a 9×13 greased pan,* place all of batter in pan first and top with cinnamon sugar mix and bake for only 35 to 40 minutes (or until cake tests done).

Kathy Greig Rowland's Fresh Apple Cake

1/2 cup margarine or oil
2 cups sugar
2 beaten eggs
1/2 cup milk
2 cups flour
2 t. baking soda
1 t. cinnamon
1/2 t. nutmeg
1/2 t. salt
1 cup nuts, chopped
1 t. vanilla
4 cups of peeled, diced, raw apples

Preheat oven to 350 degrees. Cream shortening and sugar. Add beaten eggs and milk. Beat with electric mixer until well blended. Combine all dry ingredients in another bowl and stir until blended well. Add dry ingredients to egg, milk, sugar and shortening bowl and beat just until well blended. Add nuts, vanilla and apples. Hand stir until well blended. *Note:* This batter will be very thick. Pour batter into greased 9 × 13 pan and bake for 50 to 60 minutes. Serve plain, with whipped cream or with ice cream.

Jean Boozer's Lunch Cake

1 package chocolate chips
½ cup chopped nuts (optional)
1½ cups dates
1 cup boiling water
1 t. baking soda
½ cup margarine
1 cup sugar
2 eggs
1 t. vanilla
1¾ cups all purpose flour
1 T. cocoa
¼ t. salt

Preheat oven to 350 degrees. Grease a 7 × 11 cake pan well. A 9 × 13 pan will do if you don't have this size. In a cooking pan, place cut-up dates with the boiling water and bring to a boil again, stirring for about 1 minute. Remove from heat to cool. In another bowl, cream together the margarine and sugar with an electric mixer. Add eggs one at a time and beat well. Add vanilla, salt and cocoa and beat in. Stir in soda into the now somewhat cooled date/water mixture. Alternately add date mixture and flour to the bowl of ingredients, stirring well by hand until all has been added and is well blended. Pour batter into cake pan and smooth out evenly. Sprinkle chocolate chips and chopped nuts over top of batter before baking. Bake for approximately 40 minutes, or until cake tests done.

Billy Greig's Quick Lunch Box Cake

2¼ cups of unsifted flour
  2 t. soda
  1 t. salt
  ½ t. cinnamon (optional)
  1 cup firmly packed brown sugar
  2 eggs
  ¼ cup oil
  1 can of fruit cocktail, undrained
  ½ cup semi-sweet chocolate pieces
  ½ cup nuts (optional)

     Preheat oven to 350 degrees. Mix in a bowl: oil, eggs, soda, salt, and sugar—with an electric mixer. Add fruit cocktail and juice. Stir by hand until blended. Add flour and stir until well-blended. Pour batter into greased 9 × 13 pan and smooth out. Sprinkle nuts and chocolate chips evenly over the top of the cake batter. Bake 30 to 40 minutes, until cake tests done.

Doris Greig's Sour Cream Chocolate Cake and Frosting

  2 cups flour
1¼ t. baking soda
  ½ t. baking powder
  1 t. salt
  2 cups sugar
  ¾ cup sour cream
  1 t. vanilla
  2 eggs, beaten
  ¼ cup shortening or butter
  1 cup water
  4 oz. unsweetened chocolate

Preheat oven to 350 degrees. On top of stove or in micro-wave melt chocolate, shortening and water. Remove from heat and cool thoroughly. Stir flour, soda and salt together in a large bowl. Beat eggs together with sour cream in another bowl. Then beat sugar and vanilla into egg mixture. Stir in chocolate. Beat all into flour mixture on low speed for ½ minute, or until smooth. *Note:* This batter will be thin. Pour into greased 9 × 12 baking pan or two greased 9-inch round cake pans. Bake 30 to 35 minutes or until cake tests done. If using round pans, cool 10 minutes, turn out onto racks or plates "right side" up. Frost while still slightly warm.

Sour Cream Chocolate Cake Frosting

    3 oz. unsweetened baking chocolate
    ⅓ cup butter or margarine
    3 cups powdered sugar
    ½ cup sour cream
    2 t. vanilla

Melt chocolate with butter (this may be done on top of the stove or in a medium size plastic or glass bowl in the micro-wave). Blend in the sour cream and vanilla, beating until creamy. Sift powdered sugar and gradually beat into the chocolate/sour cream mixture.

Doris Greig's Never Fail 7-Minute White Frosting

   2 egg whites
1½ cups sugar
  ⅛ t. salt
  ⅓ cup water
   1 T. light corn syrup
   1 t. vanilla

    Place in double boiler over boiling water, and beat with electric mixer about 7 minutes, stopping a few times to scrape down sides of pan with a rubber spatula in order to be sure all sugar gets dissolved and "involved" in the frosting. Remove from boiling water when frosting stands in glossy peaks (has more body than meringue). Place top of double boiler on a folded towel on counter. Continue beating with mixer until the frosting is cool and thick enough to hold firm swirls. Makes enough frosting for two 8-inch or 9-inch layer cakes, or one 9-inch or 10-inch tube cake.

Note: To have a colored frosting, add a drop or two of red or yellow food coloring before beating the last time.

Suggestion: To make sure your double boiler does not boil dry, place marbles or pennies in the bottom. You can hear if you need to add more water to your pan! This frosting makes a pretty birthday cake, and can be smoothed out if you wish to decorate the cake as well.

Cream Cheese Frosting

   3 oz. cream cheese at room temperature
   2 cups powdered sugar
     Cream, or evaporated milk
  ½ cup chopped nuts (optional)

Cream together the cream cheese and powdered sugar, using a wooden spoon. Add a small amount of cream or evaporated milk—just enough to make a spreading consistency. Spread over a 9 × 13 cake. Sprinkle with the chopped nuts.

Texas Chocolate Sheet Cake

    2 cups sugar
    2 cups flour
    1 stick margarine
    ½ cup Crisco
    4 T. cocoa
    1 cup water
    2 eggs
    ½ cup buttermilk
    1 t. soda

Frosting:
    1 stick margarine
    4 T. cocoa
    6 T. milk
    1 lb. powdered sugar
    ½ t. vanilla
    1 cup chopped nuts

Preheat oven to 400 degrees. Mix sugar and flour in a large bowl. Bring to boil next 4 ingredients. Add liquid mixture to flour and sugar and stir well. Add eggs—well beaten, buttermilk (or ½ cup milk and 1½ t. vinegar) and soda. Stir well—until completely blended. Grease an 11 × 19 jelly roll pan, and pour the batter into the pan. Bake 20 minutes. *While sheet cake is baking, prepare icing.* Mix together and bring to a boil: margarine, cocoa and milk. Remove pan from burner and pour mixture into a bowl containing one box of sifted powdered sugar. Beat well with an electric mixer until smooth. Add vanilla and beat again. Fold in 1 cup of chopped nuts (I think pecans are best). Cover the cake with icing while it is still warm. Cut in squares and serve.

Note: This cake is a nice, quick cake and is very good served with vanilla ice cream. It has almost a brownie consistency.

Edith Elrod's Date Cake (Serves 6)
A most unusual dessert!

   1 cup brown sugar, well-packed
   1 cup flour, unsifted
   2 t. baking powder
     Pinch of salt
   1 cup (8 oz.) dates, chopped
   ½ cup milk

   Preheat oven to 350 degrees. Mix all ingredients together in a bowl. Put in a greased 8×8 pan. Sprinkle with ½ cup (or more) walnuts or pecans. Set pan aside.

   ½ cup well-packed brown sugar
   ½ cup white sugar
 1¼ cups water
   1 t. vanilla

   In a sauce pan, bring to a boil brown sugar, white sugar and water. When this mixture boils, remove from burner and add vanilla. Pour this liquid slowly on top of the batter and nuts in the 8×8 pan. Bake 40 minutes (or until medium brown in color). This cake forms a pudding-type mixture at the bottom, and is delicious served with unsweetened whipped cream. It should be cut in squares and served from the pan on dessert plates.

Easy Baked Fudge Pudding

1 cup flour
2 t. baking powder
½ t. salt
¾ cup sugar
2 T. cocoa
¼ t. cloves
1 t. vanilla
½ cup milk
2 T. melted margarine
½ cup chopped nuts (optional)
1¼ cups light brown sugar
¼ cup cocoa
2 cups hot water

Preheat oven to 350 degrees. Stir together dry ingredients in a bowl. Add milk, vanilla, margarine and nuts and stir until well blended. Turn into a greased 8×8×2 pan. Mix brown sugar and cocoa. Sprinkle this mixture over the batter. Pour hot water evenly over surface of ingredients in the pan. Bake for 40 to 45 minutes.

Note: This dessert has a cake-like top with a delicious rich chocolate sauce on the bottom. Spoon out while warm into serving dishes, sauce side up. Serve with ice cream or whipped cream

Linda Elrod Cooper's Strawberry Squares
(Serves 12 to 15)

$1/2$ cup butter or margarine
$1/4$ cup brown sugar
1 cup flour
$1/2$ cup slivered almonds
2 egg whites (at room temperature)
1 package of frozen strawberries (thawed)
$3/4$ cup sugar
$1/8$ t. salt
1 cup whipping cream
2 T. lemon juice

Preheat oven to 300 degrees. Melt butter and mix with flour, brown sugar and almonds. Spread and pat evenly into a 9×13 pan. Bake 20 minutes and cool thoroughly. Beat egg whites until they hold soft peaks. Beat in sugar, salt and lemon juice until the egg whites hold their peaks well. Fold in thawed berries until well blended. Beat whipping cream and fold into the egg white mixture. Spoon this over the cooled crumb crust. Cover. Freeze. Remove about 10 minutes before serving. Cut into squares, garnish with whipped cream and fresh berries if desired. This is a nice dessert to keep in your freezer for that unexpected company dessert! Cut only what you need and return the rest to the freezer. It keeps well for 1 to 2 months in the freezer.

Kathy Rowland's Fool Proof Pie Crust (Makes 5 crusts)

    4 cups of flour, lightly spooned into cup
    1 T. sugar
    2 t. salt
1³⁄₄ cup shortening
    1 T. vinegar
    ½ cup water
    1 large egg

In a large bowl, stir together flour, sugar and salt with a fork. Cut in the shortening with a pastry blender or fork, until crumbly. In a small bowl, beat egg, water and vinegar together. Add to flour mixture and stir until all ingredients are moistened and form a ball.

Note: 1 to 2 T. more of water may sometimes be needed— depending on the flour.

Divide the dough into 5 portions and shape with hands into flat, round patties. Wrap each in plastic or waxed paper and chill at least ½ hour before rolling out. Dough can be left in the refrigerator up to 3 days, or can be frozen until ready to use (thaw until soft enough to roll). When you are ready to use, lightly flour both sides of patty and roll out on a floured board with a floured rolling pin—or roll dough between 2 sheets of waxed paper. For baked pie shell, prick the sides and bottom of pie crust with a fork. Bake at 450 degrees for 12 to 15 minutes.

Note: If making a double crust pie, use two pieces of dough and follow directions according to your recipe.

Doris Greig's Banana Summertime Pie

1¼ cups fine graham cracker crumbs
½ cup finely chopped walnuts (optional)
5 T. butter or margarine, melted
2 medium bananas, plus 1 medium banana for garnish
1 cup sour cream
1 cup milk
1 (3¾ oz.) package vanilla instant pudding mix
1 cup whipping cream

Combine graham cracker crumbs, nuts and butter. Press mixture firmly against sides and bottom of 9-inch pie plate. Chill at least 1 hour. Peel bananas and slice into chilled pie crust. In a medium size bowl, blend sour cream and milk. Mix with pudding according to package directions. Immediately pour over bananas and refrigerate for at least 1 hour. When ready to serve, whip the cream until it holds its peaks. Spread over the pie evenly. Garnish each piece of pie with a few banana slices, if desired.

Rhoda Cathey's Coconut Cream Pie

    1 baked pie shell
    1 package plain gelatin
 1/4 cup cold water
 1/3 cup sugar
    4 T. flour (or 2 T. cornstarch)
 1/2 t. salt
 1/2 cup milk
    3 egg whites at room temperature
 1/3 cup sugar
 1/2 cup whipping cream
 1/2 t. vanilla
    1 cup flaked coconut
 1/2 cup whipping cream

Dissolve gelatin in 1/4 cup cold water. Mix sugar, flour (or cornstarch) and salt in a saucepan or microwave bowl. Gradually add milk to this mixture, stirring until smooth. Bring this mixture to a boil, stirring and boil 1 minute. (You may wish to cook this mixture in your microwave instead of on top of the stove.) Remove from heat and add gelatin, stirring until it is dissolved. Cool. Beat the egg whites in a medium bowl, gradually adding sugar. Beat until they hold stiff peaks. Using a rubber scraper, put the cooled gelatin mixture into a large bowl. Fold the egg white mixture into the gelatin mixture. Beat the whipping cream until stiff, adding vanilla. Fold in the whipped cream and flaked coconut into the gelatin and egg white mixture. Pour into baked pie shell (cooled), and refrigerate at least 2 hours. Whip 1/2 cup cream and garnish pie.

Greig Family Pumpkin Pie

   2 eggs, slightly beaten
1½ cups pumpkin
  ¾ cup sugar
  ½ t. salt
  1 t. cinnamon
  ½ t. ginger
  ¼ t. cloves
1⅔ cups evaporated milk
One 9 inch, unbaked pie shell
  ½ cup whipping cream

   Preheat oven to 425 degrees. Mix filling ingredients with an electric mixer in order given. Pour into pie shell. Bake for 15 minutes. Reduce temperature to moderate (350 degrees), and continue baking for 45 minutes, or until knife inserted into pie filling comes out clean. Garnish cooled pie with whipped cream.

Note: For two nine-inch pies, double this recipe and pour into two pastry shells. Bake as directed.

Doris Greig's Lemon Pie (Serves 6 to 8)

One 9-inch baked pie shell
  1/8 t. salt
  1 cup sugar
  6 T. cornstarch
  2 cups water or milk
  3 beaten egg yolks
  3 T. butter
  1/3 cup fresh lemon juice and about 1 t. finely grated rind

Combine in the top of a double boiler or in a heavy sauce-pan the sugar, salt and cornstarch. Gradually stir in water or milk with a whisk. Stir and cook these ingredients for 8 to 12 minutes, or until the mixture thickens. Remove from heat. Pour a little of the mixture over the beaten egg yolks, stirring constantly. Gradually add all of the hot mixture and then return the entire mixture to the double boiler. Cook, stirring with a whisk about 5 more minutes. Remove from and heat and beat in the butter, lemon juice and rind. Cool in a large bowl stirring gently to release steam about every 4 to 5 minutes until the filling is cool. Pour cooled filling into the cooled pie shell. Cover with Fool Proof Meringue (recipe follows) and bake as directed. Note: Be sure the lemon filling is cool before spreading on the meringue. This will help keep the meringue from shrinking from the sides of the pie.

Fool Proof Meringue

3 egg whites
3 T. crushed ice or ice cold water
1 t. baking powder
6 T. sugar

Preheat oven to 425 degrees. Put first 3 ingredients in a medium bowl and beat together until mixture is stiff. *To test:* Put a fork, tines first, upright in the bowl. Fork should not move, but remain upright. Beat in the granulated sugar, 1 T. at a time, until stiff. Use fork test again. Spread the meringue over the pie, making sure it covers all edges of the pie. Bake for 5 to 7 minutes until slightly brown. *Do not* bake longer than 7 minutes! Cool slowly away from drafts. This meringue will be good the second day too!

Super Meringue

1 T. cornstarch
2 T. cold water
$1/2$ cup boiling water
3 egg whites, at room temperature
6 T. sugar
  Dash of salt
1 t. vanilla

Preheat oven to 350 degrees. Dissolve cornstarch in cold water. Stir into boiling water, beating with a whisk and cook and stir until mixture boils and thickens. Remove from heat and scrape contents of pan into a large bowl, using a rubber spatula to make sure you get it all into the bowl. Cool completely before beating egg whites. Put the egg whites in another large bowl, and beat until fluffy on high speed of mixer. Gradually add sugar, 1 T. at a time, while continuing to beat, until mixture is thick and glossy. Beat in salt and vanilla. Turn mixer to medium speed and add cornstarch mixture gradually (1 rounded T. at a time), while continuing to beat. When smooth, spread on pie filling, making sure it is sealed to edges of pie. Bake for 20 minutes, or until evenly browned. Cool slowly, away from draft.

Angel Lemon Pie

    4 eggs, at room temperature, separated
  1/4 t. cream of tartar
1 1/2 cups sugar
  1/4 cup lemon juice
      Fine grated peel of 1/2 lemon
    1 cup heavy whipping cream

Preheat oven to 275 degrees. Separate egg whites from yolks. Beat egg whites until frothy. Add cream of tartar and beat until firm. Add 1 cup sugar gradually to the egg whites, beating after each addition until all is added and the mixture is stiff. Spoon into a 12-inch pie plate, spreading meringue thickly on the sides. Bake at 275 degrees for 20 minutes, then at 300 degrees for 40 minutes. Remove from oven and cool on rack on the counter. *In the meanwhile,* beat egg yolks and add remaining sugar (1/2 cup). Add lemon juice and peel to the egg yolks, and cook on top of double boiler over simmering water until thick, about 20 minutes. Use a whisk to stir this while cooking. Remove top of double boiler and place on rack for mixture to cool. Whip cream until it holds its shape. Then fold it into the cooled egg yolk mixture. Spoon the egg yolk/cream mixture into the cool baked meringue shell and chill. This will keep 2 or 3 days in the refrigerator. Cut and garnish with whipped cream to serve.

Doris Greig's Meringue Pie

6 egg whites at room temperature (Save yolks for scrambled eggs.)
2 cups of sugar
1 t. vinegar
1 t. vanilla
1 cup whipping cream
1 T. sugar
1 t. vanilla
  Fresh berries or peaches

Preheat oven to 350 degrees. Place egg whites in a large bowl and slowly add sugar, beating with an electric mixer at high speed until egg whites hold their shape when you lift the beaters out. Quickly beat in vinegar and vanilla. Spread meringue into two 9 inch pie tins. Bake at 350 degrees for 15 minutes, then lower oven temperature to 300 degrees for 17 to 20 minutes. Remove meringue from oven, place on rack and cool on counter. Just before serving, whip the cream. When it holds its shape, beat in 1 T. sugar and 1 t. vanilla until blended. Spread the cream on cooled meringue. Cut and serve on dessert dishes. Top with any kind of fresh fruit, such as strawberries, peaches, blueberries or raspberries.

Alternate baking directions: Line baking sheet with waxed paper. Preheat oven to 250 degrees. Draw 8 to 10 3-inch circles 2 inches apart on waxed paper. Drop meringue evenly and shape into circles swirling sides up, and making the middle lower. Bake 1 hour. Turn off oven and leave meringues in 1½ hours or overnight to completely dry. Remove carefully from paper. Store in airtight container for several weeks. Do not refrigerate or freeze.

Margie Brown's Soda Cracker Pie (Serves 6 to 8)

   3 egg whites, at room temperature
 ½ t. cream of tartar
   1 cup sugar
 14 single soda crackers
 ¾ to 1 cup walnuts or pecans
   1 t. vanilla
   1 cup whipping cream

   Preheat oven 350 degrees. Beat egg whites and cream of tartar until foamy. Gradually add sugar to egg white mixture, beating until stiff. Beat in vanilla last. Place crackers between waxed paper and roll with a rolling pin until they are finely crushed. Fold crackers and nuts into the egg white mixture. Place in 9-inch pie pan, smoothing around sides and across the bottom of the pan evenly. Bake for 30 to 40 minutes, until golden brown. Remove from oven and cool on rack at room temperature. Whip the cream and spread evenly over cooled meringue. Refrigerate at least 2 hours. Cut in wedges to serve. Fresh strawberries, peaches or raspberries make a very nice garnish for this pie, but pie is delicious as is.

Bill's Favorite Frozen Peanut Butter Pie

   4 oz. cream cheese
   1 cup powdered sugar
 ⅓ cup peanut butter
 ½ cup milk
   1 (9 oz. pkg.) non-dairy whipped topping like Dream Whip
   1 (9-inch) graham cracker crust or regular pie crust, baked
     and cooled
 ¾ cup finely chopped peanuts

In a large bowl, whip the cheese until soft and fluffy. Beat in the sugar and peanut butter. Slowly add milk, blending thoroughly into mixture. Fold whipped topping into the mixture. Pour into a baked pie shell. Sprinkle liberally with peanuts. Freeze until firm. Cover with foil or plastic wrap if not used the first day. Remove from freezer 20 to 30 minutes before serving. *Note:* This is a nice pie to keep in the freezer for surprise guests.

Walnut Creek Joy of Living Class' Easy Layered Dessert
(Serves 12 to 15)

   1 cup flour
   2 T. granulated sugar
   1 stick margarine (¼ lb.) at room temperature
   1 cup chopped walnuts
   1 (8 oz.) package creamed cheese at room temperature
   1 cup powdered sugar
   1 (12 oz.) carton Cool Whip
   3 cups whole milk
   2 small (3¾ oz. size) instant pudding mixes (either chocolate, lemon or pistachio)

   Preheat oven to 350 degrees. Mix together the flour, sugar, softened margarine and walnuts with a pastry blender or fork. Pat into the bottom of a 9 × 13 pan. Bake for 15 to 20 minutes. Cool completely. Combine the cream cheese, powdered sugar and ½ of the Cool Whip in a bowl. Beat with an electric mixer until well blended. Spread this mixture evenly over the cooled crust. Pour milk into a medium size bowl and add the 2 pudding mixes. Beat with hand or electric mixer until blended. Spread the pudding evenly over the cream cheese layer. Spread the last half of the Cool Whip over the pudding. Chill 2 to 3 hours before serving. Can be made the day before, covered and stored in the refrigerator until serving time.

Sherry Meseck's Cream Cheese Pie (Serves 8 to 10)

   4 (3 oz.) packages of cream cheese (softened to room tem-
      perature)
   2 eggs, beaten
 ¾ cup of sugar
   2 t. vanilla
      Graham cracker pie crust

   Preheat oven to 350 degrees. Whip the softened, room
temperature cream cheese with electric beater until light and
frothy. Add eggs, sugar and vanilla to cream cheese and beat
until well blended. Pour into graham cracker crust and bake for
20 minutes. Remove from oven and allow to cool for 5 minutes
on a rack. While cooling, make topping.

   1 small carton of sour cream
 3½ T. sugar
   1 t. vanilla

   Beat sour cream, sugar and vanilla together and pour over
the cheese filling. Return the pie to the oven and bake 10 minutes longer. Place the slightly cooled pie in the refrigerator and
let stand for at least 5 hours before serving.

Garnish using 1 can of cherry pie filling, spooning some on
each piece as you serve it. Fresh strawberries can also be used
for a garnish.

Graham Cracker Crust for Cheesecake

12 to 14 graham crackers
1/4 cup, plus 2 T. butter or margarine
1/4 t. cinnamon
1/4 cup, plus 2 T. sugar

Preheat oven to 375 degrees. Using a rolling pin and 2 large pieces of waxed paper, finely crumble graham crackers (enough to make 1 cup of crumbs). Melt butter or margarine in a pan on top of your stove, or use your microwave. Place graham cracker crumbs in a medium size bowl. Add cinnamon and sugar and blend thoroughly. Add the melted butter and blend. Press this mixture into a 9-inch pie plate. Place pie on middle rack of oven and bake 8 minutes. Remove from oven and cool on a rack while preparing filling.

New York Style Cheesecake (Serves 12 to 16)

1 cup coarsely ground walnuts
1 t. ground cinnamon
2 cups sugar
1 1/2 cups vanilla wafers or graham crackers, finely crushed
3 T. melted butter or margarine
4 (8 oz.) packages of cream cheese at room temperature
5 eggs
1 T., plus 1 t. lemon juice
2 t. vanilla
   Sour Cream Topping (recipe follows)
   Strawberry Glaze (recipe follows)
   Fresh strawberries (enough to garnish top of cheesecake)

Preheat oven to 350 degrees. Lightly grease 10-inch spring

361

form pan. Combine walnuts, cinnamon, ½ cup sugar and wafer or cracker crumbs with melted butter. Mix well. Press into the bottom of pan and bake for 5 minutes. Beat cream cheese (in a large bowl) until smooth. Slowly add 1½ cups of sugar. Beat in eggs, one at a time. Beat in lemon juice and vanilla. Pour over crust and bake 50 minutes, until top is firm and a light golden brown. Remove from oven. Let stand at room temperature on a rack for 20 minutes. After the 20 minutes, spoon sour cream topping over partially cooled cheesecake. Return pan to oven (350 degrees) for 15 minutes. Cool cake on rack until room temperature. Refrigerate 3 hours or overnight. (Should be thoroughly chilled.)

Sour Cream Topping

    2 cups sour cream
    ½ cup sugar
    1 t. vanilla

    Combine ingredients thoroughly.

Strawberry Glaze

    1 (12 oz.) jar seedless strawberry or raspberry jam
    2 T. cornstarch
    ¼ cup cold water
    ½ cup cranberry juice

    Heat jam in a saucepan on low. Place cornstarch in a bowl. Gradually stir in water and stir until lump free. Pour jam a bit at a time into this cornstarch mix, stirring well. Return to saucepan and add cranberry juice. Stir over low to medium heat until mixture is clear and thickened. Cool in the refrigerator about 15 minutes, stirring frequently. Remove thoroughly chilled cake from pan and place on a large plate. Remove sides of spring form pan and place bottom of pan with the cheesecake right on the serving plate. Arrange whole strawberries, pointed side up, on top of the cake. Spoon cooled strawberry topping over the berries. Chill until serving time.

Note: Canned cherry pie filling may be substituted for strawberries and glaze.

Best Egg Custard I've Ever Made!

   4 eggs
   1/4 t. salt
   2 cups milk
   1/2 cup sugar
   1 t. vanilla
      dash of nutmeg (optional)

   Preheat oven to 325 degrees. Beat all ingredients at low speed, except nutmeg, just until blended. Place in 6 to 8 custard cups. Fill cake pan 1/3 full of hot water and place custard cups in the pan. Sprinkle a bit of nutmeg on the custard if you like. Bake 40 to 45 minutes, until it tests done.

Note: For carmel custard, melt 12 carmels in 1/4 cup of milk in top of double boiler, or in the microwave. Divide and pour over custard.

Cookies and Bars

Lindy Elrod Cooper's Trail Cookies

1¾ cups flour
   1 t. baking powder
  ½ t. salt
   1 cup butter or margarine
  ½ cup chunky peanut butter
   1 cup white sugar
   1 cup brown sugar
   2 eggs
  ¼ cup milk
   1 t. vanilla
2½ cups oatmeal
   1 small package chocolate chips
  ½ cup raisins
  ½ cup broken pecans or walnuts

Preheat oven 350 degrees. Sift together flour, baking powder and salt. Set aside. Cream butter, sugars and peanut butter together in a separate bowl, using wooden spoon. Beat in the eggs one at a time. Add milk and vanilla and stir well. Add flour mixture to the other ingredients, and beat until blended. Add the oatmeal and blend well by hand. Last of all, add chocolate chips, raisins and chopped pecans. Drop in rounded teaspoons on ungreased cookie sheets. Bake 10 to 12 minutes—just until lightly browned. Remove and cool on rack.

Snickerdoodles—Cookies for Kids to Make!

   1/2 cup margarine or butter (room temperature)
   1/2 cup shortening
1 1/2 cups sugar
   2 eggs
2 3/4 cups of flour
   2 t. cream of tartar
   1 t. soda
   1/4 t. salt
   2 T. sugar
   2 t. cinnamon

Preheat oven to 400 degrees. Mix butter, shortening, sugar and eggs with electric mixer. Blend in cream of tartar, soda and salt with electric mixer. Beat in flour gradually. Shape dough by rounded teaspoon into balls. Mix sugar and cinnamon and place in a bowl. Roll cookie balls in this mixture. Place cookies 2 inches apart on ungreased cookie sheet. Bake 8 to 10 minutes. Immediately remove from cookie sheet and cool on racks.

Dwan Walter's Ginger Snaps (Makes 4 dozen)

   3/4 cup shortening
   1 cup of brown sugar, packed
   1 egg
   1/4 cup molasses
2 1/4 cups flour
   2 t. soda
   1 t. cinnamon
   1 t. ginger
   1/2 t. cloves
   1/4 t. salt

Mix thoroughly the shortening, brown sugar, egg and molasses with an electric mixer. Blend in spices, salt and soda with electric mixer. Blend in flour with mixer, or by hand. Cover bowl and chill in refrigerator for 1 hour. Preheat oven to 375 degrees (after dough has been chilled for one hour). Shape dough by rounded teaspoons into balls, and dip tops into white sugar. Place balls, sugar side up, 3 inches apart on lightly greased baking sheet. Bake 10 to 12 minutes. Immediately remove from baking sheet and cool on racks.

Jeanne Boozer's Diamond Cookies

   1 cup sugar
   1 cup shortening
   2 eggs
   1/2 cup molasses (light or dark depending on your preference)
   1 t. soda
   1 t. cinnamon
   1/2 t. cloves
   1/2 t. ginger
   3 cups flour
   1/2 t. salt

Preheat oven to 350 degrees. Mix the sugar, shortening, eggs, molasses, soda, cinnamon, cloves, ginger and salt with electric beater in a large bowl. Stir in the flour, one cup at a time by hand. Divide dough into six portions and grease three cookie sheets. Grease your fingers and pick up one portion of dough at a time, shaping it to look like a long loaf of French bread. Place on greased cookie sheet the long way, and pat and shape a bit more into the form of a "flat French loaf." Do this with another roll and put parallel to the first one on the cookie sheet. Put two more rolls on the next cookie sheet, and the last two rolls on the third cookie sheet. Wet the top of these cookie rolls with water, using your fingers, and sprinkle liberally with sugar. If you prefer, shape dough into walnut size balls, dip top in sugar, and place on greased cookie sheets. Bake 20 minutes (if you shape dough into balls, bake less time—about 10 to 12 minutes). Remove from oven and cut cookies diagonally, as though you were cutting French bread, while they are warm. Remove the cookies to racks to cool.

Liz Anderson's Almond Shortbread

    1 cup of butter
    1 cup of sugar
    1 egg yolk
    2 cups of flour
    1 t. almond extract
    1 egg white
    ½ cup chopped pecans or sliced almonds

Preheat oven to 325 degrees. Allow butter to soften until it is at room temperature and can easily be mixed in to the sugar and flour. Beat egg yolk with almond extract in a medium size bowl. Add sugar and butter to the bowl and beat with electric mixer. Stir in the flour one cup at a time, using a spoon to blend well. Pat the dough into a greased jelly roll pan. It will be a thin covering of dough. Beat egg white until stiff, and spread over the top of the cookie dough. Sprinkle with ½ cup sliced almonds or chopped pecans. Bake 30 minutes, until slightly brown. Cut while hot into squares, and let cool in the pan. Remove cookies from pan when cool, and store in an airtight container.

370

Eleanor Doan's Date Balls (Makes 6 to 7 dozen)

1 (8 oz.) package of dates—about 24 dates
2 sticks butter
1 cup sugar
2 t. vanilla
1 cup chopped nuts
2 cups Rice Crispies

Quarter the dates. Melt butter with sugar and dates. When sugar has dissolved, cook over medium heat for 10 minutes, stirring frequently. Remove from heat and add vanilla, nuts and Rice Crispies (in that order). When mixture is cool, roll into small balls and coat with powdered sugar. They freeze well.

Note: These are like candy!

Peanut Butter Balls

1 lb. butter or margarine
2 lbs. creamy peanut butter, at room temperature
3 lbs. sifted powdered sugar
1 (12 oz.) package of semi-sweet chocolate chips
½ (2 oz.) bar of paraffin wax (found in store's canning supplies)

Soften the margarine and mix together with the peanut butter. Gradually add the sifted powdered sugar, a cup at a time, stirring with a heavy wooden spoon to blend all ingredients well. Shape this mixture into walnut size balls (a melon scoop may be used to scoop out enough dough). Place balls on jelly roll sheet or in cake pans, and refrigerate. *The next day,* melt chocolate and paraffin together, and carefully dip balls into the wax. Again, place on pans in refrigerator. When chocolate is set, store in covered tins or plastic containers. Be sure to separate each layer of cookies with waxed paper.

Pat Hall's Desperation Doughnuts

Keep one or two cans of biscuit dough in your refrigerator. The "store" or "generic" brand work fine.

1. Preheat oil in your deep fat fryer or electric frypan to 425 degrees. Fill fry pan only half full of oil, and make sure that it is back from the edge of counter and that the cord is to the back, so that no one will get burned.
2. Mix some cinnamon and sugar for rolling the doughnuts in. You may use powdered sugar as another coating. Place sugar in a small paper bag to shake the doughnuts in.
3. Lay out paper towels near the frying pan to lift the doughnuts onto when browned on each side. They will drain quickly.
4. Open the number of cans of biscuits you will need. Cut with a doughnut cutter to get the hole. If you don't have a doughnut cutter then (a) cut the hole with a well washed detergent bottle lid or large thimble, or (b) cut each biscuit into 4 pie shape pieces.
5. Drop a few doughnuts at a time into the hot oil, using tongs, so you don't get burned by splashing oil. Cook doughnut holes too!
6. Turn once to brown lightly on both sides.
7. Lift out with tongs and drain on paper towels.
8. Shake a few at a time in the paper bag to coat or roll in cinnamon/sugar.
9. Serve while hot. Delicious and so easy!

Homemade Basic Cookie Mix for Greig Kids

9 cups flour
1 T. salt
3 T. baking powder
4 cups shortening
4 cups sugar
3 cups instant powdered milk

Mix flour, salt, baking powder and milk. Sift into a bowl and set aside. In another large bowl cream shortening and gradually add sugar until this mixture is very light and fluffy. Gradually add flour mixture blending thoroughly to a coarse cornmeal texture. The electric mixer works well. Store in a large canister at room temperature. This keeps for several weeks and is a great timesaver. The children can make cookies recipes that follow easily also!

Chocolate Chip Cookies (Makes 3 dozen)

4 cups basic homemade cookie mix
1 egg, beaten
2 T. water
1/4 cup firmly packed brown sugar
1 1/2 t. vanilla
1 (6 oz.) package semi-sweet chocolate chips
1 cup chopped nuts (optional)

Preheat oven to 375 degrees. Blend all ingredients with electric mixer except chips and nuts. Stir in chips and nuts by hand. Drop by teaspoonful on ungreased cookie sheet. Bake for 10 to 13 minutes.

Oatmeal Cookies (Makes 4½ dozen)

    2 cups basic homemade cookie mix
    1 cup (old fashioned) oatmeal
    2 T. firmly packed brown sugar
    1 egg, beaten
 1½ t. vanilla
  ½ t. cinnamon
  ½ t. allspice
  ½ cup chopped nuts (optional)
    1 cup raisins
  ½ cup raisin water

   Preheat oven to 375 degrees. Cover raisins with water and simmer 5 minutes. Drain raisins, reserving ½ cup liquid. Combine raisins, water, cookie mix, oatmeal, brown sugar, egg, vanilla, cinnamon and allspice. Mix well. Stir in chopped nuts and well drained raisins. Drop by teaspoon on ungreased cookie sheet. Bake for 13 to 15 minutes.

Peanut Butter Cookies (Makes 3 dozen)

    4 cups basic homemade cookie mix
  ½ cup firmly packed brown sugar
    1 cup peanut butter
    1 egg, beaten
 1½ t. vanilla
    1 T. water (a bit more if needed)

   Preheat oven to 375 degrees. Cream all ingredients together until well blended. Make small balls of dough (about a rounded teaspoon). Flatten balls with a fork on the ungreased cookie sheet. Bake for 10 to 12 minutes.

Homemade Brownie Mix

4 cups sifted flour
4½ cups sugar
1 cup baking cocoa
1½ cups nonfat dry milk
1½ T. baking powder
1½ t. salt

Sift together all of the above ingredients *three* times. Store in an airtight container.

For one batch of brownies you will need:
1¾ cups brownie mix
¼ cup warm water
¼ cup cooking oil
1 t. vanilla
1 egg
¼ cup chopped nuts (optional)

Preheat oven to 350 degrees. Combine mix, warm water, cooking oil, vanilla and egg. Beat with electric mixer for 1 minute at medium speed. Stir in nuts with a spoon. Pour into a greased 9-inch square baking pan or 9-inch round pie plate. Bake for 20 minutes, or until brownies test done. Cool in pan on rack. Cut into two inch squares or pie-shaped wedges. Makes 16 2-inch brownies.

Gary Greig's Four Minute Brownie Pie

  2 eggs
  1 cup sugar
 ½ cup butter or margarine (at room temperature)
 ½ cup flour
  3 to 4 T. powdered baking cocoa
    Pinch of salt
 ½ cup chopped nuts (optional)

Preheat oven to 325 degrees. Combine all ingredients (except nuts) in a medium size bowl. Beat with electric mixer for 4 minutes. Add nuts and stir in. Pour into a greased 9-inch pie pan. Bake 25 to 30 minutes. This will puff slightly and settle when cut. Cut in wedges and serve with ice cream. Best when served warm. *Hint:* Mint ice cream is good!

Greig Family Favorite Brownies (Makes 2 dozen)

  2 (4 oz.) packages of German Sweet Chocolate
  6 T. butter
  2 (3 oz.) packages of cream cheese
  4 T. butter or margarine
 ½ cup sugar
  2 eggs
  2 T. flour
  1 t. vanilla
  4 eggs
1½ cups sugar
  1 cup sifted flour
  1 t. baking powder
 ½ t. salt
 ½ t. almond extract (optional)
  2 t. vanilla extract
  1 cup chopped walnuts or toasted almonds

Allow cream cheese and 4 T. butter to stand in a bowl until they are room temperature. Preheat oven to 350 degrees. Combine chocolate and 6 T. butter and melt in a 2 quart saucepan. Cool to room temperature. Cream cheese and 4 T. butter in a large bowl with an electric mixer. Add ½ cup sugar to cream cheese mixture. Blend in 2 eggs, 2 T. flour, vanilla and almond extracts into the cream cheese mixture. In another bowl, beat 4 eggs until foamy. Gradually add 1½ cups of sugar, beating slowly until mixture is a creamy color. Sift together 1 cup of flour, 1 t. baking powder and ½ t. salt and add to the above egg and sugar mixture. Blend in cooled chocolate mixture and nuts. Reserve 2 cups of the chocolate batter. Spread the remaining chocolate batter in a well-greased 8¾ × 13 pan (or an 8 × 14, or 2 smaller pans 8 × 8 square). Spoon the cream cheese batter evenly all over the chocolate batter, smoothing out as much as possible. Spread the 2 cups of reserved chocolate batter evenly over the cream cheese layer. Bake 25 minutes. Cut in 2-inch squares.

Peanut Butter Crackles

1½ cups flour
1 t. baking powder
½ t. salt
½ cup margarine
½ cup chunky style peanut butter
½ cup sugar
½ cup packed brown sugar
1 egg
1 t. vanilla
1 lb. candy kisses or M & Ms (optional)

Preheat oven to 375 degrees. Stir together flour, baking powder and salt in a medium size bowl. In a large bowl, mix the softened margarine and peanut butter until smooth. Beat sugar and brown sugar into margarine mixture. Beat the egg slightly, and then add egg and vanilla to the peanut butter/sugar mixture. Add the flour a bit at a time, and beat by hand until well blended. Shape dough into 3/4 inch balls; about the size of walnuts. Roll in sugar. Place on ungreased cookie sheet. Bake for 10 minutes. Remove from oven and quickly press chocolate candy firmly in the top of each cookie. Cookie will crackle around the edges. Remove to cooling rack.

Note: I prefer to use candy kisses.

Billy Greig's Easy Peanut Butter Cookies
(Makes about 3½ dozen)

    1 package yellow cake mix
    2 eggs, beaten
 ½ to ¾ cup creamy or crunchy style peanut butter (the more the better), at room temperature
 ½ cup shortening

Preheat oven to 350 degrees. Add beaten eggs, peanut butter and shortening to cake mix. Stir by hand until well blended. Bake on greased cookie sheets approximately 8 to 10 minutes, until done. Cool on a rack.

Note: This is a nice, easy cookie recipe for children to make.

Jane Greig's Chocolate Cookies

   1 (18½ oz.) package chocolate cake mix
  ⅓ cup oil
   2 eggs
   2 T. water
   1 (6 oz.) pkg. semi-sweet chocolate chips

    Preheat oven to 350 degrees. Combine oil, eggs and water. Beat in cake mix by hand. Add chocolate chips. Drop dough two inches apart on greased cookie sheet. Bake 10 minutes or until cookies don't show a fingerprint. Cool on a rack.

Bobby Stanick's No-Bake Peanut Butter Munchies
(Makes 36 to 40)

1¼ cups graham cracker crumbs
  1 cup unsifted powdered sugar
  1 cup plain or crunchy peanut butter, at room temperature
 ¼ cup butter or margarine
 ½ cup walnuts, chopped fine

    Melt butter and place in medium size bowl. Stir in powdered sugar and peanut butter. Add graham cracker crumbs and blend well. Shape into balls the size of walnuts. Then roll balls in nuts to cover (flaked coconut may be used instead). Refrigerate until serving time or make ahead and store in plastic container in the freezer.

Note: These are so good you will have to hide them!

Pecan Graham Crisps (Makes 4 dozen)

12 graham crackers (2½ × 4 inch)
1 cup (½ lb.) butter or margarine
1¼ cups brown sugar, firmly packed
1 cup chopped pecans or walnuts
1 t. vanilla
1 (6 oz.) cup chopped semi-sweet or milk chocolate, or 1 cup semi-sweet chocolate chips.

Preheat oven to 375 degrees. Fit crackers side by side in a single layer in a 10 × 15 baking pan. In a 2 to 3 quart heavy pan or iron Dutch oven, melt butter over medium heat. Stir in brown sugar and nuts. Cook, stirring often, until mixture comes to a boil. Continue to boil until mixture is 238 degrees on a candy thermometer, about 2 minutes. Remove from heat, stir in vanilla and pour evenly over the crackers. Spread to cover completely, using a rubber spatula. Bake to crisp crackers (topping should not darken), 8 to 10 minutes in 375 degree oven. Remove from oven and at once sprinkle with chocolate. Let stand about 10 minutes. If desired, spread the melted chocolate over the topping, using a rubber spatula. Cut into 24 squares, then cut each square in half diagonally. Let cool in pan. Serve, or store.

Note: These keep about 3 days. Store them at room temperature in a covered container.

Children love to *help* make these cookies! These require adult supervision for younger ones.

Desperation Cracker Cookies (Makes 10 to 12)

   1 egg white
      pinch of salt
   4 T. sugar
   ¼ cup chopped nuts
   10 to 12 crisp soda crackers

   Preheat oven to 350 degrees. Beat egg white until stiff, and then beat in salt and sugar gradually. Fold in nuts. Drop meringue by spoonfulls onto crackers. Bake on ungreased cookie sheet at 350 degrees for approximately 15 minutes.

Note: You can multiply this recipe to fit a crowd! Children love
      helping you prepare these cookies.

Children's Treats
the Greig Family
Enjoyed Making Together

Fruit Popsicles

In a blender place 5 peeled oranges, 2 cups of pineapple juice and 2 cups of sugar. Blend until oranges are thoroughly chopped. In a bowl, mash 5 bananas and add the juice of 2 lemons. Add the contents of the blender and stir well. In a pitcher, mix 1 can of frozen orange juice (12 oz.) with the water as directed on the outside of the can. Pour this juice into the bowl and blend well with the banana and orange mixture. Fill paper cups or Popsicle containers with this mixture and freeze.

Greig Family Frozen Yogurt Pops

1 (6 oz.) can frozen orange or grape juice concentrate
1 (6 oz.) can water
1 cup unflavored yogurt

Combine all ingredients in blender. Cover and whirl until combined. Pour into Popsicle cups or 3 oz. paper cups. Freeze partially and add plastic spoons for sticks to hold. Freeze firmly. Makes 8 nutritious yogurt cups.

Note: I always tripled the recipe so I had plenty on hand for the children and their friends!

Homemade Fudgesicles

Use 1 large box of instant chocolate pudding mix. Add milk as directed, plus one additional cup of milk. Fill Popsicle molds or paper cups, and freeze.

Note: This can be done with any flavor of instant pudding mix.

Flavored Yogurt Popsicles

Buy your child's favorite flavored yogurt and freeze in Popsicle containers.

Hot Chocolate Mix

2 cups granulated sugar
1 cup powdered sugar
3 cups instant dry milk powder
3 cups coffee creamer powder
1 cup cocoa

Sift together all ingredients and store in a closed container. Use 3 or more teaspoons per cup, according to your taste. Add boiling water and stir. You can top with whipped cream or marshmallows for a special treat.

Note: Artificial powdered sweetener may be used if you prefer. Omit powdered sugar and let each person sweeten their own cocoa.

Hot Chocolate Mix (Another variety)

3 cups powdered milk
3/4 cup sugar
1/2 cup cocoa
    Dash of salt

Sift together all ingredients and keep in an airtight container. Use 4 T. of mix, plus 8 oz. of hot water for 1 cup of cocoa.

Note: Add 1/2 cup powdered nondairy creamer or 2 T. malted milk powder for a richer flavor.

Orange Julius Counterfeit

½ to 1 cup of powdered milk
1 small can of frozen orange juice
3 cans of water
2 cups of ice
¼ cup of sugar (⅓ cup if you like it sweeter)

Mix in blender and serve immediately. Add an egg or two to this drink, if you wish.

Doris Greig's Crazy Cake

For an 8- or 9-inch square pan:
1½ cups flour
1 cup sugar
¼ cup cocoa
¼ t. salt
1 t. soda
1 T. vinegar
⅓ cup salad oil
1 cup water
1 t. vanilla

For a 9 × 12 inch pan:
3 cups flour
2 cups sugar
½ cup cocoa
½ t. salt
2 t. soda
2 T. vinegar
⅔ cup salad oil
2 cups water
2 t. vanilla

Preheat oven to 350 degrees. Sift dry ingredients directly into the baking pan. (No need to grease pan.) Make three wells in the dry ingredients. Pour vinegar in one, oil in another and vanilla in the third. Pour water over all and mix until well blended with a fork. Smooth batter out evenly in the pan. Bake for 25 minutes. Frost with favorite frosting, or serve with vanilla ice cream. This is a fun cake for kids to make.

Note: This cake can be mixed in a bowl and baked as cupcakes (24), using cupcake liners in muffin tins. Fill ½ full and bake at 350 degrees for 20 to 25 minutes.

For frosting baked on cupcakes: Fill cupcake liners only ⅓ full.

Soften 16 oz. cream cheese and combine with 2 beaten eggs and ⅔ cup sugar. Add 2 cups of chocolate chips and stir by hand. Put about 2 T. cream cheese mixture on top of each cupcake. Bake in preheated oven 20 to 25 minutes at 350 degrees.

Popcorn Cake

    1 cup butter
    1 (1 lb.) package of marshmallows
    4 qts. popped popcorn
    1 cup peanuts
    1 cup candy coated chocolate pieces
    1 cup gumdrops

    Mix popcorn, peanuts, candy chocolate pieces and gumdrops in a large, deep bowl. Melt butter and marshmallows over low heat in a large saucepan or in a microwave. Add warm butter/marshmallow mixture to popcorn mixture and stir well. Pack into greased 9-inch or 10-inch tube pan (angel food pan).
Note: Line the bottom of the cake with waxed paper.

Cool in refrigerator. Using a knife or spatula, loosen sides and center of the cake. Remove from pan and cut into wedges. Dip a sharp knife in cold water before cutting each piece.

Punch, Dessert Toppings, Granola

Liz Anderson's Favorite Punch

1 bottle cranberry juice (medium size)
1/2 cup lemon juice
3/4 cup orange juice
1 t. almond extract
1 qt. chilled gingerale

Combine cranberry, lemon and orange juice, and the almond extract and chill. Just before serving, add one quart of chilled gingerale. Delicious and different!

Doris Greig's Cranberry Punch (Serves 25, 1/2 cup each)

2 quarts Cranberry Cocktail (chilled)
1 (6 oz.) can frozen lemonade (thawed—and add cold water as directed on can)
1 qt. Gingerale or Lemon-lime soda, chilled

Mix cranberry juice and lemonade, *but* add Gingerale or Lemon-lime just before serving.

To Make an Ice Mold: Use distilled water and sliced lemons and cherries in the mold. The distilled water stays clear, whereas tap water looks frosty and not crystal clear and icy. Pour enough distilled water to just cover the bottom of the ice mold. Arrange lemons and cherries (or orange slices) in the mold. Freeze. Add distilled water to fill mold and complete freezing process again.

Note: This is a *tart* punch.

Diane Rietveldt's Punch

12 oz. frozen orange juice
12 oz. frozen lemonade
12 oz. frozen limeade
2 (32 oz.) Lemon-Lime Soda or Gingerale

Chill Lemon-Lime Soda or Gingerale well. Mix the concentrate juices according to their container instructions, making sure to use ice cold water. Add ice cubes, or frozen lemonade or limeade cubes to the punch bowl. Add the soda or Gingerale just before serving. If you use diet soda, this will be a low calorie punch! Serves one large punch bowl. Good and tart!

Banana Ale

6 cups of water
4 cups of sugar
5 oranges
4 lemons
5 bananas
1 (46 oz.) can of pineapple juice
1 bottle of Gingerale (*per* 8 to 10 people), chilled

Select a large cooking pot and place in it the water and sugar. Bring this mixture to a boil, stirring frequently. Boil 3 minutes. Let the sugar/water mixture cool. Add juice and pulp of 5 oranges and 4 lemons to sugar/water mixture. Mash bananas well, and stir into the sugar/water mixture. Add pineapple juice to the sugar/water mixture. Mix all ingredients together. Store in a large plastic or other covered container in the freezer for 24 hours. Remove from freezer and add some in each serving glass. Return the rest of the Banana Ale to the freezer. Fill the rest of the glass with Gingerale and serve with straws.

Note: If you are going to serve all of the Banana Ale at one time, chill 3 or 4 bottles of Gingerale.

This is a nice beverage for a shower, or a children's treat on a hot day. The Banana Ale will keep well in the freezer until you use it all up!

Charlotte Shackelford's Russian Tea

Blend all of the ingredients well together and store in a tightly covered container or jar with a tight fitting lid.

1 (12 oz.) package of Wyler's Lemonade Mix
1 (1 lb. 2 oz.) jar of Tang
1 cup Instant Tea (plain or lemon-flavored Nestea)
1½ cups sugar (or use artificially sweetened iced tea mix)
1½ t. ground cloves
4½ t. cinnamon
1½ t. ground ginger
2 T. dried lemon peel and 2 T. dried orange peel, optional

Pour boiling water into a cup and mix 1 slightly rounded teaspoon of Russian Tea into the cup, or more, according to your taste. This may be mixed in a preheated teapot by adding hot water, keeping track of the number of cups, and adding the Russian Tea accordingly.

Note: This makes a nice hostess gift.

Liz Anderson's Hot Fudge Sauce (Serves 6 to 8)

     2 cups sugar
     2 squares (2 oz.) baking chocolate
    ²⁄₃ cup milk
       Dash of salt
     2 T. butter or margarine
     1 t. vanilla

   Place sugar, baking chocolate, milk and salt in pan and
heat. Stir occasionally until mixture begins to boil. Then turn
burner down slightly. As mixture boils, begin to test for the soft-
ball stage. As soon as the soft-ball stage is reached, remove pan
from burner and add margarine and vanilla. Stir until margarine is melted and then pour from pan into a pitcher for people
to help themselves to the amount they want on their ice cream.
Any left over hot fudge sauce heats very nicely in the microwave and can be used at least one more time this way.

Luebke's Butterscotch Sauce

1½ cups light brown sugar, packed well
   ²⁄₃ cup Karo syrup (light color)
    2 T. butter
    1 (6 oz.) can Carnation milk
    1 t. vanilla

   Bring brown sugar, syrup and butter to a rolling boil. Take
off burner and cool. Pan can feel warm to hand, not hot. Add
Carnation milk and vanilla, beating into cooked ingredients
gradually. Serve warm or cold. Store in the refrigerator, covered.

Homemade Granola

Preheat oven to 300 degrees. Mix together in a large roasting pan or kettle:

1½ boxes (63 oz.) oatmeal (old fashioned)
- 2 cups sliced almonds
- 2 cups sunflower seeds
- 4 cups powdered milk
- 2 cups soyflower
- 4 cups all bran cereal (you may also add 2 cups of raw bran if you wish)
- 3 cups wheat germ to be added later

In a separate bowl, mix:
- 2 cups vegetable oil

1½ cups honey (or 1 box of brown sugar plus ¼ cup brown sugar)
- 2 cups boiling water

Stir this mixture until sugar or honey dissolves and is well-blended with vegetable oil and water. Pour this mixture over the grains and mix well. Spread this granola mixture thinly on jelly roll tins and bake about 1½ hours (or until slightly browned), using approximately 6 jelly roll tins or other pans. Cool on cookie tins and then crumble. Add wheat germ. Store in 3 lb. coffee tins. Makes 3 large tins, plus a 1 lb. coffee can size. Serve with raisins, cut up dried apples, apricots, or any other dried or fresh fruits. Delicious on top of cottage cheese or yogurt!

"German Style Granola" (Smaller Recipe)

    6 cups Old-Fashioned Oatmeal
  ¾ cup sliced almonds
  ¾ cup sunflower seeds
    1 cup raw bran
    1 cup wheat germ

   Bake as directed for Homemade Granola, about 1 hour. Add 1 cup wheat germ to cooled cereal.

Helpful Household Hints!

In the Kitchen

Cooking Bacon: Cook bacon in your microwave in layers. Just put bacon on paper towels in a baking dish. Add paper towels and more bacon, until the whole pound is stacked up. Rotate dish half-way through cooking time. Watch carefully to see that it is done just the way you like it.

Baking Ahead: When making cookies, bars or quick breads that will freeze, always make a double batch and freeze half or more. Saves a lot of time and energy! Great for "drop in" guests too!

Cake Flour: Spoon lightly into cup all-purpose flour. Remove 1 T. flour and sift remaining flour with 1 t. cornstarch.

Over-ripe Bananas: Sometimes these have been a problem, until I decided to mash and measure them in separate packages containing just the right amount for the banana bread recipe I always use.

Burned Pot: Add baking soda to water and boil until the burned crust softens. Clean with a stainless steel "chore boy."

Another method is to dampen the spot and sprinkle the burned crust with baking soda. Pour a little vinegar over this and let stand 20 minutes. Then scrub clean.

Black heel marks on vinyl floors? Remove with a cloth or paper towel and a bit of cigarette lighter fluid.

High Speed Barbecue. Microwave chicken parts or ribs for half the total cooking time listed in your microwave cookbook. Then finish cooking on the grill.

Shaping Hamburger Patties Easily. Wash the outside of a Number 2½ can. Press down on the pattie and trim off the excess. This is a quick and uniform method. I like to freeze patties, layered on a cookie sheet with waxed paper in between. When frozen, I remove patties from the sheet and put them individually in plastic sandwich bags. Then place them in Ziploc bags and replace them in the freezer. For a quick dinner, get out the number of patties needed. They thaw fast.

"Potlucks." Make sure you get your serving dishes back by writing your name and address with a permanent ink marking pen. Stick tape to the bottom of your casserole, cake pan or other serving dish.

Tie colored rickrack or thread around the handle of your serving pieces, or mark them with little colored adhesive dots which can be purchased in the ten cent store or stationery supply store.

Spices and Seasonings. Arrange them alphabetically in

a drawer, or on the shelf, so you won't have to hunt each time you need something.

To Simmer Spices. Place spices in a teaball or a coffee filter tied together with string. This makes whole spices and garlic buds easy to remove.

Ground Meat Timesaver. Precook ground meat in microwave by placing in a colander over glass microwave-safe bowl. Cook 3 to 5 minutes until meat loses its pink color. Halfway through cooking, break up meat with fork and stir. Drippings will collect in the bowl under the colander. Use brush to wash meat from colander.

To Remove Price Tags from Glass or Plastic. Use cigarette lighter fluid on a cloth or paper napkin after you have pulled off as much of the tag as possible.

To Substitute Unsweetened Chocolate. For each square, use 4 T. cocoa and 1 T. shortening.

To Make Catsup. Use 8 oz. can tomato sauce plus ½ cup brown sugar and 2 t. vinegar.

To Make Sour Cream for Cooking. For 1 cup, use 1 T. lemon juice, 1 T. cooking oil and enough evaporated milk to make 1 cup.

To Make Brown Sugar. For ½ cup brown sugar, blend ½ cup white sugar with 2 T. unsulfured molasses. Make according to your need. No need to pre-blend sugar and molasses if combining with other ingredients in a recipe.

Around the House

Cloudy Vases. Fill with water and drop a denture tablet into them. Let stand. Should do the trick! Repeat if necessary.

Removing Decals from Enamel Tubs. (Not for use on fiberglass tubs) You may use a pre-wash spray on the edges of the decals. Let stand 30 minutes and then gently pull up sides of the decals. Use a razor to loosen, if necessary. Blowing hot air from a hair dryer helps to hurry the softening of the glue. If a stain remains, scrub it with automatic dishwashing soap and hot water, using a stiff bristled brush.

Doilies. Do you have old doilies that are too fragile to iron? Wash by hand. Roll in a towel to remove excess moisture. Lay on the kitchen counter and pat out to smooth and remove wrinkles. Spray with a spray-on starch and let dry flat on the counter. You will not have to press. Lift carefully when dry and put in the place you want to use it.

Dusting Problems. A feather duster is an invaluable piece of equipment for a quick clean up! Ostrich feather dusters are best.

Mel Zimmer's Jewelry Cleaner. Use a small jar with a lid. Add equal parts: Water, Household ammonia, Liquid detergent for dishes. Soak jewelry overnight and then brush it with soft brush (toothbrush). Rinse under clear water. *Do not soak* pearls, opals, turquoise, coral, shell cameo, or other soft stones—they may be immersed briefly—5 minutes, and then brushed and rinsed. This solution needs changing only when it appears dirty. Use it one or two times a week to keep your jewelry sparkling clean!

400

Cleaning the Lint Trap in the Dryer. Save the fabric softener sheets and just grab a used one to wipe the lint away.

Mending or Handwork. Keep things in a basket and carry it with you to the phone while you visit with a friend, and while you watch the news on TV with your family. You will be amazed at how much you can accomplish during these times!

Rug Stains. A rug salesman told me about this trick, and it really works! He guaranteed it would not harm the rug, and it doesn't. Spray Formula 409 on the stain and rub well with a clean, beige or light colored, old terry towel. Repeat until the spot disappears. Be sure the terry towel is a beige or light color that will not fade onto your carpet!

Scratches on Furniture. Rub with "almond stick" purchased at a hardware store, or grab a pecan nut, break it in half and rub it across the scratch. This really works! An eyebrow pencil of the same color will work too!

Water Rings on Furniture. Blend mayonnaise with toothpaste. Rub in well. Let stand for a while and then wipe off and polish with a soft cloth. Repeat if necessary.

Silver Polishing. When you polish silver, never use the liquid cleaner. It removes the oxidizing, and really ruins the finish on your silver. When polishing silver, an old toothbrush can be used on the patterns that are elaborate. Make sure it is a soft brush. Use the brush to clean between fork tines too. It is really great for this! Make sure your silver is dry before storing. Moisture causes pits or deeply darkened spots which often cannot be removed, even by professional buffing.

After silver has dried, at least overnight (approximately 10 to 12 hours), store it in a silver chest lined with tarnish proof cloth, or line a box or drawer with this cloth. This can be purchased at a jewelry store, or they can tell you where to buy it. Large pieces, such as silver trays, bowls, pitcher, etc. can be stored in clear plastic sacks in your cupboard. Voila! When you have a dinner party, they are all ready for use. Then, polish them up again after dinner as you wash the silver, and let them dry on your counter overnight. Replace in plastic bags the next morning and store. They will be all ready for your next dinner party. Plastic garbage bags can be used for silver too. Store each piece individually, so it won't scratch another piece.

Storage Containers for the Freezer. Cottage cheese and yogurt cartons make excellent storage for soups, spaghetti sauce, etc. Just use a permanent ink marker to put the contents and date on the side of the carton where you can see it. These make great throw aways after you remove the contents. No dirty dishes to wash!

Scorched Fabric. Use a combination of lemon juice and salt and place in the sun until the spot disappears. Wash and iron carefully with medium heat setting on the iron.

Window Cleaner. Make a solution of 2 T. rubbing alcohol, 2 T. ammonia and 1¾ cups water. Pour solution into a spray bottle and use like a glass cleaner. To distinguish from other cleaners add a drop of food coloring.

With the Family

Pets. Does your dog or cat have fleas? Use about 2 to 3 tablespoons of Pinesol per gallon of water, and dip your pet in this solution. Kills not only fleas, but the eggs! If you have fleas in the house, flea bomb your rooms before dipping your pets. This always took care of the problem at our house! Spray your yard with Malathion to kill fleas and eggs.

School Mornings. These are nearly always frantic! Solve part of your problem by having a small box in each child's room in which they place school papers, books, and whatever else needs to be taken to school in the morning. Thus, the details are taken care of the night before and each child needs only to gather his things from his own box. This is a great time and emotion saver! This box is a great place to put a "love note" of affirmation and love for your child from time to time too!

Special Events. Anniversaries and Birthdays—In December, list all the dates on your new year's calendar and keep it posted in your kitchen, so you won't forget anyone! Buy cards ahead so you always have one to send and don't have to make an extra trip to the store.

Memory Boxes for Children. Use a cardboard box or a file box. Put in it all special drawings, handwritten notes, family photos (with dates, names and ages on back), school pictures, report cards, sports awards, etc. Let the children enjoy their memory box, sharing it with family and friends. Don't worry about the "no rhyme, nor reason" organization. You are building memories that will be passed on at a later date.

Concluding Thoughts

I have included a lot of my favorite recipes; there are many more that I could give you. Yet, I feel that each one of us needs to find and develop our own traditional family favorites to pass on from one generation to the next.

Also, as you look for recipes you will find those that are easily prepared and enjoyed most by your family. Therefore, these are just simply ideas to trigger your imagination for your own families and to help you to extend your hospitality to your children's friends, your husbands' and your friends, and to strangers whom God sends your way.

Marjorie Holmes said in her *Calendar of Love and Inspiration:* "Hospitality doesn't depend on size or supply. If the heart is big enough, so is the table and so is the house." How true that is!

> *Don't forget to be kind to strangers, for some who have done this have entertained angels without realizing it.*
>
> —Hebrews 13:2, *TLB*

Recipe for the Soul

Take: 1 chapter of the Bible and read earnestly
Add: 1 measure of prayer
                      and
         1 measure of thoughtful meditation
Add: A generous measure of thanksgiving
Season generously with:
                      love and kindness
Let simmer slowly all day on the hearth of your heart. Garnish with a smile and serve daily with God's blessing.

FAVORITE RECIPES

FROM MY COOKBOOK

Recipe Name	Page Number